# Negotiating Hostage Crises with the New Terrorists

# NEGOTIATING HOSTAGE CRISES WITH THE NEW TERRORISTS

Adam Dolnik and Keith M. Fitzgerald
*Foreword by Gary Noesner*

**PRAEGER SECURITY INTERNATIONAL**

Westport, Connecticut • London

**Library of Congress Cataloging-in-Publication Data**

Dolnik, Adam.
   Negotiating hostage crises with the new terrorists / Adam Dolnik and
Keith M. Fitzgerald.
     p. cm.
   Includes bibliographical references and index.
   ISBN 978–0–275–99748–9 (alk. paper)
1. Terrorism.   2. Hostage negotiations.   3. Crisis management.   I. Fitzgerald, Keith M.
II. Title.
   HV6431.D634   2008
   363.325′181—dc22     2007038553

British Library Cataloguing in Publication Data is available.

Library of Congress Catalog Card Number: 2007038553
ISBN-13: 978–0–275–99748–9

First published in 2008

Praeger Security International, 88 Post Road West, Westport, CT 06881
An imprint of Greenwood Publishing Group, Inc.
www.praeger.com

Printed in the United States of America

The paper used in this book complies with the
Permanent Paper Standard issued by the National
Information Standards Organization (Z39.48-1984).

10 9 8 7 6 5 4 3 2 1

**Copyright Acknowledgments**
The authors and publisher gratefully acknowledge permission for use of the following
material:

Material first published in "Negotiating the Impossible: The Beslan Hostage Crisis" by
Adam Dolnik. RUSI Whitehall Report 2-07 (London: Royal United Services Institute, 2007).

Excerpts from *Understanding Terrorist Innovation: Technology, Tactics and Global Trends* by
Adam Dolnik, pg. 104–111 (London: Routledge, 2007). Reprinted with permission.

Excerpts from "The Moscow Theater Incident: Perpetrators, Tactic, and the Russian
Response," *International Negotiation*, Volume 8, Issue 3, 2003. Koninklijke Brille N.V.
Reprinted with permission.

*In the memory of all innocent victims of*
*terrorism and counterterrorism*

# CONTENTS

# FOREWORD

September 11, 2001, left an indelible mark on Americans and on much of the world. Terrorists had done the unthinkable. Through the global span of the news media, the entire world community shared the unforgettable images of brutal terrorism in its most brazen and audacious form. This act left us shocked and confused. It turned our perception of safety and security upside down. Where else could terrorists strike? What drove these individuals to such hatred and inhumanity? How can we protect ourselves against such fanaticism and reckless savagery? Citizens of the world asked these questions and more, as did their leaders and elected officials. In response, nations have undertaken steps to combat terrorism, to uncover its support network and structure, initiated efforts aimed at preventing terrorist acts, and finally they prepared to effectively respond to those incidents that do occur despite the best prevention efforts. While perhaps not the most likely act of terrorism today, the taking of hostages by terrorists seeking to gain worldwide attention or force substantive concessions from governments is an ever-present danger. How prepared are nations to confront and effectively resolve such incidents? *Negotiating Hostage Crises with the New Terrorist* addresses the key challenges any nation will face when attempting to peacefully resolve attacks in which terrorists hold the lives of many hostages in the balance.

Authors Adam Dolnik and Keith M. Fitzgerald have undertaken a landmark study of several key hostage-taking dramas to examine the conduct of the "new terrorist" and to analyze the impact of the governmental responses on the resolution of the incidents. Focusing primarily on the Beslan School and Moscow Theater hostage crises, the authors undertake a detailed examination of the planning and execution of these horrific acts of terrorism. Their research is meticulous in identifying the behaviors, goals, and negotiation skills of the terrorists. In both incidents, many lives were lost, primarily after Russian authorities decided that they had to use force to resolve the situation. Important questions are raised concerning the need to use force. Were proper negotiations first undertaken that would have lowered the potential for a violent resolution? Might such efforts have yielded a safe and peaceful resolution, or at least secured the release of a larger number of hostages, thereby saving those fortunate ones from the inevitable fate that so tragically befell so many others? The critical question is whether or not the authorities exercised good judgment and proper negotiation skills when confronting these challenging situations.

As nations seek to combat terrorism and eliminate terrorists, are they carefully weighing the consequences of their actions? The authors provide ample evidence to support the belief that punishing the terrorists became the primary objective of the Russian authorities, with the safety of the hostages a distant secondary concern. Were their decisions driven by a lack of understanding about negotiation principles? Did their preconceived notions about terrorist behavior leave doubt in their mind that the terrorists could be effectively dealt with through negotiations? Did a tactical resolution strategy become a singular approach, with negotiation efforts simply viewed as a stalling tactic until force could be applied? The answer to these questions seems to be a clear "yes."

This book provides a strong case for the application of negotiation skills in even the most challenging and desperate hostage sieges. While terrorists may be willing to die for their cause, there is ample information to suggest that they are just as ready to embrace a resolution that provides them with some sense of accomplishment or victory. In short, they are willing to die but would prefer to live another day in all but the most extreme cases. The authors make a good argument that terrorists simply bent on death and destruction have no need to barricade themselves with hostages and press for demands. Yet, the perception on the part of most authorities is that negotiations will not work. This view helps drive decision-making toward an inevitable attempt to resolve by force what has not been fully attempted through negotiation.

In my lengthy FBI career as Chief of the FBI Crisis Negotiation Unit, I know very well the importance of negotiations as a key component to stabilizing any crisis conflict. De-escalation of any incident through the use of communication skills can foster meaningful dialogue and create a channel of contact through which alternatives to violent resolutions can be explored. In addition to buying time and gaining important intelligence, the negotiation process provides much-needed time to assemble tactical teams and prepare them for their critical mission if the negotiation process does not ultimately succeed in securing a peaceful surrender. We also know that in many cases, despite loss of life and unobtainable demands, the negotiation process is almost always successful in securing the safe release of at least some of the hostages during the ordeal. In addition, when given support by Command decision makers, a flexible and creative negotiation strategy is often successful in preventing further loss of life and has a good chance of bringing the incident to a safe resolution. Sadly, key Command decision makers, be they police officials or government representatives, do not often understand the capabilities of negotiation teams. Not understanding the methodology and skills of the negotiation team often leads such decision makers to unduly interfere with the strategy, play to an external political audience, or make unhelpful press statements that only make the situation worse.

During the FBI's fifty-two-day management of the Branch Davidian siege in Waco, Texas, in 1993, effective negotiations were often stymied by an ill-prepared on-scene Commander whose anger and frustration at the manipulations of David Koresh led to counterproductive decisions that hindered successful negotiations. When the negotiation team was able to secure the release of some individuals the Commander would say that not enough had come out. In his anger and inexperience, he ordered tactical movements of armored vehicles that nullified the progress achieved by the negotiation team. Watching my negotiation team secure the safe release of thirty-five individuals and then have that success thwarted by poor Command decision-making was heartbreaking. As with the Beslan incident, at Waco many children died in part as a result of poor decision-making on behalf o the leadership. While the hostage takers are ultimately responsible for the outcome, governments must ensure they do not undertaken actions that make a dangerous situation even worse. Fortunately, the FBI learned from its mistakes at Waco, and three years later during the eighty-one-day siege of the Freeman militia group in Jordan, Montana, the negotiation team was given the time, total support, latitude, and flexibility to resolve the incident peacefully, with no loss of life, and not a shot was fired. At one point the FBI even allowed one of the Freeman leaders to leave the compound and meet with other leaders who were in jail, then return into the crisis site. While not in any negotiation handbook, this unprecedented but successful and creative initiative played a key role in securing a nonviolent resolution.

Clearly, negotiators and their teams must undertake greater efforts to better understand today's "new terrorist" so aptly described in this book. Negotiators must understand the group they are confronting, its goals and objectives, its prior history of incidents, and its modus operandi. This "new terrorist" is a different challenge than the one faced by law enforcement negotiators in classic hostage/barricade/suicide incidents throughout the world today. The lessons learned in those cases may have to be altered in order to be more effective in dealing with the "new terrorist." Being creative in finding ways to open and maintain effective communications is critical. Yet, perhaps the biggest challenge for negotiation teams is really negotiating with law enforcement and political leadership, convincing them to support a thoughtful and creative negotiation process. We used to call this challenge the "crisis within the crisis." As a negotiation instructor of many years, I would begin my instruction by saying that the most important aspect of negotiations is "self-control." If a negotiator cannot control his or her own emotions, how then can they be expected to influence an emotionally distraught individual or a desperate terrorist? In this regard, police decision makers and politicians must understand the importance of controlling their own emotional state in the decision-making process. They need to trust and rely on their negotiation team to conduct meaningful negotiations, not just to buy time for an assault, but to actually seek out an accommodation to resolve the incident peacefully, as recommended by the authors in this book.

In 1996, I flew to Lima, Peru, in response to the MRTA's takeover of the residence of the Japanese Ambassador. That 120-day long siege was the longest in history. The terrorists came to negotiate, yet President Fujimori initially refused to talk with them and presented a tough public stance against terrorism for his domestic audience. Despite Fujimori making one poor management decision after another, the MRTA did not respond by killing hostages, although they had a huge supply of victims to choose from; rather they continued to seek negotiations. Under pressure from Western governments Fujimori finally allowed a form of negotiations to proceed, yet his entire focus was to prepare for a tactical assault. He wanted to punish the MRTA. After 120 days, Peruvian commandos entered the residence through tunnels and succeeded in killing all of the terrorists. One hostage and one commando died in the effort. While Peruvians took much pride in this heroic and successful rescue operation, was it necessary? Might misfortune have turned the operation into a total tragedy resulting in a significant loss of hostage lives? Perhaps a group of terrorists with superior preparedness might have been able to repel the rescue operation, or through their determination made it more costly in terms of loss of life. The "new terrorists" described by the authors have demonstrated that they have learned from past operations. Their commitment and adaptations could make casualty-less hostage rescues less likely to succeed in the future. While success was achieved in Lima, would the Peruvians have been wise to have seriously pursued a less risky strategy that attempted to achieve a peaceful resolution through quality negotiations? In managing a conflict, governments and law enforcement officials can make bad decisions yet still achieve success, but does that mean they made the correct decisions? The old adage about "better lucky than good" should not be the guide when innocent lives are at stake. As the risk of catastrophic outcomes increases as a result of tactical operations, it is essential that governments understand and place appropriate emphasis on alternative approaches.

Finally, the authors rightfully question the wisdom of governments declaring they will not "negotiate with terrorists." While this tough position helps win popular domestic support for a politician, does it have a practical application in the effort to save hostage lives in a dangerous situation? Would the FBI not negotiate with hijackers on a plane that landed in Washington or New York? Of course they would. Politicians need to understand that tough statements, especially during an incident, are often inflammatory and unhelpful to seeking a peaceful resolution. This book should be read by all officials in law enforcement and government who play a role in such matters. If officials have a responsibility for managing a terrorist hostage siege, they need to learn the lessons of the past so that they can avoid the common mistakes made by others. For those who do not learn from history are destined to repeat it. As I used to tell my negotiation students, "don't get even, get your way." Being tough is fine for elections, but we must be smart and flexible in saving lives. Only when key leaders come to appreciate and fully support the negotiation process, will we avoid the tragic incidents profiled in this book.

Gary Noesner
Chief, FBI Crisis Negotiation Unit, retired

# ACKNOWLEDGMENTS

My deepest thanks go to all of my mentors of past and present, in particular to Rohan Gunaratna, Jason Pate, Alex Schmid, Bruce Hoffman, William Monning, Amin Tarzi, Amy Sands, Stephen Garrett, Clint Blandford, James Wirtz, Kumar Ramakrishna, Richard Pilch, Eric Croddy, Raymond Zilinskas, William Potter, and Anna Vassilieva. Without your knowledge this book would have never come into existence.

For their continuing support I also wish to thank my present colleagues in Wollongong, Doug MacKinnon, Luke McNamara, Margaret Sheil, Jeff Penrose, Duncan Chappell, Peter Ridgway, Mark Loves, Gregor Allan, Sandy Gordon, Paul Schwerdt, Hugh Dixon, Alaeldin Maghaireh, Tracy Wood, Jessica Lopez, Rebecca Georges, and Violeta Trajcevska.

Special thanks go to friends and fellow travelers from Afghanistan and the Northern Caucasus: Petr Lebeda, Adela Kubickova, Elena Pavlova, and Kelly McEvers. Thank you for the memories.

My deepest gratitude goes to Ismail, whose courage and loyalty helped me return from Chechnya safely. I will never forget you.

This book would not have been possible without the insights of the many negotiators, investigators, hostages, journalists, victims, relatives, and witnesses, who were kind enough to share their insights. In particular, I would like to thank Larisa Kudzieva, Larisa Mamitova, Ala Ramonova, Anneta Gadieva, Susanna Dudiyeva, Lydia Tsaliyeva, Vera Solbieva, Andrei Soldatov, Madina Shavlokhova, Anna Politkovskaya (in memoriam), Grigory Shvedov, Mairaj Ariff, Valery Dzutsev, Regina Dzutseva, Ruslan Aushev, Usam Baisaev, Timur Aliev, Dina Alborova, Ekaterina Sokirianskaia, and many others who cannot be named here. Thank you for your courage to speak.

I am also thankful to the many crisis negotiators who have inspired me to undertake this project, in particular Jack Cambria, Heidi Nieboer, William Hogewood, Jan Dubina, William Kidd, Stephen LaPlante, John Mills, Tom Moyer, Timothy Sloan, and others. I hope it is useful.

For his vital contribution to this book, I am immensely grateful to my coauthor Keith—hands down the best negotiator I have ever met. This world needs more people like you.

Last but not the least, I would like to thank my family, without whose encouragement and support, this book would not have been possible. For their affection, and for teaching me to rise above challenges and never give up, I thank my parents Vladislav and Jana, and my brother David. For their love and enduring patience, I thank my wife Katerina and our children Tatiana and Max.

Adam Dolnik
Wollongong, 2007

Firstly I must thank my longtime mentor and friend, Professor Roger Fisher, who taught me as much about human nature as he has about negotiation and conflict management. Thank you for the many opportunities you afforded me. Any good I may do in the field of negotiation will be thanks to you; I pray always to live up to your example.

Thank you also to the rest of my brilliant colleagues at the Harvard Negotiation Project and Conflict Management Group; I carry your sage voices with me wherever I go. Dr Landrum Bolling and Howard Raiffa, thank you for your impressive, lifelong commitments, and for being true role models. Bruce Allyn, Scott Brown, Diana Chigas, Mauricio Duarte, Horacio Falcão, Mark Gordon, Arthur Martirosyan, Michael Moffitt, Rob Ricigliano, John Richardson, Tom Schaub, and Anthony Wanis-St. John— a finer team of negotiation professionals has never been assembled. I shall always be proud to have worked with you all, and to have learned so much from each of you. Bruce Patton, Shelia Heen, and Douglas Stone, your work on *Difficult Conversations* is saving lives in places you've never even seen in ways you probably never imagined.

I would not have sought the experiences that allowed me to contribute to this work without the guidance and friendship of Sherman Teichman, Heather Barry, and my friends at EPIIC at Tufts University. Amid the complexities of the world's conflicts and crises, conventional wisdom has a way of turning into a pillar of salt. We find only one conundrum after another; there are no easy answers, yet still we must ask the questions and question our assumptions. Crisis negotiators learn to appreciate that more than most.

Thanks also to my partners in conflict, crises, and counterterrorism; Moty Cristal in Herzliya, Joe Felter at West Point, Mike Fenzel at CENSA, Harsha Fernando in Colombo, Rohan Gunaratna at the International Centre for Political Violence and Terrorism Research in Singapore, and Hekmat Karzai, Director of the Center for Conflict and Peace Studies in Kabul. I'm honored to call you friends, and working with you continues to be a pleasure, and an ongoing education.

To my colleagues at *Sea-Change*; especially Tan Tay Keong, Scott Fritzen, Nick Clayton, and Trevor Clark, for your friendship and support throughout this and so many other projects.

Thanks to my coauthor, Adam, who took on the lion's share of this book and the research that went into writing it. I am grateful for your patience, your hard work, your attention to detail, and for inviting me to work with you. I shall look forward to doing so again.

Lastly, thanks to Carol Fitzgerald, for the gifts of life, patience, and kindness, and for the most important lesson every negotiator should learn that when two children are fighting over a ball, the problem isn't the ball ...

Keith M. Fitzgerald
Singapore, 2007

# INTRODUCTION

The question of negotiating with "terrorists" virtually always leads to divisive debates. Unfortunately the focus of the discourse is usually misplaced and becomes framed as an argument over "legitimizing" terrorism by talking with terrorists or being tough on terrorism by refusing to talk. Ultimately, the question of whether or not to negotiate with terrorists hinges not on our opinion of terrorism, but on our *definition of negotiation*. Presidents and prime ministers who "refuse to negotiate with terrorists" are taking a tough stance that is intuitively (and emotionally) understandable, and invariably, politically popular. But in essence, these leaders do not actually mean that they will not *negotiate*. What they are really saying is that they will not make *deals* with terrorists, make *concessions* to terrorists, *compromise* with terrorists, or *reward* terrorists' behavior. One of the key reasons why leaders often make the mistake of declaring that they will not "negotiate" is simply their limited understanding of what negotiation is. Like most people, they mistakenly equate negotiation merely to bargaining, compromise, and deal making.

To be sure, bargaining (the practice of offers and counter-offers) is by far the most common *process* used when negotiating. In addition, some negotiations are indeed expected to end with compromises (each side getting less than what they want), and negotiation is also frequently conducted with the purpose of making deals (sales, contracts, treaties, etc.). But while these procedures frequently constitute parts of the negotiation process, they are certainly not synonymous with the term itself. *If one assumes that negotiation is only about bargaining, making deals, or concessions,* then of course we should not negotiate with terrorists, as this action is likely to ultimately lead to some rewards for their bad behavior. However, if one understands that negotiation, ultimately, is *the use of communication to exercise influence in order to change someone's thinking, behavior, and decision making,* then negotiating with terrorists does not necessarily require making foolish concessions, nor is it rewarding and further incentivizing bad behavior. Unfortunately, this fine point is frequently missed, often resulting in the a priori dismissal of "negotiations" as an option.

One question we always ask political leaders who "refuse to negotiate with terrorists" is: How does *not talking* to them (rebels, militants, hostage takers, hijackers) help the situation? They never seem to have an answer. *Who* should do the negotiating is another question, and—in most cases—we would not recommend that heads-of-state talk directly with terrorists in the midst of a terrorist incident.[1] But in order to effectively influence the outcome of a crisis, it is absolutely essential to overcome this debilitating assumption that negotiation means "giving in," making concessions, compromise, or making deals, and that negotiation is a "weaker" approach to terrorism than tactical operations, such as assaults, raids, and rescue operations. Tactical tools and influence tools are two parts of the same toolkit; we cannot afford to throw half of that toolkit away by being too quick to discard negotiation during hostage crises. This is especially true in the era of "new terrorism," where the terrorists are increasingly effective in making tactical responses to barricade incidents both more costly and less likely to succeed. In fact, many of the "new terrorists" are *counting on* us to respond to their provocations with force. The "new terrorists" are changing the game; we can no longer depend on outsmarting or tricking hostage takers:

- They have read our manuals and studied past incidents, so they know most of the standard tricks, and they have real-time access to multiple sources of information;
- They have direct lines of communication with colleagues and others beyond the location of the incident;
- They are tactically savvy, well armed, well prepared, and quite willing to die; making coercive threats and "hard bargaining" far less effective (or completely useless) as negotiation tactics;
- In fact, they are often turning traditional tactical strengths against us, by setting traps and provoking authorities into "homicide-by-cop" scenarios, where the authorities will share the blame for disastrous outcomes.

In this new reality, is it still really preferable to respond by force? Do other less costly and more productive options exist? What about using communication to exercise influence in order to change the terrorists' thinking and behavior?

It is undoubtedly difficult for us to accept the idea of negotiating with terrorists, especially ones who engage in the more extreme acts with which we have become familiar in recent years. The epitome of this frustration came in September 2004 when a group of Chechen and Ingush militants seized a school and took over 1,200 hostages—many of them young school children—and rigged the building with explosives. The world's first reaction to the news of the Beslan siege was to declare: "you can't negotiate with people who could do such a thing." It is precisely one of the reasons why we have selected Beslan as an important case study for this book, because even in the most extreme cases, effective negotiation is much more useful a strategy than most people think.

The Beslan school hostage crises was an unprecedented terrorist attack, not only in lethality (331 people killed, 176 of them children), but also in scale and targeting. It was not only the largest ever terrorist takeover of a school,[2] but also the third deadliest terrorist attack in world history. Consider the setup:

- more than 1,200 hostages, most of them children;
- a team of some fifty to seventy well-trained hostage takers strategically positioned around the school and apparently ready to die;
- unconditional demands that seemed impossible to meet;
- 127 explosive devices set up around the school that could be activated with a single button;
- security cameras installed by the terrorists around the school to monitor all entrances;
- gas masks and two sentry dogs in place to help detect and counter a possible use of incapacitating gas;
- twenty-one hostages already executed and a dozen more killed during the initial takeover;
- the hostages inside suffering from immense heat exhaustion and lack of fluids; and
- outside, a group of angry parents armed with guns, threatening to shoot the rescue team members if they attempt to storm the school.

Quite simply, this was a nightmare scenario that would present an unprecedented challenge for *any* response team in *any* country in the world. Ominously, there are indications that such incidents may be on the rise in the future. Firstly, footage filmed in al Qaida training camps in Afghanistan has captured the group's recruits training in the urban setting for various types of operations, including hostage taking. And while al Qaida's signature modus operandi has so far focused almost exclusively on high-casualty synchronized suicide bombings, some of al Qaida's Internet sites have recently featured calls on the mujahideen to place a greater emphasis on hostage-taking operations.[3] In addition, globally distributed terrorist manuals suggest that our adversaries have been taking notes and have undergone a considerable learning curve from past barricade hostage incidents such as Beslan. For instance, the tenth issue of al Qaida's online manual Camp *al Battar*, features a highly analytical guide to hostage taking written by the late Abdul Aziz al Muqrin, the former leader of al Qaida in Saudi Arabia. In this manual al Muqrin provides detailed instructions on every aspect of carrying out a high profile barricade hostage incident, from the selection of team members and their training to treatment of hostages and conduct of negotiations. The *al Battar* manual as well as recent hostage crises such as the Moscow theater, Beslan school, or the Oasis residential compound in Khobar, Saudi Arabia, are a clear indication that barricade hostage taking will henceforth entail a much greater willingness to execute hostages, will feature large teams of willing-to-die hostage takers who will have the capability to effectively repel a possible rescue operation, and who will also have detailed knowledge of the hostage negotiation and rescue teams' "playbook." If we are to keep up with the challenge, we must also learn from lessons of past attacks and adjust our response strategies accordingly.

From the first glance, it is obvious that we are not prepared. While there are many trained crisis negotiators around the world, only very few of them have ever had contact with a terrorist hostage-taking incident. This is especially true in regard to the terrorists of the "new" breed, who have become less discriminate, more lethal, and better prepared. Further, many of the paradigms and presumptions upon which the traditional practice of hostage negotiation is based, simply do not reflect the reality of Beslan-type incidents. That being said, it must be acknowledged that some of the world's top hostage negotiation units[4] have been quick to respond to this challenge by pioneering new efforts to increase the overall capability of negotiators to deal with "new terrorist" incidents. Nevertheless, there is still an urgent need to educate the larger crisis negotiators' community about the dynamics of such incidents, and perhaps even more importantly, to increase the awareness among decision makers of the advantages and possibilities of the negotiation approach in managing such cases. It is our hope that this book can contribute to this important effort.

## ABOUT THIS BOOK

Historically, terrorists have utilized three main types of hostage incidents: barricade hostage attacks, kidnappings, and air/land/sea hijackings. The major difference between these scenarios is that unlike in barricade incidents, where the hostage takers are surrounded in an enclosed area, the location of the hostages and their captors in kidnappings is unknown. Air/land/sea hijackings are then a combination of the two scenarios, in the sense that the capturing of a vehicle—especially an airplane—provides the terrorists with a mobile platform.

The fact that kidnappers are not effectively cordoned off to an enclosed area and threatened with a violent resolution, results in considerable differences in how these incidents are handled.[5] While in kidnapping cases the authorities tend to perceive their position to be one of having no choice but to negotiate, the possibility of rescuing the hostages by force in barricade scenarios creates the dilemma of having to choose between unattractive options of either audaciously risking the hostages' lives, or being seen as legitimizing the terrorists by talking to them. It is specifically this dilemma that makes barricade hostage crises so threatening to governments, and thus highly attractive to terrorists. This is also one of the main reasons for why this book will specifically target barricade hostage incidents, in which hostage takers are situated along with their captives in a known location, in a territory under government control. This specific focus on barricade scenarios does not mean, of course, that many of the principles outlined in this book are not applicable to kidnappings as well. But the key reason behind our specific focus on barricade hostage crises is their unique aptitude to put governments in the existential position of having to act decisively in the face of acute pressure, highly unattractive options, incomplete information, tremendous stakes, and intense public scrutiny. In other words, the way a government handles a barricade hostage crises can have a direct impact on its very survival.

Built on nearly forty years of historical experience, crisis negotiation protocols for managing barricade hostage incidents are well established, and their standard application has, over the years, yielded a staggering 95 percent success rate.[6] However, the fact that the lessons and paradigms upon which these procedures are based draw mainly on the lessons of nonideological incidents involving poorly armed individuals without a premeditated plan, results in a situation where the mechanical application of standardized guidelines to incidents involving the "new terrorists" is likely to yield undesirable outcomes.

Regrettably, there is a common tendency in law enforcement and military organizations to resist change, and to resort to a rigid application of established rules and procedures, even in cases where these were never intended to be more than general guidelines. Ironically, even the negotiation practice, which places great emphasis on creativity and on thinking out of the box, has in this rigid setting been impacted by the common tendency to treat crisis negotiation manuals collectively as the "bible," essentially leading to the emergence of another "box" outside of which crisis managers do not dare to step. And while the standardized approach of "dos" and "don'ts" has been strikingly effective in routine situations for which abundant experiences exist, the historical rarity of incidents involving the "new terrorists" leaves us vulnerable and unprepared to deal with these largely untested hostage scenarios.

In recognition of this deficiency, the purpose of this book is to explore in detail the distinct dynamics of "new terrorist" barricade hostage incidents, with the objective of drawing lessons and generating guidelines that will aid negotiators in managing such incidents in the future. This will be achieved in a three-step process. Firstly, the book will outline some of the key characteristics of the phenomenon known as "new terrorism," followed by an analysis of the likely impact of these characteristics on future hostage incidents. Secondly, the book will explore several case studies that have carried some of the core characteristics of this phenomenon—such as a high level of preparation for the attack, highly absolutist or religious rhetoric on behalf of the perpetrators, credible suicidal posture, and the willingness to kill hostages at deadlines or during a rescue attempt—in order to test the applicability of standard crisis negotiation approaches and analytical tools to such incidents, and to examine whether the assumptions made about this "new terrorist" model indeed reflect the reality. In the course of assessing the case studies, particular attention will be devoted to an analysis of the events that had taken place in terms of negotiability, in an attempt to provide an analytical perspective on the possible alternatives that were available to the respective authorities in charge as the crises progressed. A critical inquiry into recent historical incidents is especially important, as lessons learned from past hostage crises are an invaluable tool in developing future response frameworks. The final portion of this book will critically reassess the contemporary crisis negotiation guidelines and assessment tools, with a specific focus on their (in)applicability to barricade hostage incidents involving the "new terrorists." The book will conclude by offering some alternative guidelines and suggestions.

Many of the historical cases that will be critically evaluated throughout this book had ended tragically, and it is thus perhaps not surprising that our commentary is sometimes highly critical of the respective authorities that were in charge. We should emphasize here, however, that our focus on pinpointing specific mistakes and failures is not motivated by the desire to ostracize the respective decision makers and responders for incompetence, but rather to facilitate an effective learning process which we could all benefit from in the future. We fully recognize the fact that the disastrous results were in some cases caused by imperfect decisions based on the incomplete information, and that much of the useful detail that we have at our disposal today (i.e., specific conversations that took place between the hostages and hostage takers) was simply unavailable to the decision makers at the time of the crisis. That being said, in order to prevent unnecessary loss of life in the future, we have the obligation to critically evaluate our past response strategies and to ask ourselves how things could have been done differently to achieve a better outcome.

Learning from past failures is not always easy, given the fact that official versions of hostage ordeals are frequently inspired less by actual events and more by the authorities' need to justify their actions in order to minimize the negative fallout from their own mishandling of the given crisis. Especially in the aftermath of high profile hostage standoffs that result in a large number of casualties among the hostages, there is a tendency to engage in a bipolar discourse about the legitimacy of the governments' response to the incident. And while this tendency to justify the respective course of action is understandable at the political level, the authorities' frequent maneuvering of facts to fit this purpose does more than protect individuals; it effectively inhibits the possibility of learning from mistakes, thus brining about their likely repetition in the future.

Politically motivated maneuvering of facts has been one of the reasons why despite their global notoriety, both Moscow theatre and Beslan school incidents still remain a widely misunderstood phenomenon. Ominously, we have witnessed that the same common misperceptions about these incidents that dominate the "open source" arena extend to the "classified" world as well, and that even some of the most renowned crisis response units around the world are essentially drawing the wrong lessons from these case studies simply because of ignorance of crucial details. Understanding the fine points is, of course, essential to any analysis of barricade hostage crises, as even small and seemingly insignificant details can provide a crucial piece of the puzzle that has the capacity to completely change our perspective with regard to the prospects of a negotiated outcome. For instance, a single interaction of a hostage taker with a hostage can provide invaluable insights into the acuteness of the terrorists' willingness to kill hostages in cold blood, the authenticity of their suicidal posture, or the sincerity of their negotiation approach. Not infrequently is it the case that incidents, which in a retrospective analysis of official versions would clearly be diagnosed as "nonnegotiable," actually start appearing in a very different light once more details begin to emerge.

Given the importance of specifics to the overall analysis of negotiability of hostage incidents, meticulous attention to detail constitutes one of the main strengths of this book. The vast majority of the smaller case studies discussed here are based on a comprehensive review of available open source accounts supplemented by interviews with actors directly involved in the attack, and further checked for accuracy by individuals involved in the respective investigation. The Moscow theater and Beslan school hostage crises are then based on exhaustive open source research in three languages, examination of thousands of pages of witness testimonies and court transcripts, analysis of available video footage, and extensive field research in Moscow, Beslan, Chechnya, and Ingushetia, including the inspection of the target locations and dozens of detailed interviews with hostages, eye-witnesses, negotiators, investigators, and relatives and friends of some of the perpetrators. The sheer amount of data collected in this massive effort has made it impossible to include all of the fascinating details of both crises in this book. Instead, only information that was somehow relevant to our analysis of the negotiations will be featured here.

Despite being described as one of this book's strengths, the importance of detail to the overall analysis of negotiability of hostage incidents also accounts for one of its greatest limitations, stemming from the fact that most available accounts of practically any hostage crisis differ significantly in their description of virtually every aspect of the given incident. This is frequently further complicated by government secrecy, vested interests, media censorship, as well as the fact that even eyewitness accounts are often contradictory, and tend to further mutate over time. Despite our efforts to ensure the reliability of witness testimonies by conducting a second wave of interviews six months after the first round, some details will inevitably remain disputed, inhibiting our ability to determine some aspects of the case studies at hand with absolute certainty. For the sake of completeness, alternative interpretations of the discussed events or our comments on uncertainty of certain pieces of information are included as endnotes. For a complete picture, it is important to pay particular attention to these.

This book will be organized in the following manner. Chapter 1 will outline the characteristics of the "new terrorism" with the specific goal of identifying the ways through which this phenomenon is likely to influence the blueprint and conduct of future barricade hostage crises. Chapter 2 will then survey several historical case studies which carried many of the characteristics of this model, in order to draw lessons with regard to the applicability of the traditional crisis negotiation approaches to such incidents. Further, this chapter will also include several more recent instances of terrorist operations and plans that have been alleged to have a barricade hostage component, and will provide an analysis of al Qaida's instructional manual on hostage-taking operations. Chapters 3 will then reconstruct and analyze in detail the first of the two most prominent examples of "new terrorist" hostage operations—the Moscow theatre crisis. The next chapter will subsequently analyze the ideological, operational, and strategic evolution of the Riyadus-Salikhin Suicide Battalion (RAS) that took place in the Moscow theatre incident aftermath, with the goal of demonstrating the dynamic nature of the terrorist group's strategic thinking and operational planning based on past experiences, and shifting strategic goals and objectives. Specific attention will be devoted to the developments in RAS' strategic mind-set that carried lessons and implications vital to the management of the Beslan attack. Chapter 5 will then analyze the myths and facts of the Beslan school hostage crisis, with the clear purpose of identifying the successes and failures of the negotiation approach. And finally, Chapter 6 will bring together the lessons of the case studies surveyed in this book, by identifying specific limitations of the "old-school" crisis negotiation manuals, and by offering alternative negotiation guidelines and approaches for dealing with hostage crises involving the "new terrorists."

# Chapter 1

## "New Terrorism" and the Dynamics of Barricade Hostage Crises

Throughout history, barricade hostage incidents have always constituted one of the most influential terrorist tactics. The live on-the-scene broadcasts, minute-by-minute updates, dramatic scenes featuring hostage pleas and terrorist threats, and the possibility of instantaneous forceful resolution tend to keep the viewers up on their toes. Further, the reality-show-like nature of the coverage, along with the opportunity for the terrorists fully to explain their grievances, are factors that usually succeed in generating a wide public debate about the moral dilemmas involved in the options available to the government. From the media perspective, barricade hostage incidents provide probably the best advertisement and propaganda benefits of any terror tactic, which is the main reason why the majority of historically groundbreaking terrorist events have involved this component.[1] In addition, from a strategic perspective, barricade hostage crises constitute a direct challenge to national governments by forcing them to choose among unattractive options. With the rare exception of extremely successful rescue operations such as Entebbe, Mogadishu, or Lima, governments are practically *always* criticized for their response, either for "giving in" to the terrorists, thus encouraging similar acts in the future, or for storming the location and thus being held responsible for any casualties among the hostages. In short, barricade hostage crises provide terrorists with an extremely effective tool directly to challenge the very legitimacy of their enemies.

On the downside, barricade and hijack cases are high-risk operations in which the outcome is never certain and the safety of the hostage takers is under constant threat—only the reluctance to risk the lives of the hostages is there to keep the security forces from storming the location and killing the terrorists. Aware of this disadvantageous position, terrorists traditionally attempt to compensate by making the assault as difficult as possible by booby-trapping the entrances to the location as well as by the repeated declaration of their determination to die during the incident.

Another variant of the barricade hostage crises scenario are skyjackings, which on top of the benefits outlined above carry several additional advantages. Firstly, the ability of hijackers to relocate from the site where they are surrounded by security forces to a friendly territory due to occupying a mobile platform allows the hijackers to deny threat level to the government, thereby strengthening their own bargaining position.[2] Secondly, the existence of national airlines has traditionally provided terrorists with a highly symbolic target, which had the capacity to speak for itself with regards to the message the terrorists were trying to convey. Thirdly, the hijacking of an airplane was, until recently, achievable with a minimum amount of force, as documented by the fact that successful hijack weapons have included items such as razor blades, colored water, sharpened toothbrushes, colon bottles, ropes, dining knives, and cigarette lighters. Since the airplane at a high altitude can easily be crashed killing everyone on board, gaining control over it gives terrorist threats considerable credibility. Furthermore, the fact that the aircraft is several thousand meters above ground eliminates the need for concern regarding potential hostage escapes or the threat of an immediate rescue operation. On the downside, the flying aircraft needs periodic refueling which can effectively be refused by denying landing rights via the blockage of runways. This is why skyjacking requires a greater determination to kill and die during the incident than any other type of hostage event. Also, during refueling stops the plane is vulnerable to government action, which usually consists of piercing the aircraft tires via sniper fire, effectively transforming the incident into a barricade scenario. Thus, unless the terrorists can relocate to a friendly country, the incident will eventually come to an ending identical to that of a barricade hostage crises.

In recent years, terrorist hostage takings have experienced several concurring developments. The first general trend has been the rising number of international kidnappings associated with the decline of state sponsorship of terrorism since the end of the Cold War, which has forced many violent organizations driven by a political agenda to adapt to self-financing. Kidnappings for ransom then became one important source of income. In contrast, barricade hostage takings and skyjackings, which have not been incorporated into the financial infrastructure of most terrorist groups, have in recent years witnessed a declining trend. Some of the reasons behind this development have also been of a practical nature, such as the implementation of security enhancements at embassies and airports, several successful high-profile hostage rescue raids, the increasingly tougher stance of many governments on the issue of granting concessions to terrorists,[3] as well as the declining willingness of potential hostages to cooperate with their captors on hijacked flights in the aftermath of 9-11.[4]

But arguably an even more important reason behind this shift in operational preferences of terrorist organizations has been the emergence of the so-called "new terrorism." There are several key characteristics that make the global rise of this phenomenon an unprecedented challenge, especially in the context of mass casualty attacks. These characteristics will be discussed in the upcoming pages, followed by an analysis of the impact of the "new terrorism" on the future of terrorist barricade hostage incidents.

## THE "NEW TERRORISM"

Terrorism as a form of political violence is as old as mankind itself. But despite the fact that the phenomenon by definition involves killing and destruction, most terrorists have traditionally practiced a considerable level of restraint on their violent activities. Traditional terrorists had not necessarily been interested in killing a lot of people, but rather in spreading fear among the general population by killing relatively few. In this respect, perhaps the best definition of terrorism is the ancient Chinese proverb "kill one, frighten ten thousand," or alternatively, renowned terrorism scholar Brian Jenkins' observation that "terrorists want a lot of people watching, not a lot of people dead."[5] The "old terrorists" typically showed little interest in indiscriminate killing of innocents on a large scale, as such action was seen as potentially counterproductive with regards to attracting popular support—an essential component of the fulfillment of traditional terrorist goals, such as the creation of an independent homeland or the implementation of social justice norms within the targeted state. In light of this dual objective, the ability of barricade hostage incidents to attract worldwide attention while at the same time avoiding the potentially politically damaging act of murdering innocents has turned barricade hostage takings into an ultimate terror tactic.

While this traditional interpretation of terrorism has been the consensus for decades, many authors have observed that over the past twenty years, the phenomenon has experienced disturbing new trends. First, there seems to be a steady trend toward an increasing lethality of terrorist acts. While the deadliest incidents prior to the 1980s involved "only" dozens of fatalities, in the 1980s and 1990s the most lethal attacks were counted in the hundreds, and in the new millennium the plateau has reached to the thousands for the first time in history. The process of increasing lethality of terrorist operations has been accelerated even more by the events of 9-11, mainly because of the confirmation that even some acts of mass-casualty terrorism can receive enthusiastic endorsement on behalf of the perpetrating group's constituency. So, while in the fifty years prior to 9-11, only fourteen terrorist operations had resulted in more than hundred fatalities, in just five years since this date this number has more than doubled. Quite simply, terrorism has become a significantly more lethal phenomenon than in the past.

There are several reasons behind this trend. One is the terrorists' natural tendency to "out-do" their previous attacks, stimulated by the perception that if the present level of violence has thus far failed to succeed in forcing a radical change in the status quo, the campaign needs to be intensified. Another reason is the fact that no matter how horrific a terrorist campaign might be, the intended audiences become desensitized to the current level of violence over time, forcing the terrorists to escalate further in order to maintain or heighten the atmosphere of panic and fear among the general population, and to stay in the spotlight. An escalation in terrorist violence is also sometimes stimulated by the actions of other organizations with which the given group competes for power or popularity. Another reason for the gradual escalation of overall terrorist violence over time has been the formation of new groups. Upon emergence, new violent organizations usually do not undergo the full step-by-step process of radicalization, but rather pick up at the level of violence where other organizations active in the same struggle have left off. Alternatively, many existing organizations can give birth to new formations through the process of splintering, which usually results in the new entity being more radical and more violent than the core group.

Possibly the most important reason behind the increasing lethality of the "new terrorism," however, has been the rise of violent activities motivated by a religious imperative, as opposed to the still lethal but arguably more comprehensible motives of ethnic nationalism and revolutionary ideologies. Bruce Hoffman, one of the most influential scholars on the subject, has identified the rise of religious motivation among terrorist groups as the primary cause of the higher number of casualties per attack in the modern era, by pinpointing several core characteristics of religious terrorists that allegedly set them aside from their secular counterparts.[6] These have included mainly the radically different value systems of religious terrorists, the different mechanisms of legitimization and justification, concepts of morality, mechanisms of victim dehumanization, and an overall worldview. According to Hoffman, the aims of "religious political" terrorists are defined as the attainment of the greatest possible benefits for themselves and for their coreligionists only, as opposed to the indiscriminately utilitarian goals of secular terrorists.[7] This allegedly further widens the gap between ends and means; "where the secular terrorist sees violence primarily as a means to an end, the religious terrorist tends to view violence as an end in itself."[8] Another implication defined by Hoffman is that religious and secular terrorists also differ significantly in their constituencies:

> Whereas secular terrorists attempt to appeal to a constituency variously composed of actual and potential sympathizers, members of communities they purport to "defend," of the aggrieved people they claim to speak for;

religious terrorists are at once activists and constituents engaged in what they regard as a "total war." They execute their terrorist acts for no audience but themselves. Thus, the restraints on violence that are imposed on secular terrorists by the desire to appeal to a tacitly supportive or uncommitted constituency are not relevant to the religious terrorists. Moreover, this absence of a constituency in the secular terrorist sense leads to a sanctioning of almost limitless violence against a virtually open-ended category of targets—that is, anyone who is not a member of the terrorist's religion or religious sect.[9]

Another closely related characteristic of the "new terrorism" has been the perpetrators' declining political sensitivity in relation to the perceived adverse effects of indiscriminate violence, which has led to the expansion of targeting categories to include targets that had traditionally been considered "off-limits." Crucial in this regard has been the "new terrorists'" desire to "share their pain" and to make a target group "feel"—or otherwise appreciate—the consequences of a war for which their government may be responsible, but from which many in the general population are detached. Some groups see themselves as representing populations that are—or feel—brutalized as part of a larger war, and they desire to punish those they see as responsible. While this logic is endemic to terrorism in general, some of the "new terrorist" groups are now including even the most innocent segments of the general public in the list of those responsible for making war on them, considering them "legitimate" targets.

Besides the increasing lethality and reduction of "taboo" targets, the third important component of the "new terrorism" has been the terrorists' greatly enhanced striking power,[10] caused primarily by the "democratization of destruction," a by-product of the proliferation of advanced technologies. Possibly most influential in this regard has been the boom of the Internet in the mid-1990s, which became instrumental in significantly aiding the efficiency of terrorist operations. This has included the facilitation of easy access to astonishing quantities of instructional material that enables the terrorists to acquire useful skills, such as knowledge on how to manufacture explosives and poisons from dual use materials, or the specifications of buildings, power plants, and other potential targets. Information technologies have also aided the "new terrorists" in studying their enemies' investigative capabilities and operational procedures, and thus providing the aptitude to identify and exploit potential weaknesses and vulnerabilities. As a result, terrorists now have a greater capacity to organize sophisticated operations, adding yet another component to the list of factors responsible for the growing lethality of terrorist violence.

The developments in communications technologies are also closely associated with the fourth critical characteristic of the "new terrorism"—the transformation of terrorist organizational structures from the hierarchical, political party-like formations into more loosely knit networks of cells operating without any real central command.[11] The characteristics of the worldwide network we know as al Qaida, or the concept of "leaderless resistance" embraced by the North American Christian Identity and animal rights movements, provide good examples of this phenomenon, which in many ways represents one of the downsides of globalization. Today's terrorists can easily communicate via e-mail, using commercial encryption programs and coded messages posted on various Web sites and chat rooms, a fact that has resulted in an unprecedented international reach of terrorist networks and the proliferation of operational know-how among groups through knowledge sharing. Further, the sheer size of traffic on the Internet makes monitoring such communications difficult, and even in the event of tracing a sender's IP address, the terrorists' practice of using public computers and Internet cafés makes their subsequent identification and capture nearly impossible. Overall, the advancements in communication technologies have made the contact between groups safer, faster, and more efficient. And finally, the proliferation of the Internet has also led to the rise of the so-called "home grown terrorism," or the emergence of active *jihadi* terrorist networks in the West. This opening up of ranks of terrorist organizations to volunteers that have never gone through actual training or formal organizational acceptance has also contributed to the increasing lethality of the "new terrorism." Today one can theoretically become a "member" of a terrorist group simply by embracing its ideology, gaining operational knowledge through manuals accessed from the Internet, and carrying out attacks in the group's name via its signature modus operandi and general targeting guidelines. Since members of such ad hoc groups operate without any moderating influences from the more politically aware central leadership, this decentralization of decision making has also contributed to the deterioration of restraint that traditionally played a role in the planning of spectacular attacks.

The final component of the "new terrorism" has been the striking emphasis on suicide operations, which constitute the most rapidly proliferating terrorist tactic in the world today. Since the commencement of this practice among modern terrorist groups in 1981, the phenomenon has spread around the world at an unprecedented pace—at the time of writing in 2007, there have been over 900 suicide bombings carried out by at least 30 organizations in 31 different countries. Significantly, more than 70 percent of these attacks have taken place in the five years since 9-11. What makes suicide operations so popular? The first obvious benefit of suicide operations is their tactical advantages over other forms of attack, which results in their remarkable effectiveness in terms of delivering a high number of casualties. According to data from the Rand Corporation's chronology of international terrorism incidents, suicide attacks kill on average four times as many people as other terrorist acts.[12] But perhaps even more important than these tactical advantages is the message such operations convey. The first target audience is the international community, which is shocked by the images of desperation and commitment to sacrifice. Further, the seeming irrationality of suicidal operations is useful in attracting extensive media coverage. In turn, that coverage may prompt popular, indeed even global, interest in understanding and investigating the motivations behind such an act. As a consequence, the terrorists' cause might be perceived as just, as people question how their plight—and that of the constituency they represent—could be so humiliating and so unacceptable that for them death becomes preferable to life under such conditions. The second target audience is the enemy, who is supposed to embrace the message that since the terrorists are not afraid of death they cannot be deterred; the only way to end their campaign of violence then is to concede to their demands and objectives. Finally, since suicide operations tend to set an organizational precedent leading to the establishment of a culture of martyrdom in which death on behalf of the group becomes an attractive proposition, organizations that initiate such a campaign typically do not have to worry about a lack of future volunteers for such operations.

## IMPLICATIONS FOR HOSTAGE CRISES

There are several key implications of the rise of the "new terrorism" for future trends in barricade hostage incidents. As mentioned earlier, in the era of traditional terrorism these incidents constituted one of the most influential terrorist tactics, mainly due to their spectacular nature and curiosity-inspiring "reality show" effect. The ability of barricade hostage incidents to attract wide international attention provided groups with not only a highly suitable platform for the expression of grievances, but also the capacity to create pressure on the enemy government without necessarily being associated with the potentially politically damaging act of killing civilians. Quite simply, the idea of taking hostages and placing the responsibility for their fate into the hands of the opposing government was a highly effective tool in attracting international sympathy for the terrorists' cause.

With the rise of the "new terrorism," barricade hostage incidents seem to have assumed a much less prominent role in the tactical repertoire of terrorist organizations. One of the main reasons behind this development has been the "new terrorists'" increasing emphasis on lethality, which has led to the deflation of perceived benefits of casualty-less operations. In short, with the almost universal causal relationship between the number of fatalities and media attention, barricade hostage incidents in which no one dies have become less attractive. An even more crucial factor has been the changing nature of the "new terrorists'" goals associated with the religious nature of their ideologies. As today's terrorists allegedly place less emphasis on politics in favor of religion, they presumably find themselves in less of a position to issue realistically accomplishable demands. This fact in combination with the allegedly decreasing dependence on "earthly" constituencies as well as the absence of an ambition to take responsibility for governance upon eventual victory of the struggle has decreased the "new terrorists'" restraint associated with political considerations that characterized their secular counterparts in the past. According to this argument, the rise of the "new terrorism," characterized by the tendency to "view violence not as a means to an end but an end in itself," has logically led to the global decline of *instrumental* terrorist tactics such as barricade hostage taking.

While this declining importance of such incidents may lead us to the conclusion that these operations no longer constitute a major threat, hostage crises such as in Beslan or the Moscow theatre, as well as *jihadi* manuals such as al Qaida's "Camp *al Battar* Magazine," indicate that we might be witnessing a comeback of this tactic with a "new" face. Unlike traditional terrorists who have rarely resorted to killing hostages, the "new terrorists'" increasing emphasis on killing, along with the decline in political constraints accompanied by the power of religious sanction, will likely lead to a greater willingness of the "new terrorists" to execute their captives. In addition, the proliferation of the culture and ideology of martyrdom is in all probability going to lead to the perpetrators' assumption of a more unconditional suicidal posture, presenting a situation in which the terrorists will possess an attractive best alternative to a negotiated agreement (BATNA), increasing their leverage. Further, the availability of modern communication technologies and increasingly entangled networks among terrorist formations is likely going to result in the terrorists' prior knowledge of the operational "playbooks" of hostage negotiation and response teams, which will strengthen the terrorists' negotiating position even more.

In addition, the increased ability to learn from past experiences of groups in other countries, as well as the ability to conduct more detailed casing and analysis of possible targets, will probably lead to the terrorists' greater preparation aimed at eliminating any possibility of a successful rescue operation. Such measures will likely take the form of employment of large teams of hostage takers armed well enough to repel a possible raid, strategic positioning of snipers, use of surveillance technology and booby traps to monitor and obstruct possible entry points, and the deployment of potent explosive devices among the hostages to make any attempt to rescue them by force as costly in terms of loss of human life as possible. By disrupting the authorities' monopoly on destruction, the terrorists will decrease the attractiveness of their opponents' BATNA, resulting in an even greater strengthening of their own bargaining position.

In addition to shifting the traditional balance of power in the hostage takers' favor, the proliferation of communication technologies will probably also strongly influence the very process of negotiation itself. Firstly, the terrorists' immediate ability to consult with their leadership via mobile phone will deprive the negotiators of much of the influence they typically strive to gain by disrupting the hostage takers' chain of authority, thus forcing the perpetrators to make their own decisions in isolation from their leadership. And while terrorist hostage takers of the past had often gone on operations with minimal instructions from their leaders, and thus frequently found themselves in a position of having to make decisions on their own, today's technological reality that gives the terrorists immediate access to their superiors has radically altered the situation. Since the leaders—unlike the hostage takers—will not be confined to the location under a constant threat of immediate forceful resolution, the processes that form the baseline foundation of the contemporary practice of crisis negotiation will not take place, making the task of lowering the terrorists' expectations much more difficult. Further, the availability of surveillance technology that can potentially aid the terrorists in eavesdropping on communication channels used by the security forces will also introduce new challenges. And finally, the global reach of the Internet will present the terrorists with an independent communication channel to the media and the outside world, which will allow them to present their own version of events along with documentary evidence, making censorship and media manipulation a much less effective or even counterproductive incident management tool than in the past. Moreover, in such a situation, providing access to the media as a minor concession used to initiate trades will also become a decreasingly important instrument in the negotiators' toolbox.

As is clear from this breakdown, barricade hostage crises in the age of the "new terrorism" are going to present us with many new challenges. It is obvious that we are not adequately prepared for this reality. While there are many trained crisis negotiators around the world, only very few of them have ever had contact with a *terrorist* hostage-taking incident. Similarly, with the exception of some of the world's top hostage negotiation bodies such as the FBI Critical Incident Negotiation Team, Scotland Yard's Crisis and Hostage Negotiation Unit, and New South Wales Police Negotiation Unit, the majority of today's crisis negotiators—not to mention operational commanders and political leaders—are not prepared to handle crises involving issues such as ideology, religion, or the differing set of objectives and mind-sets of ideological hostage takers.[13] This is especially true in reference to terrorists of the "new" breed, who have become less discriminate, more lethal, better prepared, and more operationally savvy. Unfortunately, the consensus within the larger crisis negotiators' community has been that terrorist cases are not substantially different

1. The use of time to increase basic needs, making it more likely that the subject will exchange a hostage for some basic need.
2. The use of time to collect intelligence on the subject that will help develop a trade.
3. The use of time to reduce the subject's expectation of getting what he wants.
4. Trades can be made for food, drink, transportation, and money.
5. Trades cannot be made for weapons or the exchange of hostages.
6. The boss does not negotiate.
7. Start bidding high to give yourself room to negotiate (ask for all the hostages).
8. Quid pro quo: get something for everything.
9. Never draw attention to the hostages; it gives the subject too much bargaining power.
10. Manipulate anxiety levels by cutting off power, gas, water, etc.

**Figure 1.1   FBI Guidelines for Crisis Negotiations**

*Source:* McMains and Mullins, *Crisis Negotiations: Managing Critical Incidents and Hostage Situations in Law Enforcement and Corrections* (Dayton, OH: Anderson Publishing, 2nd ed., 2001) p. 37.

from any other hostage incident, and that the "current set of negotiation strategies and tactics available to law enforcement provides viable alternatives from which to choose, whatever the motivation for the taking of hostages."[14] But while this still holds true with regards to the basic principles of barricade crisis negotiations summarized in Figure 1.1, many other paradigms and presumptions upon which the contemporary practice of hostage negotiation is based no longer apply in the cases involving the "new terrorists." As a result, a mechanical application of traditional approaches and diagnostic tools to these incidents could potentially lead to disastrous consequences. Some of the differing characteristics of hostage crises involving the "new terrorists" will be explored in the following section.

## NEW CHALLENGES

Although the practice of crisis negotiation was originally designed to fit hostage situations involving political extremists, over the years its focus has gradually shifted in favor of non-terrorist incidents. In fact, only about 18 percent of situations to which crisis negotiation teams are called today involve any hostages at all, with the vast majority of those cases consisting of interrupted criminals, domestic violence cases, "suicides-by-cop," and mentally disturbed individuals. The one distinct element that such cases have in common is the low level of preparation on behalf of the hostage takers. This works in favor of the negotiator, as an unprepared counterpart is more likely to question his or her decision to take hostages with passing time. In contrast to this scenario, one of the challenges of negotiating with politically or religiously motivated hostage takers is the fact that they have prepared their actions in advance, and that the individuals involved have actually chosen to be in the given situation. Another factor working against the negotiator is the frequent availability of more than one individual to handle the communications, which presents an obstacle to the negotiator's ability to form a rapport with his or her counterpart during the crisis.

A further dynamic that makes the mechanical application of today's crisis negotiation framework to terrorist incidents precarious is the fact that up to 85 percent of today's barricade hostage takers are mentally disturbed individuals.[15] This has led to the increasing emphasis on "psychologization" of the negotiation practice, consisting of a tendency to assign individual hostage takers to one of the identified diagnostic categories (i.e., inadequate personalities, drug or alcohol users, antisocial personalities, paranoid schizophrenics, depressed individuals, etc.)[16] and to subsequently follow the specific negotiation guidelines attached to each category. And while the category of extremist hostage takers also exists, negotiators still maintain that they encounter "normal" people only rarely.[17]

In contrast to the average negotiators' experience of dealing primarily with psychologically deranged individuals, psychiatric enquiry into the field of terrorism has found no solid evidence of any psychological idiosyncrasy universally present among the terrorist population. In fact, some studies have even concluded that "the outstanding common characteristic of terrorists is their normality."[18] As a result of this finding, the contemporary emphasis on "psychologization" of hostage taker categories has many problems when applied to incidents involving the "new terrorists." For instance, the highly religious rhetoric used by the "new terrorists" lends itself to being psychologized along the lines of the anecdotal evidence used in crisis negotiation literature to draw a connection between heightened religious fervor and paranoid delusions.[19] This mechanical application would then lead to a completely unrealistic assessment of the subject as delusional, thus shifting the analytical emphasis from causes to symptoms.[20] Such an oversimplification of perpetrator motives will result in an incomplete picture with regards to the hostage takers' real interests, which in all likelihood will lead to the selection of a negotiation strategy that will not only have little chance of success, but will even possess the capacity to make the situation all the more volatile.

One successful way to deal with politically motivated incidents in the past has been for the negotiator to stress the widespread attention the perpetrators' cause had already received. Since publicity has usually been one of the main goals the terrorists strove to achieve in barricade hostage incidents, the captors could often be persuaded that they have succeeded in their mission, and that killing hostages would only hurt their cause in the eyes of the public.[21] Since most terrorist movements use the rhetoric of liberation from oppression and inhumane treatment, the same language could be used to reiterate the innocence and suffering of the hostages, in order to appeal to the moral beliefs of the captors. And while these standards were typically automatically deflected, their pronouncement still played an important role in the effort to humanize the victims to their captors as much as possible, in order to make cold-blooded execution of hostages psychologically more difficult.[22] The stressing of the attention the terrorists' cause had already achieved in combination with a guarantee of a free passage for the terrorists has historically been the most frequent formula for the negotiated resolution of politically inspired barricade incidents. Such outcome is sometimes called the "Bangkok Solution," referring to the 1972 incident in which members of the Black September took over the Israeli embassy in Thailand, but after nineteen hours of negotiations agreed to release their hostages and drop all other demands in return for safe passage out of the country.[23]

In the era of the "new terrorism," the situation will probably be much more complicated. Firstly, the terrorists' overt pronouncements of "love of death" and "desire for martyrdom" will make the question of a free passage a highly delicate matter, as such a proposal will likely be interpreted as an offensive second-guessing of the fighters' commitment to God, possibly only escalating the situation. Secondly, the terrorists' prior knowledge of the processes that typically make it difficult for hostage takers to kill in cold blood will possibly lead the terrorists to the conscious obstruction of these dynamics, which in combination with the advanced level of enemy dehumanization associated with religious sanction of their actions will almost certainly make the moral appeals on the terrorists' conscience unsuccessful. And thirdly, the alleged absence of a politically mindful constituency on behalf of the "new terrorists" will likely make the negotiation emphasis on the success associated with high level of publicity already achieved a much less persuasive argument. Overall, the management of barricade hostage crises involving the "new terrorists" will probably be even more challenging than the high-pressure terrorist standoffs of the past.

## THE PEOPLE INVOLVED

Some of the most influential researchers in the field of crisis negotiations have cited convincing anecdotal evidence debunking the myth that terrorists undergo extensive and detailed training for hostage-taking operations. In fact, these authors argued that terrorist hostage takers "are unsophisticated, uneducated, and ill-trained young men."[24] One of the possible reasons for this finding seems to be the fact that the people involved in organized hostage incidents tended to be fairly low in their organization's ranks since death or arrest of the perpetrators was a likely outcome, and most groups were reluctant to risk their senior operatives for such high-risk operations.[25] But while at the time of its writing in 1990 such an observation was certainly correct, today's reality no longer reflects this paradigm (as the respective authors would be the first ones to acknowledge). Still, even in 2006 some of the most influential figures in the field of crisis negotiation research and practice have maintained that "[terrorists] might have planned to take hostages, but do not have a clue about negotiating tactics or techniques."[26] The clear inapplicability of this conclusion to the era of the "new terrorism" will be demonstrated in the cases of the Moscow theatre and Beslan, as well as the al Qaida hostage-taking manual analyzed in Chapter 2. In fact, the superior preparation for a hostage-taking incident, which now includes detailed casing of the target, advanced infiltration, and a high level of knowledge of the crisis negotiation "playbook," is one of the key characteristics of the "new terrorist" hostage takers identified earlier. As a result, the common dismissal of terrorist hostage takers as unsophisticated is a highly dangerous proposition, which can lead to the underestimation of the threat. Negotiators must realize that the terrorists' advanced planning and common lack of authority to make autonomous decisions will make it a much more difficult task to convince the hostage takers to release the hostages and surrender. As a result, negotiators need to adjust their own expectations accordingly, in order to avoid escalating the situation by applying too much pressure too early.

## MEANS OF COMMUNICATION

Effective means of communication is the precondition of any successful negotiation. In barricade incidents, establishment of a line of communication is the first action that takes place after the perpetrators' location has been secured. In most incidents, negotiations are usually conducted through a direct phone line or via a field "throw telephone." The direct communication setting helps the negotiator in building rapport through which he or she tries to influence and later change the hostage takers' behavior.[27] It is the task of the negotiator to persuade the captors that they are in a no-win situation. As time elapses, the abductors' primary needs such as hunger or thirst tend to replace other, hierarchically lower sets of needs.[28] This opens up a wide range of opportunities for the negotiator to trade items such as food, water, or tobacco for the release of a hostage or some other favor on the part of the hostage taker. Elapsing time also helps in reducing the subject's expectations of having his or her demands fulfilled. From a tactical perspective, prolonging the incident also provides more time to gather intelligence and to prepare for an assault.

One of the key differences in dealing with barricade hostage incidents in the era of the "new terrorism" has to do with the aforementioned technological reality of the attack executioners' ability to consult with their leadership throughout the incident via mobile phone. This in many ways introduces a key obstruction to the currently established practice which relies on the prolonged isolation of the hostage takers from their organization in an attempt to weaken their sense of obligation to the group. Much like in the case of an interrogation of terrorists in jail, the isolation of hostage takers from their support system can decrease the subjects' resolve, thus increasing the influence of the negotiator.[29] However, today's terrorist hostage takers are likely to have constant contact with their support system throughout the incident, which will effectively negate this process. Under these circumstances the responders will need to take into consideration the executioners' representative identity and the fact that just like the negotiator, the terrorists answer not only to themselves but to a higher authority, which is not necessarily influenced by the pressures excreted at the crisis scene.

To respond effectively in this situation, the negotiators will need to expand the scope of their analysis past the subjects they are actually dealing with, to also include the organization on behalf of which the terrorists are acting. This is another area where the traditional approach to crisis negotiation is deficient, given its overwhelming focus on "individual identity" over "group identity."[30] In the "new terrorism" setting, it will be absolutely essential for the negotiators and decision makers to analyze the group's worldview, grievances, evolving strategic mind-set, leadership, and tactics, in order to correctly identify the underlying interests and goals of the particular hostage-taking incident from the perspective of both its planners as well as its executioners. In the absence of this analysis, responders may be lured into proceeding with a counterproductive course of action that will effectively fulfill the terrorists' hidden strategic goals.

## DIAGNOSTIC TOOLS

The "new terrorists'" likely knowledge of our response protocols and strategies is not the only aspect that will present dramatic new challenges. Even more important in this regard is the realization that some of the diagnostic tools traditionally applied to barricade hostage crises are unsuitable for analyzing incidents involving the "new terrorists." For example, Figure 1.2 summarizes the characteristics of a "negotiable incident," which are currently used by the various crisis negotiation bodies as the basic guideline for assessing the likelihood of success of the negotiation approach. Additional checklists and criteria are used as well. As we have seen in the analysis of the characteristics of the "new terrorism,"

---

1. The desire to live on the part of the hostage taker.
2. The threat of force by the police.
3. The hostage taker must present demands for release of hostages.
4. The negotiator must be viewed by the hostage taker as someone who can hurt but desires to help.
5. The negotiator needs time to develop trust with hostage takers.
6. The location must be contained and stabilized to support negotiations.
7. The hostage taker and negotiator must have a reliable means of communication, either by phone or face-to-face.
8. The negotiator must be able to 'deal' with the hostage taker who controls the hostages and makes the decisions.

---

**Figure 1.2   Characteristics of a negotiable hostage incident (FBI)**

*Source:* McMains and Mullins, *Crisis Negotiations: Managing Critical Incidents and Hostage Situations in Law Enforcement and Corrections* (Dayton, OH: Anderson Publishing, 2nd ed., 2001).

most of these conditions will be less applicable in future terrorist incidents, and numerous additional obstacles and indicators of volatility will also be present. Does this mean that any terrorist incident involving the "new terrorists" is universally nonnegotiable? Certainly not, since there is plenty of evidence to suggest that negotiation with political/religious hostage takers can be successful.[31] But ominously, in such cases, the contemporary checklists used to determine the negotiability of barricade hostage incidents, could quickly lead inexperienced decision makers to prematurely discard the chances of a negotiated settlement, setting into motion the decision to proceed with a violent resolution. From this point onward, negotiators would be moved into a supporting role tasked with stalling for time while the hostage rescue team prepares for the assault. One of the dangers of such a quick, mechanical analysis is the use of already incomplete information to further simplify the incident to fit a standardized typology, which in itself is based on past experiences that do not necessarily reflect the realities of this new scenario. Such an analysis would be fundamentally flawed, and would run a high risk of producing unwanted results. Moreover, experience has shown that once the decision to proceed with an assault has been taken, a point of no return is reached in which any subsequent successes in the negotiation process suggesting the possibility of a nonviolent resolution are typically ignored. As we will see in later chapters, such a decision can have tragic consequences due to the likely capability and possible intent of the "new terrorists" to make the storming as costly as possible in terms of loss of human life. In a situation like Beslan, how does one proceed with a rescue operation if there are more than 1,200 hostages inside, the opposition is ready for death, and has the capability to kill all hostages at will? Under such conditions, is a full breach really the preferable option, or even a plausible worst-case alternative? Do other, less volatile means exist? Probably yes, but in order for responders to be able to reach such a conclusion, their analytical toolbox needs to be critically reevaluated to reflect the experience of incidents involving the "new terrorists." This issue will be discussed in more detail in Chapter 6.

Similarly, we need to reevaluate the way we view the issue of terrorists' negotiating position and options. In most hostage crises, the options of barricade hostage takers are rather limited and their ability to force compliance is relatively weak. While the perceived position of power allows them to dictate demands and deadlines, very few tools are at hand for the hostage takers to enforce their prompt fulfillment. Once the deadline approaches, the perpetrators have only two options: let the deadline pass or carry out their threat and kill hostages. But in the traditional sense, this is essentially a "no-win" situation, as passing of the deadline weakens the perpetrators' leverage by exposing their possible reluctance to kill, while killing of hostages is likely to trigger a forceful resolution of the incident. The fact that the negotiator operates from the position of strength, due to being backed by security forces, is one of the key factors that make the current practice of crisis negotiations work. The hostage takers' knowledge that they face "assured destruction" in the event of hurting hostages ensures compliance, thus minimizing risks to hostages.

However, in the era of the "new terrorism" the strength of both parties' negotiation positions has been significantly altered. The first component of this changing dynamic is the increased destructive power on behalf of the terrorists, which in many ways removes the authorities' monopoly on a violent resolution. The "new terrorists'" high numbers and superior preparation and training result in a situation in which hostage takers actually have a viable chance of successfully repelling an assault or a rescue attempt. In the situation where rescue teams can no longer overcome their adversaries at will, the threat of a forceful resolution will be reduced significantly, thus strengthening the terrorists' negotiating position. In combination with the aforementioned greater readiness to die in the incident, and the overall decline in political sensitivity associated with killing innocents, this situation has essentially converted the barricade hostage scenario into a potential "win-win" situation for the terrorists. If the hostage takers achieve their demands they win. If the government troops storm the location and the terrorists are killed in the shootout (along with many hostages) then the outcome of dying a martyr's death is also perceived as a victory.

In contrast, the negotiator's position has been significantly weakened. With the removal of the immediate threat of a forceful resolution, the terrorists can effectively resort to executions of hostages without immediate sanction. This in combination with the terrorists' perceived religious blessing of their actions and the associated high level of dehumanization of their victims will again likely lead the terrorists to take advantage of this option and conduct pressure executions. How should we respond? The traditional theory still upheld by many hostage rescue teams worldwide holds that executions of hostages outside of the initial stages of a hostage incident provide "evidence of a deprived mind" on behalf of the hostage taker. Based on the rationale that since the captors are psychopaths who will kill again, some responders would conclude that negotiations do not have chance of resolving the incident, and the center of gravity would shift toward a (violent) tactical resolution.[32] But if it is clear that a rescue operation has a limited chance of success, and even if it does succeed, it will result in a very large number of hostage casualties, we must ask ourselves: Is it better to risk more deaths resulting from the rescue, or to continue negotiations? Does the execution of several hostages really constitute a reliable and absolute sign of nonnegotiability? What is there to be gained from dismissing an incident as nonnegotiable? On utilitarian grounds, decision makers need to ask themselves: Which approach can maximize the chance of a good outcome or at least result in the deaths of fewer people—storming of the location or further negotiations? All of these questions need to be analyzed and the premises upon which the traditional hostage rescue "playbooks" rest need to be reevaluated. This will be the objective of this book.

# Chapter 2

# THE CHANGING FACE OF THE THREAT

In the previous chapter we have identified the key characteristics of the "new terrorism" and discussed some of the challenges through which this phenomenon is likely to influence the dynamics of future terrorist hostage crises. In this regard, we have so far focused mainly on a hypothetical situation of what a barricade hostage incident involving the "new terrorists" might entail. In this chapter, we will explore several historical cases that carried some of the aforementioned characteristics of this model in order to survey what lessons can be learned, and to examine whether the assumptions made about this hypothetical model indeed reflect the reality. The main criterion for inclusion of the particular cases presented here is a combination of some of the characteristics of the "new terrorism," such as a high level of preparation for the attack, highly absolutist or religious rhetoric on behalf of the perpetrators, credible suicidal posture, and the willingness to kill hostages at deadlines or during a rescue attempt. Following the description and brief analysis of these historical cases, this chapter will also include several more recent instances of terrorist operations which have been alleged to have a barricade hostage component. Finally, this chapter will analyze al Qaida's instructional manual on hostage taking operations.

## KIRYAT SHMONA, MA'ALOT, HOTEL SAVOY

Probably the most influential historical incident that caught the imagination of the world with regard to the drama involved in a terrorist barricade hostage incident was the infamous Munich Massacre, in which eleven Israeli athletes were killed by members of the Black September Organization during the 1972 Olympic Games in Germany. Two of the hostages died during the initial assault, with the remaining nine killed by the terrorists during an incredibly botched rescue attempt at the Munich Airport.

This event was in many ways pivotal, not only due to its high media exposure, but also because of the virtually unprecedented willingness of the terrorists to go ahead with killing their hostages, albeit during a rescue operation. It was also this incident that shifted the focus of security services to exploring options for peaceful resolution of hostage crises, prompting the development of specialized hostage negotiation teams in many countries of the world.

Throughout the 1970s, additional Palestinian groups crossed the threshold of killing hostages during standoffs, especially after the 1973 defeat of Syria and Egypt in the Yom Kippur War and the associated intensifications of divisions and operational competition within the Palestinian camp. While Yasir Arafat's PLO and allied groups advocated a negotiated settlement with Israel, a block of rejectionist groups formed arguing for the struggle to continue. Among these groups was Ahmed Jibril's Popular Front for the Liberation of Palestine (PFLP-GC), which will always be remembered as one of the most spectacular terrorist groups in history. On April 11, 1974, only several days after Arafat appealed to all Palestinian groups to stop attacking Israel from Lebanese territory, three PFLP-GC terrorists entered Israel precisely via the Lebanese border and attacked an apartment complex in the border town of Kiryat Shmona.[1] Going from apartment to apartment, the attackers fired indiscriminately, killing eighteen people and wounding sixteen more. Following a brief standoff with the security forces, all three terrorists were killed. A PFLP-GC communiqué following the attack stated: "Our men carried out their instructions. They set off explosive belts they wore for the operation when the enemy stormed the building they were holding. They died along with their hostages."[2] What makes this attack interesting for the purposes of this book is that according to some sources the original plan was to take hostages at a nearby school and demand the release of dozens of Palestinian prisoners from Israeli jails. But since the school was unexpectedly closed due to the Passover holiday, the attackers then allegedly improvised and switched targets, perpetrating one of the most brutal attacks Israel has ever witnessed.[3]

Throughout 1974, the PFLP-GC was not the only Palestinian group to initiate hostage-taking operations with the aim of securing the release of Palestinian prisoners. On 15 May, three members of the Democratic Front for the Liberation of Palestine (DFLP) launched a similar raid in the town of Ma'alot, taking over the Netiv Meir elementary school where about a hundred teenage members of a quasi military organization *Nahal* were sleeping during their fieldtrip to the Golan Heights.[4] On their way to the target, the terrorists dressed in Israeli Defense Forces (IDF) uniforms first attacked a van killing two women, before raiding an apartment in Ma'alot and slaughtering its residents. Following this action the terrorists took over the school, killing three people in the process and immediately wiring the location with explosives.[5] On the next morning the terrorists released two hostages who were ill, and then sent out two more people with a list of twenty-six prisoners they demanded to be freed from Israeli jails. In the negotiations, the hostage takers specified that they wanted the prisoners to be flown to Damascus, where their release was to be verified by Romanian ambassador Ion Covaci and French ambassador Francis Hure. Following a confirmation of the prisoners' release conveyed by a public announcement containing a prearranged code word, the terrorists promised to free half of their hostages. The other half would then accompany the terrorists to an Arab capital in order to guarantee the terrorists' safe passage.[6] The hostage takers also stated that if the freedom of demanded prisoners was not confirmed by the two ambassadors by 6:00 P.M., they "would not be responsible for the consequences."[7] At 3:00 P.M., after hours of official silence, the Israelis publicly agreed to negotiate. In reality, however, they allegedly deliberately prevented the French ambassador from arriving on time, obstructing any possibility of negotiations actually taking place.[8] After the terrorists allegedly refused to extend their 6:00 P.M. deadline, just fifteen minutes before its expiry, the elite *Sayeret Matkal* unit launched a desperate raid, initiated by a failed sniper attempt to kill one of the terrorists.[9] Although the assault was relatively quick, one of the surviving terrorists managed to kill at least a dozen hostages before himself being eliminated.[10] Overall, twenty-one hostages were killed and sixty-five injured in one of the most influential events of the Israeli–Palestinian conflict.[11]

The effects of this failed operation on the Israeli psyche were devastating, and created a fertile ground for successful hostage-taking incidents in the future—since the Israeli Government could hardly afford another Ma'alot; it could be more effectively forced to concede to terrorist demands than ever before. The PFLP-GC was quick to react to this new situation, and on June 13, 1974, four of the group's operatives again slipped across the Lebanese border and attacked the settlement of Kibbutz Shamir. The alleged plan was to take hostages at a nursery and again demand the release of Palestinians from Israeli jails. According to the leaflets carried by the militants, the demands would include the release of 100 prisoners including Kozo Okamoto, the only Japanese Red Army (JRA) terrorist to survive the 1970 Lod Airport Massacre, whose release had also been demanded in Ma'alot. However, the takeover of the settlement did not go as smoothly as expected, and in the initial gun battle six armed settlers killed one of the attackers. The surviving trio then ran into a factory building where they were surrounded, and after a brief shootout, the attackers followed the path of their comrades from Kiryat Shmona and blew themselves up with grenades and explosives.[12]

Finally, on March 5, 1975, eight Fatah terrorists sailed in a rubber dinghy to Tel Aviv, with the alleged plan to attack the Municipality Youth

Center.[13] After they were spotted and alarm was raised, the terrorists retreated to Hotel Savoy, where they barricaded themselves in the top floor with about a dozen hostages. After a ninety-minute gun battle, the terrorists forced one of the hostages, Kochava Levy, to convey their demands through the window. The terrorists demanded the release of ten of their colleagues from Israeli jails, including Greek Archbishop Capucci, who had been imprisoned for smuggling guns to Fatah.[14] The group also demanded a plane to Damascus, and ambassadors from the Vatican, France, and Greece to serve as mediators, attaching a four-hour deadline.[15] After only about an hour into the incident, the situation seemed to have progressed in a positive direction after the terrorists reduced their demands to a sole condition of a free passage to Damascus, and released one of the hostages who had earlier been injured. But despite this promising development, the Israelis continued to insist on an immediate and unconditional surrender. Just four hours and forty-five minutes into the standoff, Prime Minister Rabin ordered the *Sayeret Matkal* troops to storm the building. During the fifteen-minute rescue operation, the terrorists retreated to a room on the third floor where they blew themselves up. One terrorist was captured alive, while eight hostages and three soldiers were killed, and twelve others were injured.[16]

There are many characteristics of the above cases that make them seemingly unsuitable for inclusion in an analysis of the dynamics involved in barricade hostage crises involving the "new terrorists." None of these Palestinian cases were driven primarily by a religious motive, nor did they involve meticulous preparation or a very large number of hostage takers or hostages. Further, the demands set forth by the hostage takers were quite specific, and despite their political unattractiveness to Israel, they constituted a starting position that brought an acceptable negotiated outcome within reach. What made these specific hostage crises important from the perspective of this book was the atypical combination of the hostage takers' suicidal posture, indiscriminate targeting, and the willingness to kill hostages, albeit during a rescue operation. And while none of these cases had featured pressure executions of hostages at deadlines, these attacks provided an early indication of the escalatory direction in which terrorist barricade hostage crises would be heading in the future.

## MECCA

The first hostage crisis to bear multiple characteristics of the "new terrorism," as described earlier, took place in Mecca, Saudi Arabia, in 1979. On November 21 of that year (the first day of the year 1400 in the Islamic calendar), at 4:30 A.M., more than 50,000 Muslims gathered near the Grand Mosque in Mecca on the *hajj* pilgrimage. Among them was a group of mourners carrying coffins on their shoulders. Since bringing the dead for the final blessings to the Grand Mosque was not unusual, nobody paid much attention to these "pilgrims" until they threw the coffins to the ground and brandished automatic weapons and grenades.[17] After making their way to the Qa'ba, the leader of the group, former member of the Saudi National Guard, Juhaiman ibn Muhammad ibn Saif al Utaibi, grabbed the microphone and delivered a speech in which he denounced the royal family's "un-Islamic ways" and introduced Muhammed ibn Abdullah Qahtani as the *Mahdi*, or the "final messiah." After the mosque's imam declined to ratify the new *Mahdi*, the attackers reportedly sprayed the crowd with gunfire killing dozens of worshipers.[18] The attackers also killed one guard and seriously injured two more, while completing the takeover of thousands of people by chaining the gates to the courtyard. Shortly thereafter, Juhaiman selected out several dozen pilgrims as hostages, releasing everyone else with instructions to spread the message of the takeover throughout the city.

From the very outset it was clear that the Saudi authorities had no intention of negotiating with the hostage takers. The kingdom's leadership was deeply embarrassed by such a bold attack conveying a message that was highly uncomfortable for the royal family, especially given the presence of several former Saudi National Guard members (including a colonel) among the hostage takers. As a result of this embarrassment the Saudis' top priority was to end the crisis as quickly as possible. In the first step, all of the kingdom's transportation and communication links with the outside world were severed, in order to prevent the spread of the news of the takeover past the kingdom's borders. This secretive approach resulted in the proliferation of many myths and rumors, some suggesting Iranian, and others American, involvement in the attack. These speculations in turn led to violent assaults on American embassies and corporations in India, Pakistan, and Libya, in which four people were killed.[19]

By noon of the second day the kingdom's communications with the outside world were reestablished, in order to facilitate the government's attempt to mobilize the Islamic world in support of the idea of resolving the crisis by force.[20] As a part of this strategy Interior Minister Prince Naïf denied any possible political motive behind the attack, claiming the hostage takers were common criminals.[21] Another step was to secure the religious backing at home, which entailed the need to convince Saudi religious authorities to issue a formal permission to allow the bearing of arms and the shedding of blood inside a holy place.[22] For this purpose, the government turned to the Council of Ulema, which eventually issued a *fatwa* in support of armed action on the basis of the need to fight "atheist influences."[23] Coincidentally, the head of the Council was Abdul Aziz al Baz, a highly conservative blind sheikh and one of the country's most powerful leaders, who had ironically been Juhaiman's mentor during his studies at the University of Medina.[24]

Having secured the necessary religious sanction for the attack, the national guardsmen finally proceeded with the assault, blasting the gates to the mosque and storming the location. However, the hostage takers relatively easily repelled the storm, which was called off after the commander of the mission was killed.[25] Several additional attempts to retake the mosque by force followed, but despite the use of tanks and heavy artillery the hostage takers were still able to retain control.[26] On the fourth day of the siege the self-proclaimed *Mahdi* was killed, and his body was shown to photographers in order to prove to the masses that he was not a messiah chosen by God.[27] On the next day the terrorists decided to retreat to the underground catacombs beneath the complex, where it was even more difficult to flush them out.[28]

Recognizing their limited experience with similar operations, the Saudis looked for international assistance, and on November 23, Captain Barill and three other noncommissioned officers from the elite French GIGN (Groupe d'Intervention de la Gendarmerie Nationale) counterterrorist force arrived at the site.[29] In order to overcome the religious prohibition for non-Muslims to enter the city of Mecca, the royal family again had to turn to the religious establishment, which resolved the issue by declaring the commandos "honorary Muslims." On December 3, more than two weeks since the initial takeover, the next phase of the attempt to retake the mosque took place, in which unidentified asphyxiating gas was used in order to force the attackers out of the underground passages. According to some sources the Special Forces also deliberately flooded the Grand Mosque, and electrocuted the hostage takers by placing high voltage cables in the water.[30] The final casualty counts are clouded in mystery, with reported figures ranging between 127 and 10,000 fatalities.[31] The official version of events indicated that 270 people were killed, more than 550 wounded, and 170 terrorists were captured.[32] On January 9, 1980, sixty-three of these arrested militants were publicly executed in the squares of eight cities in an attempt to send a message to the opposition movement inside the kingdom.[33]

Was it possible to end the Mecca hostage crisis without violence? From the beginning there were a number of discouraging signs. First, this was the largest hostage crisis in history initially featuring thousands of hostages and a very large group of more than 300 attackers, most of them Saudis but also including Yemenis, Iraqis, Pakistanis, Egyptians, Sudanese, Kuwaitis, and Bangladeshis.[34] Further, it was clear that the attackers had made meticulous preparations for the operation, having smuggled weapons inside the kingdom from South Yemen,[35] and having stocked food, water, and ammunition at the target location. Interesting in this regard was the role of the Bin Laden Construction Company, whose trucks were used to smuggle in arms and provisions prior to the raid.[36] In the trucks the police later also found maps of the underground passages beneath the mosques,[37] leading to the arrest of Marhous bin Laden, one of Osama's half brothers.[38] Osama himself was strongly influenced by the event, and later used the violation of the Grand Mosque by the Saudi National Guard as evidence of the evil nature of the royal family, arguing that "all that was needed was time … to resolve the incident without bloodshed."[39]

Perhaps an even more ominous sign than the large numbers of hostages and the high level of preparation on the side of the attackers was the hostage takers' alleged apocalyptic plan to overthrow the monarchy and replace the king with a *Mahdi*, a final messiah whose emergence would signal the coming of the end of the world. The figure of *Mahdi* is described in detail in various *hadiths*, which specify that the messiah would be proclaimed on the first day of the year 1400 (November 21, 1979),[40] as "people will perform hajj together and gather without an Imam. The Hajjis will be looted and there will be a battle at Mina in which many will be slain and blood will flow until it runs over the *Jamra al-'Aqaba*."[41] It is further specified that the *Mahdi's* arrival would come "when the existing corrupt environment is extremely intense and severe" and that "a star with a luminous tail [would] rise from the East before the *Mahdi's* emergence."[42]

Ominously, the Mecca attack appeared to be an enactment of this doomsday Islamic prophesy. The attack took place exactly on the first day of the Islamic year 1400, and the hostage takers justified their actions by proclaiming that the "Al Saud had lost its legitimacy through corruption, ostentation, and mindless imitation of the West." Further, just nine months before the attack, the world witnessed the high-profile appearance of the Halley's Comet, which could be interpreted as the "star with a luminous tail [that would] rise from the East" to signal the *Mahdi's* emergence. In addition, some *hadiths* specify that at the time of the *Mahdi's* coming "religious prohibitions [would be violated] and big sins [would be] committed near the *Qa'ba*,"[43] a condition that was fulfilled when the attackers killed several people during the takeover, thereby committing what was seen as an act of major desecration of the holiest site in Islam. This apparently apocalyptic mind-set of the hostage takers made the prospect of a negotiated settlement seem impossible. How could one possibly negotiate with terrorists that want to bring about the end of the world while interpreting their own actions as fulfilling God's will?

At this point however, we must remind ourselves of the common tendency of governments to maneuver the story in a direction that fits their objectives. The Saudis' primary goal in this instance was the regime's survival, and the official version of events was strongly geared toward this aim. As a part of the campaign to gather widespread support in the Islamic world for its delicate action of using violence in the holiest site in Islam, it was in the royal family's interest to trivialize the motivations of the hostage takers. It is thus no surprise that the Saudi leadership initially described the terrorists as "ordinary criminals" and "atheists," later changing this label to an even more abhorrent image of irrational apocalyptic fanatics. But in reality, the hostage takers' goals oscillated around political grievances that were very real. According to interrogations of surviving terrorists, the attack was supposed to be a part of a larger uprising against the Saudi regime, which besides violent action in Mecca and Medina was also supposed to comprise protests and strikes of foreign workers at the oilfields.[44] In his speeches that could be heard on the Grand Mosque loudspeakers mounted throughout the city, Juhaiman also attacked the royal family for traveling in the West, drinking alcohol, and for using the country's greatest natural resource for purchasing personal luxury. The attackers also declared that they sought reversal of Saudi modernization, and the abolishment of television, professional soccer, and employment of women outside their homes.[45] Additional tenants of the hostage takers' ideology could be found in several pamphlets written by Juhaiman prior to the attack including the *Saba Rasail* ("Seven Letters"). These included the imperative to emulate the Prophet's example— revelation, propagation, and military takeover; the necessity for the Muslims to overthrow their present corrupt rulers; the duty to reject all worshipers of the partners of God; and the duty to establish a puritanical Islamic community which protects Islam from unbelievers and does not court foreigners.[46]

From this perspective, proclaiming a *Mahdi* (expected one) was simply a political tool used to religiously legitimize the uprising in order to mobilize the masses. The general demands made, while being highly religious in nature, were not necessarily irrational or idiosyncratic, as documented by the fact that many of them were actually adopted by the government after the siege was over, partly in an effort to weaken the political appeal of the opposition and partly as a concession to the conservative religious leaders for their support of the king during the crisis. Following the attack, the royal family banned women from television, forbade the broadcasting of music over the radio, imposed a rule closing all stores during the five daily prayers, and symbolically empowered the religious police for stricter enforcement of these rules.

Besides the political nature of the demands which runs contrary to the apocalyptic interpretation of the terrorists' actions, it also seems that the attackers were far from suicidal, introducing yet more doubt about the version suggesting their alleged inherent expectation of the end of the world. On the one hand, according to some accounts the attackers insisted on repaying their debts to their friends and relatives right before the attack, in order to clear their accounts for martyrdom.[47] On the other hand, the target selection itself is highly suggestive of a desire on the part of the terrorists to insure their own safety during the standoff. Firstly, counting precisely on the religious prohibitions against violence in holy places as well as the royal family's likely fear of physical destruction of the holiest site in Islam, the attackers apparently did not assess the likelihood of a violent resolution as very high. In addition, it later transpired that a part of their plan was also to capture King Khalid, who was scheduled to visit the Grand Mosque on the day of the attack but had cancelled the appearance due to illness.[48] Had this plan worked as anticipated events would have likely turned out differently, as the authorities probably would not have launched an indiscriminate armed rescue operation fearing for the king's safety. And finally, the fact that no less than 170 of the attackers eventually surrendered also seems to suggest the desire to live on behalf of at least some of them.

In conclusion, the Mecca hostage crisis bore all the characteristics of "new terrorist" ideology, including highly religious rhetoric combined with apocalyptic symbolism. At the same time the hostage takers' objectives were primarily of a political nature. And while that in itself is hardly a guarantee of success, the demands issued by the terrorists provided plenty of room for the implementation of crisis negotiation strategies in order to attempt to bring the ordeal to a peaceful end. However, the political realities inside the House of Saud insured that no such solution would be acceptable, leading to the violent encounter and the deaths of hundreds of people. In the end, Juhaiman's selection of the Grand Mosque as the target was a gross strategic error, as instead of insuring the attackers' safety, it triggered a horrified reaction by Muslims around the world, which ultimately ended up strengthening the Saudi Government in its decision to proceed with a violent resolution.[49] In the attack's aftermath, the terrorists' motives were trivialized and delegitimized via the portrayal of the terrorists as irrational religious fanatics. As we shall see in Chapter 5, this would be just one of the parallels between the crisis in Mecca and the attack in Beslan twenty-five years later.

## MALTA

On November 23, 1985, a group of three well-dressed terrorists belonging to the Abu Nidal Organization[50] rose from their seats twenty-two minutes after takeoff on board Egypt Air Flight 648 flying from Athens to Cairo, and brandishing guns and grenades they quickly took control of the aircraft, demanding for the pilot to fly to Libya. Shortly thereafter, they started collecting passports from the hostages in order to divide them by nationality.[51] One of the passengers, a plain-clothes sky marshal, instead of providing his passport took out a gun and shot, and seriously wounded the lead hijacker. Three additional sky marshals were on board, but since their guns were locked away in the overhead compartment, they stood by as the two remaining terrorists shot and badly injured their colleague in retaliation.

The hijacking had gone utterly wrong. The hijackers had not only suffered a significant disruption of their chain of command, but had also broken the threshold of violence against hostages. Perhaps even more importantly, during the shootout, twenty-seven bullets had penetrated the fuselage, causing the plane to lose cabin pressure, thus forcing the pilot to descent to 14,000 feet in order to avoid disaster. Flying at such a low altitude significantly increased fuel consumption, forcing the terrorists to abandon their original destination and attempt an emergency landing in Malta.[52] Initially, the Maltese authorities denied permission to land and shut off the runway lights, but at 10:16 P.M. the desperate pilot landed the aircraft despite this obstacle at the Luqa Airport in Valletta.

Shortly after landing, the hijackers opened talks with the control tower, where the negotiations were handled personally by Maltese Prime Minister Carmelo Mifsud Bonnici who spoke to the terrorists over the radio via an interpreter. The hijackers communicated indirectly via Captain Hani Galal, but one of them was always present in the cockpit to monitor the conversations. Curiously, the hijackers put forward no political demands of any kind, demanding only enough fuel to reach Libya, a doctor, and an engineer to inspect the plane.[53] Bonnici agreed to provide the latter two in exchange for some hostages, but refused to refuel the airplane unless all passengers were first released.[54] Shortly before midnight the hijackers freed two wounded flight attendants as a sign of good faith, followed quickly by the release of another eleven women[55] in exchange for a doctor to come on board to examine Salem, the injured hijacker. The doctor found Salem to be dead, but determined that the sky marshal was still alive and in need of immediate treatment. The hijackers agreed to his evacuation, but as the sky marshal was carried on a stretcher to the front door, Rezaq Omar Ali Muhammed, the terrorist that had taken over command following Salem's death, shot the man several times with his gun, killing him instantly.

The fired-up Rezaq then firmly repeated his demand for the plane to be refueled, and after the Maltese Government again refused to comply unless *all* passengers were first released, the terrorists responded with a threat to kill a hostage every fifteen minutes until their demand was fulfilled. The authorities at this time assessed the threat to be a bluff,[56] and after waiting for several hours they again stubbornly expressed their absolutist position on the issue of providing fuel. Inside the plane Rezaq lost his patience and yelled out the name of Israeli passenger Tamar Artzi. Apparently convinced that she was about to be released, Tamar identified herself willingly. But once she reached the stairs Rezaq shot her in the back of the head and pushed her body onto the tarmac. Five minutes later, the terrorists called out the name of another Israeli woman, Nitzan Mendelson, and after identifying her by a passport photo, they took her to the front exit. "Another passenger is being prepared for execution . . . I demand fuel! ... " "He's killing another one!" Galal shouted desperately over the radio as the hijacker fired two shots into the woman's head.[57] Following the next execution of Patrick Scott Baker, an American, the authorities responded by surrounding the plane with troops (who however had not been issued any bullets), justifying their action to the hijackers as "protection from a possible attack by American commandos." Simultaneously, the authorities explained to the hijackers that they had no chance of getting away even if fuel were provided, citing the *Achille Lauro* precedent as evidence that American fighter jets based at the nearby Sigonella U.S. Naval Air Station would intercept the plane and force it to land.[58]

With their backs against the wall, in the early morning hours of November 24, the hijackers proceeded with the execution of two American women, Scarlet Rogencamp and Jackie Pflug.[59] In the meantime, the terrorists also made a demand for food, which the authorities granted in exchange for the hijackers' permission to approach the plane and collect the bodies of the executed passengers.[60] Throughout the day the hostage takers grew increasingly aggressive, "waving guns and shouting in everyone's faces,"[61] as the Maltese authorities turned down their demand for more food until all nine children present among the passengers were released.[62]

By this time, a decision had already been made to storm the plane and rescue the hostages by force. Since Malta lacked a special hostage rescue commando unit, the attack was to be carried out by the fifty-five-men-strong Egyptian *Al-Sa'iqa* (Thunderbolt) 777 Combat Unit that had been flown in at 8:30 A.M. The original plan called for the prolonging of negotiations and the storming of the plane when food was to be taken onboard the aircraft by soldiers dressed as caterers.[63] However, without consent from Maltese authorities, the Egyptians independently initiated the strike at 7:10 P.M., about ninety minutes before the agreed time.

From the beginning, the rescue was bound to become a colossal failure. Firstly, the Egyptians did not use any eavesdropping devices or debriefs of released hostages to acquaint themselves with the situation inside. Secondly, they never rehearsed the operation and even telegraphed its start by accidentally shutting off the runway lights.[64] Thirdly, the commandos attacked by placing a large explosive device near the luggage compartment doors, triggering a massive blast that not only blew out the last six rows of passenger seats, but also caused fire and detonation of oxygen tanks located in the back of the aircraft.[65] And finally, when the commandos actually entered, they fired indiscriminately, killing several additional hostages in the process. Remarkably, the rescue operation killed fifty-six passengers and two crewmembers, while succeeding to eliminate only one (!) hijacker, who died in the initial blast. Autopsies revealed that eight of the victims had died from the effects of the explosion; seven had been shot to death (four of them by bullets fired from guns carried by the commandos); and no fewer than forty-four died from burns and smoke inhalation.[66]

The Egypt Air Flight 648 tragedy carries several key lessons for the future. The first such lesson is that the disruption of a hostage taking team's chain of command by eliminating the leader can sometimes result in making the incident even more volatile. After Salem was killed by the sky marshal on board, the command ended up in the hands of muscle hijacker Rezaq, who was described by the hostages as psychologically unstable. For instance, in the words of Jackie Pflug who miraculously survived her execution, Rezaq "seemed like a crazy person. I could see in his eyes that something was wrong with him."[67] While Rezaq's other colleague allegedly even apologized to the hostages when he led them for execution, Rezaq coldly carried out the killings without emotion. Later during his trial Rezaq claimed that he was legally insane at the time of the incident due to posttraumatic stress disorder, a claim that was confirmed by a number of psychiatric experts but eventually rejected by the jury.[68] In any case, it is quite possible that had Salem led the operation until the end, events might have turned out differently.

Another key lesson of Malta is associated with the unsound approach to negotiations. Firstly, Prime Minister Bonnici's direct involvement in the negotiations was a great strategic mistake. When handling demands in a hostage crisis, one of the things negotiators strive to achieve is the perceived position of an intermediary between the authorities and the hostage takers. If the demands issued are difficult to satisfy, the negotiator can stall for time by pointing to the difficulty of locating a key decision maker or some other objective obstacle to meeting the terrorists' deadline. Further, the negotiator's lack of decision-making authority also allows him or her to effectively disassociate him or herself from the official refusal to comply, while empathetically validating the reasonable component of the demand and promising to keep trying to convince the authorities in favor of its fulfillment. This strategy is useful in stalling for time, decreasing the expectations of the hostage takers, and creating a bond between the negotiator and the suspect. In a situation where the negotiations are conducted directly by the head of a country's executive branch of government, every refusal to comply with a demand is likely to be perceived more absolutely, as in this context, the negotiator does not have the option of deferring responsibility for the decision to anyone above himself. In the absence of a believable explanation for why a particular demand has not yet been satisfied, the hostage takers are audaciously pushed into a corner, thereby increasing the likelihood of their resorting to more extreme measures. In this regard, Bonnici's direct involvement was thus a giant mistake, especially given the instrumental nature of the terrorists' demands. As we shall see later, the direct involvement of high government officials in hostage negotiations can play a crucial role in reaching a peaceful settlement, but only in extraordinary circumstances that require a political decision at the very top. Given the absence of any political demand, lack of insistence on behalf of the terrorists to speak with a high official, as well as the Maltese unconditional refusal to comply with a simple instrumental demand to refuel the plane, the prime ministers' direct negotiating role in the Egypt Air Flight 648 case became highly counterproductive, perhaps even to the level of directly contributing to the executions of hostages.

The final obvious lesson from the Egypt Air Flight 648 tragedy has to do with the storming of the plane. In a situation where the opposition consisted of only two hostage takers, the sledgehammer approach to the rescue operation is simply mind-boggling. This is especially the case given the fact that by the time the assault was launched, the authorities already knew that the terrorists had only very limited firepower, using homemade ammunition, the impotency of which had been demonstrated by the fact that three of the five executed hostages survived their injuries, some despite being shot multiple times. The executions also demonstrated the terrorists' overall poor aim, as Rezaq managed to miss two of the hostages' heads despite firing from point blank range.[69] In such a context, it seems that the elimination of the hostage takers, even if perhaps misguidedly given preference over negotiations, could have been achieved by more effective and by less costly means.[70]

## KARACHI

Less than a year after the Malta fiasco Abu Nidal struck again, this time in Karachi, Pakistan.[71] On September 5, 1986, at 5:55 A.M., four terrorists dressed as airport security personnel and armed with assault rifles, pistols, grenades, and plastic explosive belts,[72] drove a customized vehicle resembling an official car up to the boarding steps of Pan Am Flight 73 with 379 people on board.[73] The terrorists quickly entered the plane during the final preparations for takeoff, killing a crewmember who objected to the rough handling of a stewardess, and injuring two more baggage handlers in the process.[74] The hijackers then rushed inside in order to subdue the crew, but they failed to find the cockpit because its location was not at the nose of the aircraft as anticipated, but at the top of the stairway in the rear of the first class cabin.[75] This critical delay allowed the control tower to notify the crew, and the pilot, co-pilot, and flight engineer were able to escape through the cockpit hatch, thereby obstructing the terrorists' plan to take off and fly to another location.

Shortly after seizing control of the aircraft, the terrorists ordered the flight attendants to collect the passports of American passengers.[76] Several hours later, the terrorists held first telephone negotiations with the director of Pakistani Civilian Aviation Department, Khurshid Manwar Mirza, in which Naseem A. Khan, the base manager for Saudi Airlines, served as interpreter. During the talks the terrorists demanded the return of the crew in order to fly the aircraft to Cyprus, where they planned to demand the release of British, Jordanian, and Syrian terrorists convicted of killing three Israelis on a yacht in September 1985, later adding to the list a Lebanese terrorist held for the August 1986 mortar attack on a British base at Akrotiri. The authorities explored the possibility of fulfilling the terrorists' demand to be flown to Larnaca, but both Iran and Cyprus allegedly refused to let the plane fly over their airspace or land on their soil.[77]

By 10:00 A.M., the terrorists' leader Zayd Hassan Safarini became angry with the lack of progress in negotiations and forced one of the hostages to kneel with hands behind his head in the front doorway, threatening to execute him if the demand for a new flight crew was not fulfilled within ten minutes. Exactly ten minutes later, American citizen Rajesh Kumar was shot in the head and pushed out the door onto the tarmac.[78] During further negotiations, Safarini again announced that if the authorities did not satisfy his demand to provide an Arabic speaking crew by 7:00 P.M., his "revolutionary fighters [would pass] a death sentence on American intelligence officials on board."[79] At 6:30 P.M. the negotiators won an extension on the deadline by promising the hijackers that a crew from Frankfurt was already on its way to Karachi. The terrorists set a new deadline for 11:00 P.M. By that time, Pakistani authorities had already decided to end the crisis by a rescue operation.[80]

However, during the seventeenth hour of the standoff, the Auxiliary Power Unit that supplied electricity to the aircraft's lights and air-conditioning ran out of fuel, causing the interruption of radio contact with the control tower as well as the dimming and flickering of lights onboard. The terrorists interpreted this development as a sign of the beginning of a rescue attempt, and responded by herding all of the passengers into the middle of the aircraft.[81] Mirza, ran out on the tarmac with a megaphone to warn the hijackers not to panic, but it was too late.[82] When the lights went out, the leader yelled "are you ready for the final episode? *Jihad*!!!" and the hostage takers opened fire on the passengers, firing two clips of ammunition and throwing grenades into the crowd. Some passengers managed to open an emergency door and people started jumping out using an escape slide. The lead hijacker reportedly ordered one of the other terrorists to shoot him in the stomach where he had his explosive belt, but the terrorist missed, then fled.[83]

While these events unfolded, Pakistani commandos were in the process of preparing for the assault and were nowhere near the airplane. It reportedly took nearly fifteen additional minutes for them to arrive on the scene and storm the plane. To make things even worse, their action was far from perfect as the commandos lacked hostage rescue equipment such as stun guns or flash grenades, using instead high caliber weapons to fire indiscriminately into the crowd inside.[84] In the end, twenty-two people died, ten of them from gunfire, seven from shrapnel wounds, and four from injuries suffered by jumping from the plane.[85] An additional 100 passengers were injured, and three of the four terrorists were captured.

The terrorists had prepared the operation meticulously, spending three weeks on identifying ways to infiltrate what at the time was regarded by the U.S. Federal Aviation Administration (FAA) as one of South Asia's safest airports. This included the acquisition of security personnel uniforms, purchase of security badges at a local market, the painting of a rented van in official colors and adding a light and a siren on the rooftop.[86] Despite tightened security amid warnings of possible terrorist attacks against American airliners, the terrorists managed to bypass the security measures by entering the tarmac from the airport's perimeter in the early predawn hours on a Friday, when the security was most lax.[87]

Another aspect that makes this case important for our purposes besides the execution of hostages, precise preparations, and unquestionable resolve to kill as many passengers during a perceived storming as possible, is the hostage takers' apparent suicidal intent. According to Masror Hausen, a Pakistani journalist to whom the captured terrorists had passed a secret message written on cigarette packets and foils, the terrorists' true motive was to "fill up the aircraft with explosives and hit the Israeli defense ministry, using the aircraft as a missile...."[88] On January 5, 1988, the attackers admitted in court that their original plan was to negotiate the release of not only the demanded prisoners, but also another 1,500 Palestinians held in Israeli jails. Upon completing this task, the terrorists confessed that their plan indeed was to "drive the plane somewhere toward some sensitive strategy center of the Zionist enemy and blow it up with [everyone] inside ... [the hostage takers] wanted to destroy the sensitive strategic center of the Zionists through an American weapon—the explosion of an American plane."[89] Interestingly, three of the four terrorists were caught while trying to escape or hide among the hostages, introducing some doubt into the terrorists' alleged resolve to die. In addition, there are some indications that one of the terrorists might have attempted to sabotage the operation from the very beginning due to his persistent desire to live.[90] In any case, this example demonstrates that even terrorist hostage takers that assume a suicidal posture in the beginning of the incident can under extreme circumstances change their mind, especially if their plan runs into unexpected obstacles. Implicitly, the common tendency to rule out the mere possibility of negotiations in such situations is seriously deficient, and only serves unnecessarily to limit the responders' options.

## MARSEILLES

Another very similar case study that is also highly relevant with regards to the characteristics of hostage crises involving the "new terrorists" is the infamous 1994 Air France hijacking. On December 24, 1994, at 11:15 A.M., four uniformed members of the Algerian Armed Islamic Group (GIA) boarded the Air France Flight 8969 scheduled to fly from Algiers to Paris,[91] and claiming to be police officers they proceeded to check the passengers' passports. As soon as the doors were shut the terrorists revealed their real identity and ordered the hostages to close all window shutters and empty their personal belongings into a plastic bag. After taking control over the cockpit, the terrorists also changed into flight crew uniforms in order to confuse potential snipers, and instructed all women on board to cover their faces.

During the document check the terrorists identified an Algerian police officer among the passengers, and ordered him to move to the front of the plane, where despite his desperate pleas, they shot him in the head.[92] A few minutes later the hijackers made contact with the control tower at Houari Boumedienne Airport and citing the alleged intent to fly to Paris and hold a press conference, they demanded for the plane to proceed with the takeoff.[93] After their initial request was refused, the terrorists threw the body of their first victim onto the tarmac and made threats to execute another hostage if their demands were not met immediately. Indeed, following several minutes of inaction, the terrorists quickly executed another hostage, this time Vietnamese embassy attaché Bui Giang To. Later, they placed one ten-stick pack of dynamite in the cockpit and another one under a seat in the central section of the plane, connecting them with a detonator cable.[94] At one point the terrorists also took a hostage's watch with the alleged intent of using it as a timer for the bomb.[95]

At the control tower the negotiations were handled by Interior Minister Abderahmane Meziane-Cherif, who spoke to the terrorists via the cockpit radio. The hijackers refused to talk to him directly, using Captain Bernard Delhemme to communicate on their behalf. The terrorists demanded the release of Islamic Salvation Front (FIS) leaders Abassi Madani and Ali Belhadj from house arrest, and the freeing of several other militants from jail.[96] The terrorists also demanded that France cut all support to the Algerian regime and assume a neutral position on the Algerian conflict.[97] The minister responded by issuing demands of his own: "Start by freeing the women, the elderly and the children if you want us to start talking." The response was positive and about four hours into the incident the hijackers began releasing passengers. Initially, they freed nineteen people including fourteen women, one man, and four children. Eleven more hostages were released shortly, and by the end of December 24, the terrorists had freed sixty-three people, some of them in exchange for food deliveries.[98]

The next day also started on a positive note as the terrorists released additional passengers, mainly women and children.[99] Following this action the hijackers reiterated their demands from the previous day, namely, the release of Abassi Madani and Ali Belhadj. They also added to the list the names of former GIA chief Abelkader Layada, and the author of the

1992 *fatwa* authorizing *jihad* against the government, Ikhlet Cherati. Their last demand was the removal of the staircase in order for the plane to be able to take off.[100] By this point all women had been released, with the exception of several female flight attendants that remained on board.[101]

Using night vision devices, the Special Forces were able to identify the lead hijacker as twenty-five-year-old Abdul Abdullah Yahia. In an attempt to use this knowledge to their advantage, the authorities summoned Yahia's mother to the scene to try to influence her son. "In the name of God, I implore you, my son, to let all the passengers go," she pleaded directly on the cockpit radio. As an answer, Yahia fired in the direction of the control tower and replied: "Mother, we'll meet in paradise!"[102]

On December 25, at 9:00 P.M., the terrorists escalated their threats after the authorities continued to refuse their demand for the plane to take off. At this time, they threatened to execute Yannick Beugnet, a cook at the French ambassador's residence in Algiers, unless the boarding ramp was removed from the plane by 9:30 P.M. Beugnet was brought to the microphone and forced to plead to the control tower: "If you don't allow the plane to depart, they will kill me!" At 10:00 P.M., his body was thrown onto the tarmac, accompanied by a threat to kill one person every half hour until the plane was allowed to fly to Paris.

The French Government which had pleaded with the Algerians to be allowed to handle the crisis since the beginning was furious. As early as nine hours into the hijacking a team of forty GIGN troopers had even flown to Algiers, but after being denied landing rights their plane was forced to divert to the Spanish airport of Palma de Mallorca and wait.[103] But after the execution of Beugnet, a French national, the French Government lost all patience and forcefully demanded that the Algerian President give the authorization for the hijacked plane to take off.[104] Finally on December 26, at 2:00 A.M., the Algerians removed the mobile staircase and wheel chocks, and allowed the plane to leave for Paris.[105]

While some sources claimed that the terrorists demanded to fly to Marseilles,[106] it was actually the decision of the French response team to divert the plane to that location. In order to achieve this end, the air traffic controllers secretly communicated to the crew to tell the hijackers that the plane did not have enough fuel to make it all the way to Paris and needed to land in Marseilles to refuel.[107] This was a risky move, given the fact that since the plane's original scheduled destination was Paris, the story about lack of fuel to reach that destination was not easily believable.[108] Moreover, even if the terrorists did believe the story they still had other landing alternatives they could have used, which would have further complicated the situation for the French. But in the end the gamble paid off, and at 3:33 A.M. the plane touched down in Marseilles with 170 hostages still on board.[109] Tired from the long flight and the earlier forty-hour standoff in Algiers, the hijackers remained silent until 6:00 A.M. At this time, they contacted the control tower, demanding twenty-seven tons of fuel and the hosting of a press conference. Alain Gehin, the Marseilles police chief who handled the negotiations agreed, also asking for a goodwill gesture consisting of the release of some hostages. "We can release a few, go get the journalists," replied the hijackers, and subsequently freed two elderly hostages.[110] An agreement was reached for a press conference to take place directly on board the plane, and the terrorists started moving hostages to the rear of the aircraft in order to make the necessary room.

Despite the terrorists' persistent demands for staging a press conference, there was some doubt in the command centre as to whether this was indeed the hostage takers' ultimate objective. In the early stages of the incident, the AFP news agency had received a statement from Phalange of Signers in Blood (El Mouakioune Bi Eddima) saying the hijackers protested France's unconditional aid to Algeria's military regime.[111] In this sense the hijacking seemed to follow the traditional script of previous cases, in which terrorists would hijack planes to the West with the intention of conveying their grievances and political goals to a wide international audience. But the one thing that puzzled the officials in this case, was the demand for twenty-seven tons of fuel, which seemed excessive given the fact that a trip to Paris would only require nine to ten tons. This suggested that the militants might have other plans, possibly to escape to a friendly Islamic country. But according to an anonymous warning received by the French consulate in Oran, the plan was much more sinister: "the plane [was] a flying bomb that [would] explode over Paris."[112] In addition to this information, the authorities also learned from released hostages that there were explosives on board, rigged in a way to tear the plane apart if detonated in flight.

At this stage, the decision was made to launch a rescue attempt, and the negotiators' role shifted to stalling for time while the GIGN trained for the assault on an identical plane. During this process, Yahia became highly impatient and at one point proclaimed: "Listen, in my opinion, you want us to blow up everything right here! You have one and a half hours to let us take off for Paris—until 9:40." Skillfully applying the traditional principles of crisis negotiation, the negotiators used minor concessions such as food, water, vacuum cleaners, and the emptying of toilets to break through the deadline.[113] At 4:45 p.m. the Special Forces were finally ready to move in, but at the last minute their positioning had been compromised after the terrorists demanded for the plane to move within thirty meters of the tower, also issuing their "final deadline" for the plane to take off by 5:00 p.m. or "action would be taken."[114]

Inside the aircraft, the terrorists were apparently getting ready to kill two more hostages, as documented by the preparation of blankets to cover the bodies.[115] According to the hostages, the hijackers also performed a death ritual, as judged by the particular passages from the Koran they recited during prayers. At 5:08 P.M., one of the terrorists started firing at the control tower, triggering an immediate decision to proceed with the assault.[116] The GIGN troops tossed stun grenades into the cockpit and the first class section of the plane, while moving in on mobile staircases and entering the aircraft. The commandos exchanged fire with the terrorists, who tossed a homemade grenade into the first class section of the plane, which however resulted in only minimum damage. In the seventeen-minute firefight, all hijackers were killed, while eleven commandos, thirteen passengers, and three members of the crew were injured. Not a single passenger was killed in one of the most successful hostage rescue operations in history. The sense of triumph was augmented even more by the realization of the potential consequences of the fulfillment of the terrorists' original plans.

Admittedly, some questions about the actual parameters of the hijackers' plan still remain. According to some sources, the intent was to explode the plane over Paris, while other versions suggested the 9-11 scenario of crash-diving the plane into a target in the city, possibly the Eiffel Tower.[117] There is still some doubt whether this was necessarily the case. On the one hand, there was the Oran consulate warning, the request for an unexpectedly large quantity of fuel and the testimony of hostages who revealed that the terrorists' idea was to "set Paris ablaze."[118] On the other hand, if the intent was indeed to blow the plane up over Paris, why would the terrorist rig the explosives as a time bomb? In addition, the hijackers repeatedly threatened to explode the plane unless they were allowed to take off, suggesting possible intent to use the explosive on the ground as a deterrent against a rescue operation. This seems confirmed by a GIA communiqué, which later stated that the rescue succeeded not because of bravery and skill of the French Special Forces but "because of the will of Allah, [since] the four kilograms of explosives [on board] did not detonate."[119] In addition, prior to this attack, the GIA had never launched a suicide operation, so the crash-dive scenario would have constituted an unusual deviation from the group's established modus operandi. Nevertheless, there is solid evidence to believe that the terrorists' plan was indeed to use the plane as a flying bomb in some form.

The GIA, too, analyzed the lessons of the attack, identifying the decision to let the plane land in Marseilles as a key strategic mistake, given the fact that the plane actually did have enough fuel to reach Paris. "Since they were half way, the mujahideen *may have wanted* [emphasis added] to fill up the tanks of the plane for later blowing it up over Paris. These will be lessons learned for future operations."[120] In addition, the GIA also announced a "new phase" of the struggle, which they called the "martyrdom phase." Indeed, on January 30, 1995, the GIA perpetrated its first suicide attack after one of its members drove an explosives-laden car into the headquarters of the national police on Boulevard Colonel Amirouche in Algiers, killing 42 people and wounding 265. Interestingly, this remains the only GIA suicide attack to this day.

The Air France case study is absolutely crucial to the understanding of the challenges likely to be present in managing hostage crises involving the "new terrorists." First of all, the incident demonstrated that procedural agreements for the release of hostages can be achieved even in cases where the terrorists' expectation is, apparently, to die in the incident. Secondly, this case reminds us that in order to select the appropriate negotiation strategy we first need to analyze the terrorists' *real* objectives, which frequently lie outside of the scope of their own proclamations. As this case demonstrates, and as will repeatedly be emphasized throughout this book, the lack of ability to "read between the lines" and correctly assess the situation may lead to unexpected outcomes. The identification of appropriate negotiation strategies for cases involving a suspected suicidal hijacking plan will be discussed later in this book.

## BUDYONNOVSK

On June 14, 1995, Chechen warlord Shamil Basayev personally led a 162-strong commando unit for "Operation *Jihad*" in Russian territory in order to "stop the war [in Chechnya] or die." The attack occurred just weeks after a Russian bomb landed on Basayev's house in Vedeno, killing eleven members of his family including his Abkhazian wife and children. Basayev's team, allegedly composed solely of fighters who had also lost loved ones in the war in Chechnya,[121] was heavily armed, with each individual reportedly carrying 1,700 AKS cartridges, eleven hand grenades, five kilograms of TNT, three Mukha grenade launchers, and 150 Stechkin pistol cartridges.[122] Traveling disguised in three Kamaz trucks under the cover of transporting corpses of Russian soldiers back to Russia, the convoy was escorted by a police car driven by three clean-shaven Chechen fighters dressed in police uniforms.

According to officials, Basayev's original target was the Mineralniye Vody Airport, where the group allegedly planned to seize an aircraft and fly it into the Kremlin in a 9-11 style operation. For his part, Basayev claimed the convoy was heading to Moscow. In any case, the convoy made it through no less than twenty-two checkpoints[123] all the way up to the village of Praskaeva near the Russian town of Budyonnovsk, but reportedly having run out of bribe money, the group was arrested and brought to the police station in town.[124] Once there, previously undiscovered fighters emerged from the trucks and with swift action seized a number of key buildings in the city, eventually retreating with some 2,500 hostages into a hospital.[125] During the initial takeover as many as 41 people were killed,[126] a number that would reach no less than 130 dead and 415 injured by the end of the crisis five days later.

Once inside the hospital, the terrorists divided hostages into groups and moved the men into the basement, with elderly women and children being placed in corridors of the first floor.[127] In the evening, two doctors were sent outside with a list of demands which included the stopping of war in Chechnya and pullout of federal troops. The doctors also reported that the terrorists were "selecting policemen and military personnel from among the hostages and killing them at will."[128] They were apparently referring to the execution of six male hostages—three military pilots, two policemen, and an employee of a military registration and enlistment office—who were killed on the first day.[129] Although initial media reports indicated that the incident involved only about 20 terrorists and 40 hostages,[130] a list compiled by the victims themselves and sent outside on the first day featured more than 2,000 names, including 150 children.[131]

The first negotiations took place on June 15 around 8:00 A.M., when a group of three negotiators including Sharip Abdulkhazhiev, brother of one of the lead hostage takers, entered the hospital.[132] In the discussions the terrorists demanded the holding of a press conference and the *initiation* of negotiations between Russian and Chechen authorities on a pullout of Russian troops from Chechnya under international oversight.[133] After the talks, a group of more than 20 hostages was freed, bringing the figure of released hostages to over 300.

On the next day events took an ugly turn, as the terrorists executed another five captives after their morning deadline for staging a press conference had repeatedly been ignored.[134] In order to avoid further killings, the Russian authorities finally allowed a group of journalists to enter the hospital and hold a press conference inside.[135] During the event, Basayev proclaimed: "Your pilots killed my family—eleven people, including women and children. But we do not fight women and children. They will be killed by your own soldiers. Your imperial army."[136] This statement would turn out to be prophetic, as on the next day at 4:55 A.M., the Ministry of Interior (MVD) and Federal Security Service (FSB) troops indeed launched an armed operation in an attempt to free the hostages by force. Russian forces led by the elite Alpha commando unit assaulted the Chechen positions but were forced to retreat, partially due to the terrorists' use of hostages as human shields.[137] The four-hour assault was not completely without success however, as eighty-six people were rescued while the terrorists were forced to retreat from the wings into the main building.[138] Still, more than thirty hostages were killed by the rescuing troops, and the lives of the ones remaining inside came under a direct threat due to a fire that had erupted throughout the building.

After the storming ended Basayev released pregnant and nursing women, and an agreement was reached for fire trucks and emergency services to approach the building in order to collect the bodies of those killed. Negotiations continued, in which Basayev reportedly turned down an offer for a free passage via airplane to a country of his choice. This refusal then triggered yet another assault, which lasted over an hour and included the use of tear gas. At 3:30 P.M. the storming stopped, after Basayev promised to release the remaining women and children.

In the evening of June 17, there was a breakthrough in the negotiations after Prime Minister Viktor Chernomyrdin made a statement on television in which he promised to send *official* delegates for negotiations. Chernomyrdin later personally held telephone discussions with Basayev, some of which were televised. On June 18, at 3:00 A.M., Chernomyrdin promised Basayev to end military operations immediately, and also specified the names of delegates that were heading to Chechnya for peace negotiations. In the conversations, Chernomyrdin also asked about the nomination of representatives from the Chechen side, an issue that was eventually put off until later. In addition, Basayev demanded free elections in Chechnya, and specified that his men would only surrender if they were allowed to take some hostages along with them to guarantee their safety.[139] In another call seven hours later, the in-principal agreement was reached, and additional discussions were held locally to resolve the specific details of the logistics of Basayev's free passage to Chechnya. The terrorists reciprocated by releasing 186 hostages. By 5:00 P.M., the number of people set free since the beginning of Chernomyrdin's involvement in the negotiations had reached 350.

On June 18, the Russian peace delegation arrived in Chechnya and Basayev received a written letter from Chernomyrdin specifying the conditions of the settlement, as eight buses pulled up next to the hospital, along with a refrigerated truck to carry the bodies of nineteen terrorists who were killed during the standoff.[140] Additional logistical issues, such as the route of travel to Chechnya, procedures for surrender and for hostage release, protocol for media interviews, and the identity of the "safe passage" hostages, were subsequently finalized. In the end, it was agreed that the safe passage-hostages would need to include 9 MPs, 16 journalists, 9 drivers, and 114 male hostages.[141] Following a final confirmation call between Chernomyrdin and Basayev, on June 19, the convoy left for Vedeno, and after changing the route several times the buses peacefully reached the village of Zandak in Chechnya. Once there, the remaining hostages were released and the fighters escaped into the mountains.

Budyonnovsk has several important lessons to offer with regard to the management of future incidents. Most importantly this case has demonstrated that even in hostage crises involving the "new terrorists" negotiators can achieve significant gains saving lives, although many people tragically had to die in vain for that realization to occur. Secondly, Budyonnovsk is also instrumental in exposing the obsolescence of many of the diagnostic tools currently used by crisis negotiation teams to determine the negotiability of hostage incidents. The fact that hostages were killed

during the initial takeover, and the involvement of a large number of suicidal hostage takers who showed little hesitation to execute hostages to
enforce deadlines, would normally lead to the assessment that a peaceful solution is not possible, leading incident responders to initiate an attempt to rescue the hostages by force. However, as this case has demonstrated, such an assessment would be incorrect, possibly resulting in tragic
consequences—and certainly, missed opportunities. At the same time, it
must be recognized that the terrorists apparently did not originally plan
to take hostages in Budyonnovsk, which likely contributed to their eventual acceptance of a free passage offer. In addition, at this stage of the
Chechen War, Basayev still tried to attract international support for his
cause, which strongly influenced the strategy with which he approached
the standoff. However, following the events of Kizlyar and the Moscow
theatre hostage crisis, his approach to barricade incidents would assume
an ominous escalatory trajectory leading directly to the tragic events of
Beslan.

## KIZLYAR

Only six months after the Budyonnovsk incident, Russia witnessed another crucial hostage-taking event in Dagestan, where on January 9, 1996
Salman Rudayev's[142] 250-strong Chechen commando unit attacked the
military airbase in Kizlyar. The attackers' original plan was to cause significant damage at the base, but after finding only two helicopters to destroy
and encountering heavy resistance, Raduyev changed his plan and took
more than 2,500 hostages at a hospital in the city. Once inside, the terrorists wired the location with explosives and positioned snipers on rooftops
of nearby buildings, gaining strategic control of the bridge over the Terek
River. Raduyev replayed the Budyonnovsk scenario to the smallest detail.
After the Russians attempted to storm the location, he allegedly executed
a police officer and used hostages as human shields to force the troops
to abort the operation.[143] In total, some forty people were killed and fifty
wounded in the initial attack and the subsequent unsuccessful hostage
rescues.[144]

Raduyev issued superficial political demands, including the pullout of
Russian troops from Chechnya and the cancellation of the results of the
last Chechen election.[145] In order to enforce compliance, Raduyev also
threatened: "We can easily turn this city into hell and ashes. We are not
at all concerned for our own lives." At the same time, he also made it clear
that what he really wanted was a free passage back to Chechnya. In order
to facilitate this agreement, the terrorists were quite amendable to releasing some 120 hostages throughout the first day of the crisis as a sign of
good faith. Eventually, the negotiations yielded a successful outcome, and
an agreement for the release of the majority of the remaining hostages in

exchange for free passage to Chechnya was reached. In the early morning hours of January 10, a convoy of nine buses containing the terrorists and their sixty safe-passage hostages, and two lorries loaded with weapons and the bodies of two dead rebels, departed in the direction of Chechnya.

The agreement called for release of half of the hostages near the Pervo-mayskoye village on the Dagestani side of the border, with the remaining hostages to be freed near Azamat Yurt on the Chechen side. However, frustrated and humiliated by the Budyonnovsk experience, the federal authorities were determined to not let the terrorists get away this time around. A plan to assault the convoy immediately after the hostage release on the Dagestani side was drafted and troops were positioned near the key bridge over the Aksai River. But as the convoy approached Pervo-mayskoye, Raduyev spotted helicopters and troops waiting for him on the other side. Fearing for his life Raduyev changed his mind and demanded for the release of hostages to take place only after reaching his final desti-nation at Novogrozenskaya in Chechnya. After one of the helicopters fired on the first bus of the column, the convoy took a sharp turn and drove into a nearby field where the Chechens set up a defensive perimeter.

After releasing several hostages, the terrorists again demanded a free passage to Chechnya via a different route, to which the Russians re-sponded by issuing their own ultimatum for the release of *all* hostages. As the standoff progressed the terrorists retreated into the village itself, taking twenty-five more hostages in the process, and setting up trenches and burying heavy equipment into the ground in preparations for a long battle. In the evening, some of the hostages were reportedly issued with weapons and thirty-seven Dagestani policemen that were taken as addi-tional hostages at a checkpoint near Pervomayskoye were released with words: "You [in Dagestan] are not guilty of anything."[146]

On January 12, Raduyev attempted to replicate the steps that facili-tated Basayev's success in Budyonnovsk and demanded to talk directly to Prime Minister Chernomyrdin. Even after his request was denied, Raduyev followed the Budyonnovsk scenario and released four women and six children along with a request for a free passage, to be guaranteed by an escort of foreign journalists, Russian and Dagestani officials, and representatives of NGOs including Doctors without Borders. In a tele-vision interview, Raduyev clarified: "We are here in a Dagestani village. Bring us to a Chechen village . . . we will release hostages and hand over our arms."[147]

The Russians, determined to punish Raduyev at whatever the cost, re-sponded by issuing January 13, 10:00 A.M. as the deadline for the release of all hostages. "If even one hostage is killed, all of [the hostage takers] will be finished!" FSB Director Mikhail Barsukov warned.[148] On January 15, at 9:00 A.M., ten minutes after the government's extended ultimatum had expired,[149] the Russians launched a furious assault on the village.

Largely outnumbered, the Chechens were still able to hold off the Russian troops, though a good portion of luck was involved at times.[150] After a day of fierce fighting, the Russians apparently gave up on the lives of the hostages and after issuing a false statement claiming that the Chechens had already executed all remaining hostages,[151] the Russian troops leveled the village with artillery fire.[152]

On January 16, 1996, while the rebels at Pervomayskoye continued to hold off the assault, another commando unit of nine people including two Chechens, an Abkhaz, and six Turks hijacked a Black Sea ferry, the *Euroasia*, and threatened to blow it up along with the 255 hostages on board unless the Russian army stopped the Pervomayskoye siege and withdrew its troops from Chechnya.[153] In addition, yet another group of rebels kidnapped thirty employees of a Russian power plant in Grozny and issued similar demands. Finally, in the morning of January 18, the Pervomayskoye siege ended, after sixty-seven remaining hostage takers aided by reinforcements arriving from the Chechen side managed to escape from the village. Suspecting that the terrorists had followed their initial plan and retreated to the Chechen villages of Novogroznensky and Tsentoroy, the Russians indiscriminately obliterated these locations with artillery fire as well. The exact number of casualties of the Pervomayskoye siege remains unreported, although it is known that there were no less than sixty-eight fatalities among the hostages and rescuing troops. In Turkey, one day after the Russian forces finally took control over Pervomayskoye, the hijackers of the *Euroasia* called off their plan to blow up the ship and surrendered to Turkish authorities. Although they were promised a maximum jail sentence of six months, they were later all sentenced to nine years in prison.[154]

Involving hundreds of hostage takers and thousands of hostages, Kizlyar was the second largest ever hostage crisis in history.[155] At the same time, the taking of hostages in this case was purely a desperation move, the sole purpose of which was to facilitate the terrorists' survival and escape, thus creating a textbook situation in which even the standardized crisis negotiation approach may have held the possibility to resolve the incident peacefully. What makes Kizlyar more important for our purposes, however, is its role in the shaping of Russian response strategies to future hostage incidents. Following the overarching perception of the government's humiliating defeat in Budyonnovsk, the emphasis in the management of hostage crises clearly shifted away from the objective of saving as many lives as possible toward the primary goal of punishing the perpetrators at all costs, under the rationale that a strong and uncompromising reaction would discourage any Chechen hostage incidents in the future. Not only did the fallacy of this argument come to light with the barricade hostage crises in Moscow and Beslan, this shortsighted approach also directly contributed to the tragic outcomes of both incidents.

## INDIAN PARLIAMENT ATTACK

In addition to the hostage crises outlined earlier, there are also several important cases of hostage-taking operations that did not materialize. While reviewing these cases does not provide any added benefit with respect to the negotiation aspect of hostage crisis management, these examples do serve as a useful tool for analyzing the likely shape of future terrorist barricade incidents.

On December 13, 2001, at 11:41 A.M., a white Ambassador displaying Ministry of Home Affairs parking label and flashing a red light, routinely entered the Indian Parliament complex in New Delhi. Once inside, the driver calmly steered left toward the Vijay Chowk end, but the fact that the car proceeded in the wrong direction caught the attention of security officer J.P. Yadav. After his instructions for the driver to stop were ignored, Yadav raised an alarm over the walkie-talkie. The car quickly raced on, but eventually crashed into the motorcade of Vice President Krishan Kant who was getting ready to leave the building.[156] Five heavily armed terrorists dressed in military fatigues emerged from the vehicle, and firing wildly they quickly dispersed throughout the compound. A forty-five-minute gun battle erupted, in which all five terrorists, nine policemen, and a gardener were killed, and sixteen additional people were injured. One of the terrorists died in an explosion after a bullet penetrated the suicide belt strapped to his waist.[157] Other terrorists were eliminated in different parts of the compound, some only meters away from the doors to the Central Hall of Parliament, in which several senior ministers and over 200 MPs (Members of the Parliament) were present at the time.[158] Ominously, since even security guards were not allowed to bear arms inside the building, had the terrorists been able to enter the Hall and close the gates, they would have had much of India's political leadership at their mercy.

The exact nature of the terrorists' plan is subject to much speculation. Some sources have drawn a link between the Parliament attack and another similar operation that took place just six weeks prior at the Jammu and Kashmir Legislative Assembly in Srinagar,[159] in which the sole apparent object of the terrorists' attention was Chief Minister Farooq Abdullah.[160] Drawing a link between these two incidents, the Indian intelligence community speculated about a possible plot to assassinate the then Prime Minister Vajpayee, who was supposed to address the Parliament on the day of the attack.[161] Another version alleged that the plan was to ram the explosives-laden vehicle into the main entrance of the Parliament complex in a suicide operation. According to this version the plan failed after the wires attached to the thirty-kilogram improvised explosive device (IED) came loose in the terrorists' collision with the vice president's motorcade. After the bomb failed to detonate, the terrorists allegedly changed their plans and improvised.[162] It seems more likely however, that the

hierarchy of plans would in fact be in reverse order, with the suicide detonation of the car bomb being only a backup plan in case the terrorists were
stopped while trying to enter the compound through the main gate.

So, what were the terrorists trying to achieve? Available evidence suggests that the primary objective of the attack was to take hostages inside
the Parliament building and issue demands. Supporting this theory is the
fact that inside the bags carried by the terrorists was a large quantity of
dried fruits, possibly indicating preparations for a longer standoff. In addition, the terrorists also had an outside accomplice who was monitoring
the parliamentary session on television, and whose role was to advise the
attackers about the location of the most influential parliamentarians via
a mobile phone.[163] Moreover, the fact that among the equipment found
in the terrorists' possession were radio-activated detonators, two wireless
sets,[164] five cell phones with chargers, and a rope[165] also seems to point in
the direction of a possible hostage-taking plan, as does the fact that one
of the attackers had direct experience with hostage-taking operations due
to his alleged involvement in the 1999 hijacking of Indian Airlines flight
IC-814.[166]

Despite the fact that the full scope of the Parliament operation never
materialized, this case is highly ominous, not only because of the severity
of potential consequences, but also due to the sophistication involved in
its planning. After arriving in New Delhi from Kashmir, the terrorists had
found refuge in the Christian Colony, where they were frequent visitors
to Internet cafés, downloading ID cards and the Home Ministry parking
tags from the "websity" Internet site, also studying the target's blueprints
online. In addition, the terrorists were also able to obtain uniforms normally worn by Indian security forces and purchase an Ambassador, which
they had fitted with a VIP red light to facilitate their smooth entry into the
complex. To be sure, the terrorists were also significantly aided by security
lapses, which included the ability of VIP escorts to enter the Parliament
complex without a security check, the nonfunctionality of three electric
strong gates that were installed shortly prior to the attack, the absence of
two mobile commando elements normally stationed at gates 1 and 2, and
the nonappearance of staff tasked with continually monitoring the CCTV
control rooms.[167] In the end, the Indian Government was extremely lucky.
The terrorists had studied only outdated blueprints of the complex, and
thus, were not aware of the newly constructed wall between gates 10 and
11.[168] This small detail then obstructed the terrorists' timely entry into the
Central Hall, saving India from falling victim to one of the most audacious
hostage-taking plots in history.

**KHOBAR**

Another case that deserves our attention is the 2004 al Qaida attack on
the Oasis residential compound in Khobar, Saudi Arabia, which according

to official reports involved a gruesome slaughter of nine hostages. And although in reality the hostage component of this crisis was not nearly as prevalent as official versions suggest, the attack still presents many lessons useful for the purposes of this book.

The twenty-five-hour rampage began on May 29, 2004, at 7:30 A.M., when four heavily armed gunmen, dressed in military uniforms and driving a car with military markings, entered the oil industry office compounds and attacked the Arab Petroleum Investment Corporation (API-CORP) and the "Petroleum Center." Moving between the buildings, the attackers shot at people in cars killing an American, a Briton, an Egyptian, two Filipinos, an Indian, and a Pakistani, along with two Saudi employees and seven security force members. The militants then tied the body of one of the dead Westerners to a car and dragged it down the road for over a mile before dumping it near a bridge.[169] Moving up the street, the terrorists then made their way into the luxurious Oasis residential complex, which houses primarily expatriates working for oil companies. Once inside, the terrorists opened fire on the armed guards[170] killing at least two of them before firing on surrounding buildings.[171] The gunmen then went from door to door in an apparent search for Westerners. Upon encountering anyone in the compound, the terrorists checked that person's identity documents, in order to identify his or her nationality and religion. Muslims were left alone, after being lectured about the terrorists' worldview, appropriate clothing, and the "real" meaning of Islam. Encountered non-Muslims had their throats slit immediately, with one Swedish hostage being fully decapitated and his head placed on the gate of the building. The attackers also cut the throats of "Filipino Christians" and "Hindu worshippers of cows" in proclaimed support of the Muslim separatist struggles in Mindanao and Kashmir.[172]

Five hours into the attack, the assailants moved freely to a hotel located inside the compound, where according to the official version they took hostages on the top floor of the six-storied building, supposedly booby-trapping the lower levels with explosives.[173] The terrorists then allegedly separated the Muslims from the non-Muslims.[174] After releasing five Lebanese hostages, the hostage takers gave a never-aired phone interview to *al Jazeera* in which they emphasized that only "infidels" were their targets, and that Muslims would not be hurt. While waiting in vain for the interview to air, the terrorists found out through a newscast, that a rescue operation was under way.[175]

It had taken the Saudi security forces five hours to arrive at the scene. Three hours later, the National Guard finally launched a rescue operation, which was however, easily repelled by the hostage takers after they managed to kill several troops and injure many more. Although the Saudis claimed to have attempted to persuade the gunmen to release the hostages and surrender before using force,[176] no serious attempts to initiate negotiations with the hostage takers had ever taken place.[177] In fact, the terrorists never even took any hostages per se; all identified foreigners were executed immediately, and the people who accompanied the terrorists on the hotel's top floor were, in fact, Muslim employees trying to take cover from the heavy arms fire coming from the outside.

Following the first rescue attempt the terrorists located an Italian citizen, whom they forced to plead for his life in a live *al Jazeera* broadcast before cutting his throat. The next assault was not launched until the morning of May 30, when a helicopter landed on the roof of the hotel and Saudi commandos stormed the location. This time the operation was declared a success, announcing the rescue of "most of the fifty foreigners held hostage" as well as the killing of two militants and the arrest of another.[178] However, according to the terrorists' own version of events the accuracy of which was confirmed to us by a well-informed source inside the security services, the attackers had already left the location on the night before, after breaking through all six layers of the security cordon. By the time the rescue operation had taken place the militants were already watching the helicopter land on the hotel's rooftop from miles away.[179] Only one of the terrorists, Nimr al Baqmi, was killed during the escape.[180]

A group known as the "Al Qaida Organization in the Arabian Peninsula" released a statement stating: "The heroic mujahideen in the Jerusalem Squad were able, by the grace of God, to raid the locations of American companies ... specializing in oil and exploration activities which are plundering the Muslims' resources." The statement explained that the group had targeted facilities "affiliated with the US occupation company Halliburton," which was selected because of being mentioned in a recent speech by Osama bin Laden."[181] In another statement the organization also denied "false claims" of the Saudi Government that the security forces had freed any hostages. "The mujahideen did not leave any of the hostages alive; instead, the mujahideen executed every infidel and crusader they could reach," the statement said.[182]

The final casualty count included twenty-two people killed and twenty-five more injured. According to an interview to al Qaida's journal *Sawt al-Jihad*, the operation's leader, Fawwaz bin Muhammad Al-Nashami, claimed that the original plan was to have one of the terrorists drive the explosives-laden car into the gate in a suicide attack, in order to clear the way for the other three attackers. But after the terrorists captured a guard in the street and forced him to open the gate, the terrorists did not need to blow up the car and instead drove it inside the compound. On June 20, 2004, an al Qaida media production company released a fifty-four-minute video providing the general background of the operation, an audio recording of the attack and video testaments from the group's leader and the attacker that was killed.[183]

Ominously, a number of different *jihadi* web sites also analyzed the lessons of the Khobar operation, discussing ways to improve operational procedures and calling for similar attacks in the future. Although published several days before the Khobar attack itself, the most important in this regard was the tenth issue of "Camp *al Battar* Magazine," al Qaida's online manual. Written by the late Abdul Aziz al Muqrin, the mastermind of the Khobar operation and former leader of al Qaida in Saudi Arabia, the manual provides a fascinating insight into the mind-set, expectations, and operational procedures likely to be employed by the "new terrorists" in future barricade hostage incidents. Further, it provides important evidence that the once prevalent assumption that "[terrorists] might have planned to take hostages, but do not have a clue about negotiating tactics or techniques" no longer holds.[184]

## CAMP AL BATTAR #10

In *al Battar*, al Muqrin employs a strikingly analytical, almost academic approach to identifying the scope of possible purposes and goals of launching what the manual calls "overt kidnappings." These include the "shedding of light on a specific cause, forcing a government or a group to carry out certain demands, or putting governments in a politically embarrassing situation." Al Muqrin also argues that history is full of examples of very successful hostage takings, above all "the operation carried out by Commander Shamil Basayev in Moscow." Al Muqrin goes on to argue that "although not all the goals were met ... the operation was 100 percent successful, because it brought [Chechnya] back to the attention of the international scene, therefore the Mujahideen got their reward."

This breakdown demonstrates the high level of strategic calculation on behalf of the contemporary *jihadi* groups. Barricade hostage takings are designed to achieve real time comprehensible and pragmatic goals, not to simply kill hostages, as has sometimes been suggested in the context of crises involving the "new terrorists." This means that negotiations still have a prominent role to play in managing these situations. It certainly seems to be the case from al Muqrin's perspective, since his manual stipulates the necessity for the hostage-taking team to include a "negotiating group," the role of which is labeled as "extremely important and sensitive." Moreover, the manual even prescribes procedures for the release of hostages and safe evacuation of the hostage-taking team from the target location following resolution, signaling confidence in the possibility of achieving a negotiated outcome.

Further, the aforementioned objective of making a cause visible worldwide suggests that the hostage takers are not at all immune to the light in which their cause will be perceived among the population they aspire to influence. This is one of the reasons why al Muqrin considers a hostage-taking operation to have a "missionary component as well" and thus instructs hostage takers to "observe the *Sharia* at all times," and not to "look at women." He even declares: "You must keep your word, as our religion has taught us, so don't kill any hostages after the enemy has accepted your terms and is carrying them out." This suggests that perhaps it is not completely inconceivable that terrorists may keep their promises, and fulfill the conditions specified under a negotiated agreement.

With regards to the negotiation process itself, al Muqrin instructs the hostage takers to pay close attention to the enemy negotiator, who is seen as nearly a superman and a dangerous person who can "strike fear and disappointment in the hostage takers' hearts, as he works to know the personality and the psychological condition of the kidnappers and their respective morale. He would know immediately if the [hostage takers'] morale is down or whether [they] are determined and ready to carry out [their] threats." Al Muqrin also claims that the negotiator is most likely the leader of the response team, who has the authority to give the go ahead for the storming of the location. This is the one mistake that al Muqrin makes—negotiations are practically never handled by the commanding officer in order to exploit the deferment of authority strategy. Another mistake in the manual is the suggestion that buying time in the negotiations inevitably signals the planning of a rescue operation. This presents a considerable challenge to the negotiators of future incidents, who will have to work very hard to break this perception and establish at least some level of mutual trust.

For forming a team of executors for a barricade hostage operation, al Muqrin prescribes selecting only individuals that have the capacity to withstand psychological pressure and extremely difficult conditions, possess sharp intelligence and wit along with improvisational skills, as well as the ability to control the enemy effectively. Given the perceived high importance of the "negotiation element," al Muqrin states that the negotiator on the side of the hostage takers must be "very calm, with a strict personality, who does not let any feelings or emotions filter through, has the capacity to properly express himself and the demands of the group, and to explain the cause for which he has carried out such an act." In addition, al Muqrin is very specific on the point that the incident must not be prolonged since the "capability of the group gets weaker by the day and tensions rise." In order to achieve a prompt fulfillment of their demands, the hostage takers are instructed to execute hostages in the beginning of the incident to prove their willingness to carry out their threats. Especially interesting and important is the remark that executions apply to only those hostages that are "eligible for such action." This suggests that despite the acceptability of killing hostages, a certain discriminatory key for their selection is likely to exist. Elsewhere in the manual it is specified that these "eligible hostages" include the members of security services found among the hostages who "must be killed instantly ... to prevent others from showing resistance." The manual also prescribes the separation of the young men who "constitute a threat with their youthfulness." Following this line of thought, it seems that specifically young men are likely to become the next in line for executions in the event that no "security elements" are found among the hostages or if additional executions are seen as necessary. This has important implications that are consistent with some of the analysis presented earlier, most importantly the fact that executions of male hostages do not automatically translate into an increased probability of indiscriminate execution for other types of hostages. This means that even if some hostages are executed, the possibility of achieving a negotiated settlement should not be mechanically excluded. Understanding the logic for the selection of specific hostages for execution and the circumstances in which these killings occur will become vital to the analysis of whether the terrorists are indeed prepared to kill *all* of their hostages indiscriminately and in cold blood.

At the same time, it is important to note that many of the instructions in the manual also focus on disrupting the formation of the Stockholm Syndrome[185] in order to preserve the hostage takers' resolve to kill their hostages if necessary. These measures include the instructions to keep the faces of the hostage takers and the eyes of the hostages covered at all times, and to only approach the hostages in cases of emergency and necessity, keeping the distance to no less than 1.5 meters. Such measures are designed to limit interaction with the hostages, and thus reduce the chances of their humanization in the minds of the hostage takers. Consequently, executions of some hostages throughout the course of barricade hostage crises involving the "new terrorists" constitute a likely development.

Another area where the manual complicates the negotiator's job is the high level of distrust toward the authorities transparent in the claim that "in almost every case, the enemy will try to con and attack the hostage takers." As a result of this expectation, the one section that receives the most attention in the manual is operational security. Many preventive measures are prescribed including the booby-trapping of the location, division of labor, rotation of guards, strategic positioning of snipers, checking the floor plan for possible entrances, paying attention to the ventilation system, and the threat of use of gas or diversion during counterattack. The extent of attention devoted to security is remarkable, signaling that the hostage takers' personal safety is an issue of serious concern, and that despite their proclaimed desire to die and become martyrs, the achievement of demands and other political objectives seem to take priority over anything else. This is especially the case given the instructions for the hostage takers to cover their faces, speak in a language other than their own in order to conceal their identity, as well as the detailed guidelines for a safe withdrawal from the location. This suggests that the hostage takers' proclaimed desire to die does not necessarily preclude the possibility of a negotiated settlement.

## CONCLUSIONS

The case studies examined in this chapter carry a number of important lessons and implications for the future. Firstly, we have seen that historical barricade hostage incidents bearing many of the characteristics of the "new terrorism" were essentially associated with unanticipated circumstances and unexpected developments, as opposed to being the product of the terrorists' precise preparations. For instance, the killing of hostages and suicides of hostage takers tended to take place in situations where the terrorists ran into sudden obstacles to their original plan; where they were pushed into a corner by a blunt refusal of the authorities to even discuss their demands; or were violently confronted in a rescue operation. This, of course, does not in any way relieve the terrorists of their responsibility for creating the crises in the first place. At the same time, it is vital to recognize that the negative results in these instances were essentially associated with the respective governments' refusal to negotiate, principally over demands that in retrospect were not unfeasible to fulfill. This is not to suggest that the authorities should have been "soft" or that they simply should have "given in" to the terrorists. The key point to emphasize here is that even in cases where the authorities have no intention to make concessions, they can still use negotiation to influence the outcome, or at the very least, offer an alternative in the form of a well-thought-out strategy *not to negotiate*. We must realize that the tragic results of many of the cases discussed in this chapter occurred when the authorities engaged in frustrated knee-jerk reactions constituting mainly of an emotional refusal to even listen to the hostage takers, and hasty rescue operations that were launched despite the lack of preparedness and thorough contingency planning. Consequently, the *worst* possible lesson we could draw from these cases is that negotiation has nothing to offer to incidents involving the "new terrorists."

On the contrary, it appears that one of the most important implications of the case studies discussed in this chapter is that even in instances bearing all the characteristics of the "new terrorism," such as highly credible suicidal posture, executions of hostages, and a team of hostage takers capable of repelling a rescue operation, negotiation can still achieve significant gains. This suggests that despite the escalating dynamics of terrorist barricade hostage crises, there is no reason to disregard negotiations as an option automatically simply because the given scenario does not fit the model characteristics of a "negotiable" incident.

The final key lesson of this chapter is the confirmation that terrorist plots and training manuals are indeed increasingly geared toward significant operational improvements prompted by the terrorists' understanding of our operating procedures. As the "Camp *al Battar*" manual demonstrates, the "new terrorists" are indeed preparing themselves for the obstruction of many of the mechanism and dynamics that make the traditional crisis negotiation approach work, such as the use of indirect communications to disrupt the building of rapport between negotiators on both sides, minimization of interaction between the hostage takers and hostages in order to obstruct the formation of the Stockholm Syndrome, preparations designed to mitigate the effects of prolongation of the incident, and the carrying out of executions in order to pressurize the authorities and eliminate direct physical risk. This, of course, will make future barricade hostage crises incredibly challenging. An analysis of alternative approaches designed to cope with these challenges will be offered in Chapter 6, following the in-depth analysis of the two most influential barricade incidents of recent years: the Moscow theatre and the Beslan school hostage crises.

# CHAPTER 3

## NORD-OST

On October 23, 2002, at 9:15 P.M., two vans carrying a group of armed men and women arrived at the Dubrovka Theater on Melnikova Street in Moscow.[1] In the next thirty minutes, terrorists entered the theater during the performance of the popular "Nord-Ost" musical, and with swift action took 979 people hostage. The fifty-eight-hour ordeal that would ultimately be ended by a controversial rescue operation in which 129 hostages died, was about to begin.[2]

The Moscow theatre hostage crisis personified the characteristics of the "new terrorism" to a greater extent than any other hostage crisis to that date. A large team of highly experienced and brutalized fighters armed with fanatical religious rhetoric that worshiped the cult of martyrdom and called for the indiscriminate destruction of unbelievers. Terrorists who were extremely well prepared, strategically deploying snipers in key areas around the building and using mines and booby traps to secure the site. Two large explosive devices placed in the middle of the theater hall, which according to initial analysis had the potential to bring down the building thus killing everyone inside. Unconditional demands that from the very beginning seemed impossible to fulfill. From this very setup, it is clear that the Moscow theater hostage crisis is a vital case study in any meaningful exploration of the issue of negotiating hostage crises involving the "new terrorists." This chapter will reconstruct the events that took place in Moscow, followed by an analysis of the incident in terms of negotiability. Critical flaws of the negotiation approach employed in the standoff will be identified, along with an analytical assessment of the possible alternatives that were available to the Russian authorities as the crisis progressed.

### BASIC INCIDENT TIMELINE

#### Day 1

On October 23, 2002, at 21:15 P.M., a group of armed men and women dressed in plain clothes arrived at the theatre building. The two minivans were left outside with their engines still running, as the terrorists sprayed the entrance with gunfire and quickly made their way into the main lobby. Once inside the complex, the commandos changed into military fatigues and covered their faces.[3] Minutes later, shouting slogans and firing into the air, the gunmen stepped on the stage during Act II of the "Nord-Ost" musical, joined by several other team members who were disguised among the audience. At this point, few spectators realized that the emergence of armed militants was not a part of the show, which was set in World War II and filled with special effects. When the terrorists fired more shots and commanded the actors to leave the stage and join the spectators as hostages, however, it became clear that the assault was for real. The man on the stage announced that the goal of the operation was to stop the war in Chechnya, and commanded: "Get out your cell phones! Call your friends! Call your families! Tell them we've taken you hostage!"[4]

As soon as the audience and staff were subdued the militants set up booby traps around the building and declared that they would blow up the structure if Russian forces attempted to rescue the hostages by force. According to the Russian press agency INTERFAX, the Chechens installed thirty different explosive charges around the theater, the largest of which was equivalent to roughly 110 pounds of TNT. Made out of two metal containers filled with ball bearings and containing an artillery shell as the main charge, the bomb was divided into two parts, one placed in the fifteenth row of the main auditorium and the other in the balcony area. The detonator was placed in the hands of one of the female terrorists. The remaining explosive charges consisted of 6–8 pound hexogen bombs placed throughout the theater and 1.75–4.5 pound plastid suicide belts strapped around the waists of nineteen female terrorists.

About thirty minutes after the initial takeover, the president of the Russian Federation, the heads of federal ministries and the Moscow city authorities were all notified of the attack.[5] One hour later, the police and elite Alpha troops sealed off the building and nearby streets, summoning at least two armored personnel carriers, twenty police cars, five fire trucks, and a handful of ambulances to the scene.[6] Operational headquarters was established in the Veterans Hospital, which is located next to the theatre complex. Headed by the deputy director of the Federal Security Service (FSB), Vladimir Pronichev, the command centre also included representatives from the Ministry of Internal Affairs, Ministry of Emergency Situations, Ministry of Defense, Committee on Health Protection, and other agencies responsible for management of extreme situations. Almost immediately, special units of the FSB Special Operations Center (SOC) began rehearsing assault scenarios at a similar building located in another part of the city.[7]

In the meantime, inside the auditorium the terrorists called for citizens of Azerbaijan or Georgia, and anyone with small children, to approach the stage.[8] Subsequently a group of thirty people including twenty children under the age of twelve and several pregnant women were set free. Kids older than twelve would have to stay. "In Chechnya children that age are soldiers," explained Movsar Barayev, the leader of the group.[9]

### Day 2

Shortly after midnight Aslanbek Aslakhanov, State Duma deputy for Chechnya, made the first reported contact with the terrorists. At 12:40 A.M., hostage Tatiana Solnyshkina, phoned the NTV television network, begging for the security services not to storm the building. In the conversation, the journalist suggested for the terrorists to express their demands live on television.[10] The hostage takers apparently liked the idea, and an hour later Aslakhanov confirmed that the terrorists declared their intention to make a statement to the media.[11] This situation presented a clear opportunity for an early exchange of mutual favors, in which providing access to the media would have been traded for the release of additional hostages. Whether this approach was applied is unclear, but shortly after Aslakhanov's announcement, seventeen additional hostages were released without any conditions attached. Simultaneously, the terrorists announced their readiness to release "fifty to hundred more hostages" in exchange for the head of the pro-Moscow Chechen administration Akhmat Kadyrov. "If Putin wants to save the lives of fifty of his citizens, let him send Kadyrov here to negotiate with us," the hostage takers declared.[12]

Four hours into the siege, the Russian Government made its first official statement in which the authorities publicly promised not to storm the theatre unless the terrorists started killing hostages. Simultaneously, the Kremlin offered the hostage takers a "green path" to any third country if all hostages were immediately released, also categorically excluding the possibility of making a ransom payment to end the crisis.[13] This public announcement produced mixed results. While the first part of the statement was a good strategic choice that had the potential to decrease tension on all sides, the offer for a "green path" was a clear misstep. Not only was this offer made to an audience of fighters who kept repeating their desire for martyrdom and were thus likely to be insulted by the idea of their personal safety being used publicly as a bargaining chip. Even more importantly, the offer came just four hours after the beginning of the incident, at a point when the terrorists, who had been preparing for this moment for months, were at the stage of experiencing feelings of excitement and invincibility. And while the "green path" is certainly a tool that has historically been very successful in resolving barricade hostage incidents, it will only work at a stage when the hostage takers are already exhausted and have begun to modify their expectations. Making the offer of safe passage this early in the incident was unwise and only served to provoke the hostage takers. A similar effect can be ascribed to the statement ruling out the possibility of a ransom payment; not only did the terrorists not make a such a demand, the public trivialization of their motive as pure self-enrichment was bound to be highly offensive to hostage takers who saw themselves as fighting for a greater just cause. Quite simply, while the first public statement made by the authorities was designed to bring calm and stability into the situation, it achieved just the opposite.

Another attempt to stabilize the situation was made by Aslanbek Aslakhanov, a native Chechen, who made a public appeal to his compatriots living in Moscow to come to the theatre and try to influence the terrorists.[14] A considerable number of Chechens heeded this call, clearly creating uncomfortable pressure for the terrorists who responded by the threat to kill ten hostages for every member of the Chechen diaspora who offered him or herself as a substitute hostage.[15] Nevertheless, until this point the hostage crisis was progressing without any loss of life, and the terrorists independently continued to release hostages. By 4:00 A.M., the number of hostages that had either been freed or escaped had reached 150. Then shortly after 4:00 A.M. a young woman suddenly entered the auditorium. Despite warnings and repeated threats from the terrorists, she approached the stage making inflammatory remarks about the hostage takers and shouting at the hostages to flee. Following a brief moment of confusion and uncertainty, the terrorists decided to shoot the woman, later explaining that she was a spy sent by the FSB as a part an established secret services tactic previously used in the Budyonnovsk siege. In reality the dead woman was Olga Romanova, a twenty-five-year-old shop assistant, whose apartment was located inside the secure perimeter, providing an explanation for how she was able to breach the cordon.

Unlike in most hostage crises where the killing of a hostage is a highly volatile development and a serious setback to the negotiation process, inside the theatre the terrorists proceeded to prepare for the release of another group of hostages: "Everyone with foreign passports, come up!" the terrorists shouted. "Don't worry," a female Chechen assured the group. "We're starting negotiations this morning. We'll release you. This is our war, not yours."[16] This intention to release all foreigners was made public shortly thereafter in a phone call to the Chechen separatist Kavkaz Center news agency. At this time, the terrorists declared to have in their possession thirty foreign nationals, and announced the intention to release them in the morning. Simultaneously, the first specific deadline was pronounced, as the terrorists gave the government of Russia seven days to fulfill the demand of withdrawing all its troops from Chechnya.

As the morning approached, the foreign hostages were informed that their release had been scheduled for 9:00 A.M. This action was apparently the terrorists' own initiative, as the only negotiations up to this point consisted of Aslakhanov's refuted suggestion to use Chechen politician

Ruslan Khasbulatov as negotiator. In addition the terrorists were provided with a telephone number to the operational headquarters, which however, according to the hostage takers themselves, was allegedly not operational.[17] Around 6:00 A.M. the terrorists announced in a phone call to Kavkaz Center that they had killed a "drunken policeman who approached the central entrance of the theater and did not respond to warnings and threats." This death was denied by the officials at the time. Only more than a year later did the authorities confirm that the man was FSB Colonel Konstantin Vasilyev, who was killed when approaching the building on his own initiative in an attempt to exchange himself for the children.[18]

As the morning deadline for the release of all foreign hostages approached, the terrorists compiled a list of their names, which specified that there were seventy-six foreigners inside, which included citizens of the Netherlands, Bulgaria, Canada, Australia, Latvia, Moldova, Yugoslavia, Belarus, Turkmenistan, Azerbaijan, Armenia, Georgia, USA, Germany, Great Britain, Switzerland, and Ukraine. Only one condition was set for the foreigners' release—the terrorists would only hand them over to the representatives of their respective embassies.[19] But despite the arrival of embassy representatives at the crisis site, this ostensibly easy exchange never materialized. According to Alexander Machevsky, a spokesperson for the Russian crisis team, the opportunity was lost because the diplomats "did not get there on time and [thus] the agreement was broken."[20]

At 10:20 A.M. the terrorists communicated through hostage Maria Shkolnikova, their demand to hold talks with representatives of the International Red Cross and Doctors without Borders (Medecins Sans Frontieres). They also specified a condition that no Russian citizens were allowed to be among them.[21] The refusal to speak to Russian nationals was reversed only ninety minutes later, as the terrorists demanded to meet with a group of prominent Russian figures who have in the past advocated a peaceful solution to the Chechen conflict. These included journalist Anna Politkovskaya, and politicians Irina Khakamada and Grigory Yavlinsky. Following the revelation that Yavlinsky was not present in Moscow, the terrorists demanded another liberal politician, Boris Nemtsov, to take his place.

At 1:00 P.M., a politician and popular singer Iosif Kobzon entered the theatre along with Red Cross doctors. During his fifteen-minute stay inside, he was told that while the terrorists gave the government a week to retreat its troops from Chechnya, the deadline for hostage executions was considerably more imminent: "If we don't see or hear from our commander that there is some movement in *three days* [emphasis added], if only one shot is fired or one mop-up operation is carried out on Chechen soil, or if one military action is launched, we will immediately start killing the hostages," the terrorists told Kobzon.[22] After this short discussion more hostages were freed, as Red Cross representatives led out an elderly Englishman while Kobzon exited the theatre with a woman and three children. Two hours later, Kobzon entered the theatre again along with Irina Khakamada, but their efforts to achieve the release of more hostages were unsuccessful. According to Khakamada the hostage takers argued that they had already released all of the children, and that anyone over twelve years of age could not be considered a child.[23] While the failure to achieve additional release of hostages was a setback, another positive development took place during the negotiations as the terrorists renewed their proposal to release "hostages from countries [they were] not fighting." Nevertheless, despite a number of Russian authorities' promising announcements to the media, the deal again failed to materialize.

At 6:35 P.M., several shots were suddenly fired inside the theater. Minutes later it became clear that the gunshots did not signal the beginning of the threatened hostage executions but rather were an unsuccessful attempt by the gunmen to stop two women hostages from escaping the location. This high-pressure moment was followed by a relatively calm afternoon highlighted by several unsuccessful attempts to convince hostage takers to accept food for the hostages, and by an announcement from Grozny in which the separatist Chechen President Aslan Maskhadov denounced the attack.[24]

In addition, the Qatar-based Arabic channel *al-Jazeera* aired a prerecorded videotape made by the terrorists before the attack, in which one of the female hostage takers proclaimed: "We have been waiting for a just, humanitarian solution, but humanity is living in a state of slumber and does not care about the killing of innocent people. Old men, women, and children are being killed in Chechnya ... The Russian occupiers have flooded our land with our children's blood. Therefore, we have chosen this path, the path of struggle for the Chechen people's freedom." Also in the tape, the group's leader announced: "Each one of us is willing to sacrifice himself for the sake of God and the independence of Chechnya. I swear by God that we are more keen on dying than you are on living."[25] Later in the evening, Barayev would have a chance to repeat this sentence once more during an interview with Mark Franchetti, the *Sunday Times'* correspondent, whom the terrorists granted entry for about twenty minutes in the late hours of the second day.

### Day 3

On October 25, shortly after midnight, the terrorists allowed doctor Leonid Roshal to enter the building with a supply of medicines. Around 3:00 A.M. Roshal was accompanied by a group of NTV reporters and a cameraman, who filmed another interview with Barayev, his deputies, several female hostage takers, and a number of hostages. According to the journalists, Barayev declared that he was ready to release a group of children if the interview was aired on television.[26] Shortly after the reporters left, the terrorists freed one hostage, followed by the additional release of six more people an hour later. The details of the conditions of this release are unclear, but according to federal authorities all those freed were Russian citizens, adults of both sexes.[27]

In addition to this positive development, in the early morning hours of the third day, the terrorists announced that all the foreign citizens held inside the theatre would be freed as soon as their official representatives arrived to receive them personally. Yet again, the diplomats stood by as the deadline kept being postponed, until the deal was eventually called off altogether. The official explanation given by the terrorists inside was that the ambassadors again failed to arrive on time. But one of the hostages who managed to call his respective ambassador at the time, was told: "We were there, but the Russians won't allow us to go through [to] the terrorists."[28]

The repeated failure to achieve the release of all foreign nationals presented a frustrating setback. In addition, as the atmosphere inside the theatre was already becoming more tense, another volatile moment followed after a hot water pipe burst on the ground floor. The terrorists, who interpreted this development as a sign of preparations for a rescue operation, responded by threatening to start executing hostages unless the "provocations" stopped.[29] The terrorists were clearly losing patience. At this time, some of the hostages decided to make their own negotiation initiative,[30] making telephone calls to the command centre in which they suggested that the remaining children inside the theatre would be released if an antiwar demonstration took place by midday and was televised. Initially, they demanded the demonstration to take place near the command centre, but later revised the location to Red Square. The hostages also conveyed the terrorists' threat to start killing hostages the next day, unless the Russian military started pulling out of Chechnya.

Before noon a group of about thirty desperate relatives staged a short demonstration near the theatre building, but was not allowed to proceed closer through the police cordon. After long deliberations, the FSB eventually allowed another rally to take place on the Red Square, under the condition that the number of participants did not exceed twenty people.[31] Shortly after noon, a group of eight children aged between six and twelve was released into the hands of representatives of the International Committee of the Red Cross. Dimitri Rogozin, chairman of the Russian Parliament's international affairs committee, claimed that "the children were released without any conditions," in an obvious attempt to delink the protest rallies with the freeing of hostages. At 2:00 P.M., Rogozin also announced that the release of foreign nationals was only a matter of another three to four hours. This positive atmosphere subsided again shortly, however, after the NTV interview with Barayev videotaped earlier was

broadcast in a censored form showing only video without sound.[32] This
visibly upset the hostage takers, and according to the hostages, a group of
children already prepared for release was told to go back to their seats.[33]
"That's it!" one of the leading hostage takers shouted. "No more negotiations! Now we start killing hostages!"[34]

Before 3:00 P.M., another key negotiator demanded earlier by the terrorists arrived at the scene: Anna Politkovskaya, who was in Los Angeles at
the time of the takeover receiving a prize for courage in journalism for her
work on Chechnya. After entering the theatre building along with doctor Roshal, Politkovskaya held a meeting with the terrorists in which she
learned what exact actions had to be taken, and who would have to verify
the initiation of these actions in order for all of the hostages to be freed. The
first specific demand was that President Putin should publicly comment
in some way on the issue of ending the war in Chechnya. The terrorists
did not demand any written document or decree, just an oral statement.
Secondly, in the course of a day, Putin should demonstrate that his words
are not empty by, for example, taking the armed forces out of any one
Chechen district, and this action was to be confirmed with the help of an
international mediator, more specifically Lord Judd of the Council of Europe. If these demands were fulfilled the hostage takers were prepared to
release all the remaining hostages.[35]

Around 4:00 P.M. an emergency meeting was held at the Kremlin, during which an apparent decision was made to rescue the hostages by
force.[36] Immediately after the meeting, FSB deputy director Nikolai Patrushev made a public promise to "spare the lives of the terrorists" if all
hostages were immediately released unharmed. As one might expect, the
terrorists became very upset and cut off all negotiations. Not only did
the Russians again put to question the hostage takers' determination to
die and become martyrs, their last offer was an offensive ultimatum: free
all the hostages and we may not kill you.... Following Patrushev's announcement Barayev returned to the auditorium, swearing profusely in
Chechen. The hostages enquiring about what had happened were told by
one of the female terrorists: "Now we will start taking radical measures."
Later the hostages heard from a radio broadcast that the terrorists threatened to start executing ten hostages every hour, beginning at dawn.[37]

During the evening, several negotiators made desperate efforts to save
the negotiations. Between 9:00 and 10:00 P.M., former Ingush President
Ruslan Aushev, former Russian Prime Minister Yevgeni Primakov, as well
as aforementioned Member of Parliament (MP) Aslakhanov and singer
Alla Pugacheva made contacts with the hostage takers in attempts to free
at least a few more hostages. But the terrorists made it clear that this
would not happen: "We have freed everyone we could free," one of the
gunmen told *Reuters* in a telephone call. "What happens now depends
on Russia's leadership, on what agreement it can reach with our senior

representatives."[38] However, at 10:00 P.M., a group of four hostages, three women and one man, was released from the theater following a promise to release any citizens of Azeraijan made by one of the gunman, Abu Said, in a live interview on Azeri television.[39] These four people would be the last hostages to be freed.

At 10:50 P.M., Russian special services reportedly intercepted a telephone conversation between Barayev and a "foreign interlocutor" in Qatar: "Tomorrow we will go ... Work will start tomorrow and we will begin by shooting the fattest cats."[40] The situation was worsening. An hour before midnight, the terrorists received a telephone call from General Kazantsev, Putin's special envoy in Chechnya. In the phone call, Kazantsev agreed to fly to Moscow and be at the theatre by 11:00 A.M. to conduct negotiations. "Look, all I ask is don't lose your cool, don't take any unnecessary steps," Kazantsev pleaded. "Okay, we will be waiting. See you later," came the reply. According to the hostages, following this conversation the terrorists' mood suddenly changed, they acted happily and some of them took off their masks. This was a triumph; the hostage takers would get to talk to Putin's man with the authority to make decisions, and now the negotiations could finally start moving forward. Barayev informed the hostages about the good news, and told them that they could relax until 10:30 A.M.

In this quiet atmosphere, around 11:30 P.M., a man was seen walking toward the front door of the theater building. Once he was inside the terrorists intercepted the man, beat him up, and brought him to the auditorium. "Who are you, and why have you come?" Barayev asked. The man explained that he had come to fetch his son, Roma.[41] The terrorists then shouted throughout the auditorium: "Who is his son? Who here is Roma?" No response. Then they took the man to the stage in front of everyone and asked: "This means there is no such son?" "I guess not," the man replied. Suspecting another FSB spy, the terrorists led the father into the hallway and shot him. Just moments later, an overwrought male hostage leapt to his feet and charged toward the Chechen woman guarding the primary explosive, throwing a bottle at her in stride. She fired into the air and yelled for him to sit down, but he continued on. Another terrorist then fired at the man. The bullet missed its target but pierced the head of hostage Pavel Zakharov who was seated in the vicinity, and another bullet penetrated the chest of hostage Tamara Starkova.[42] The hostage takers were allegedly distraught, and told the hostages to call the Red Cross.[43] When the phone call came into the command center requesting medical assistance, the callers apparently did not describe the circumstances of the shooting, and those on the other end of the line neglected to ask.[44] One of the gunmen then took the phone from the hostages and said: "If you think that you can smother us here, you are mistaken. You are smothering your own people. At least come and get your own!"[45] It took more than an hour to convince the authorities to send medical help. The ambulances themselves did not arrive until 3:00 A.M. "Tell them it wasn't our fault you were shot," Barayev instructed Starkova as she was leaving the building.

By then the situation in the auditorium had again calmed down, as hostages understood that nothing was likely to happen until morning. At this time, Barayev called on the hostages: "Any Americans here? Call the consulate, talk to them, and tomorrow morning we'll let you go." After a phone call to the U.S. embassy, the terrorists agreed to release American Sandy Booker, his Kazakh fiancée Svetlana Gubareva, and her daughter Alexandra at 8:00 A.M.[46] But this would turn out to be too late.

### Day 4

Less than an hour into Saturday, October 26, 2002, a restricted message began to circulate among officials and reporters on the scene of the crisis— the Spetsnaz, Russia's elite counterterrorism force, was planning to raid the theater at 6:00 A.M., the Chechens' original deadline for the initiation of hostage executions. In the early morning hours, however, the alleged belief that the terrorists had already begun to execute hostages significantly truncated the raid's timeline. According to the Kremlin spokesman Alexander Machevsky, after the shooting inside and the call for ambulances, the general feeling at the command center was that the terrorists had begun carrying out their threats of executing hostages, leading to the decision to initiate the storming as soon as possible. The command center notified the city's ambulance service, and the Spetsnaz quietly moved into place.[47]

Witness accounts state that shortly after Spetsnaz forces arrived on the scene, the situation inside the theater grew tense. Apparently aware of the new developments outside, some of the terrorists rushed into the main hall of the theater, shouting to their compatriots that an assault was about to begin. This was likely triggered by the fact that the lights that illuminated the main entrance to the theatre went out. During daytime the terrorists had warned that if these lights were shut off, they would regard this development as the beginning of a storm, and would respond by shooting the hostages.[48]

It seems that the Russians' intent to use an incapacitating gas in the raid, though discussed for days prior to the actual assault,[49] only became apparent when team members entering the adjacent nightclub were spotted carrying gas cylinders.[50] Reports conflict regarding the timeframe and location of the gas' dispersal, but the consensus is that the gas was released into the air-conditioning system sometime around 5:15 A.M.[51]

Meanwhile, tensions had largely subsided within the theater. While many hostages and hostage takers alike reportedly sprawled out over the theater seats and slept, Barayev and other prominent members of the

Chechen team spent their time in the theater's sound and lighting room, editing a videotape of the raid recorded by the hostage takers themselves and by the theater's security cameras.[52]

As the gas crept into the auditorium, it drew the attention of both the terrorists and the hostages.[53] Judging by a phone call from one of the hostages to a local radio station, the people inside the auditorium knew about the assault for at least two minutes before being overwhelmed by the gas. Rebels rushed about the theater screaming "Gas! Gas!" and "Turn on the air conditioning!"[54] While some succumbed to the effects of the gas before any defensive action could be taken, others successfully donned respirators that had been brought along for the attack.[55] In addition, those terrorists situated in areas far enough removed from the point(s) of release[56] were not exposed to the gas in large enough quantities to be overwhelmed. Similarly, not all occupants of the theatre hall reacted to the gas in same way. One of the hostages walked out of the theater fully conscious after a full twenty minutes of exposure to the gas. Thus, it is certain that a significant number of the hostage takers remained conscious long enough to kill all hostages in the theater, had they truly desired to do so.

About twenty minutes after the release of the gas, the Spetsnaz forces approached the theater in three small teams. The first team took cover outside, while the second and third teams entered the "Central Station" nightclub that shared a wall with the theater.[57] Once inside the club, one team paused and made preparations to blast through this wall. The other team proceeded into the club's basement and entered a tunnel system beneath the theater, then advanced to a set of iron doors marking the orchestra pit and forced these doors open using an explosive charge.

Entry by the three Spetsnaz teams appears to have been graded. By almost all accounts and as best determined by temporal associations,[58] it was the team outside the theater that struck first, engaging the unaffected rebels in the corridor either from the outside or from within the corridor itself.[59] The sound of gunfire drew a number of those rebels not incapacitated by the gas out of the auditorium and toward the exchange.[60] At the raid's outset, Barayev was immediately located in the upstairs kitchen and killed along with the other rebel leaders.[61] As the engagement in the corridor continued, the underground team entered directly into the auditorium from the orchestra pit and began to evacuate hostages immediately, wary of the fact that the explosives could be detonated at any time.[62]

Spetsnaz forces ultimately converged on the auditorium and were successful in eliminating the primary threat.[63] By approximately 7:00 A.M., only three terrorists remained alive within the theater. They surrendered and were escorted away, while a fourth, apparently trying to blend in with a crowd of journalists, was apprehended outside. Several others were thought to have escaped in the chaos.[64] By 7:20 A.M., the siege was over and the building was declared secure.[65]

However, what seemed to be a miraculous rescue was soon revealed as something much less, as incapacitated hostages started dying in their seats, choking on their own vomit and swallowing their own tongues. Since no information was provided to doctors in the nearby hospitals about the gas, responders were inadequately prepared to treat the incoming patient load. The incapacitant utilized in the raid was in fact a derivative of the highly potent opioid fentanyl, which is commonly used in emergency rooms as an anesthetic,[66] and for which a common antidote naloxone (Narcan) exists. Had the responders been informed, and had enough doses of the antidote been stocked at the site, many hostages' lives could have been saved. In the absence of this effort, the casualty levels were catastrophic: of the 129 hostages that died, 126 were killed due to the effects of the gas used in the assault. Hundreds of other people were treated for the effects of gas exposure, many of them suffering from disabilities to this day. Forty-one terrorists were killed, some of them in their sleep, others while they were already subdued and handcuffed.

## INCIDENT ASSESSMENT

This portion of the chapter will analyze the potential of negotiations as a possible tool for the resolution of the incident. Firstly, the motivations and strategic calculus of the attackers will be examined. What were they trying to achieve? What was their best possible outcome? What were their best alternatives to a negotiated agreement (BATNA)? Without understanding these questions, it is impossible to design an appropriate negotiation strategy. Secondly, traditional analytical frameworks for assessing the negotiability of hostage incidents will be used to identify the negative indicators of volatility, as well as comparatively positive indicators of de-escalation that were also present. Simultaneously, the weaknesses of a mechanical application of this framework to Nord-Ost-style incidents will be identified. And finally, this section will analyze the successes and missed opportunities of negotiations in Nord-Ost in order to draw lessons for the future.

### The Chechen Team

Although presented to the world as Movsar Barayev, the Chechen commando unit was actually headed by one Mansur Salamov,[67] twenty-two-year-old nephew of Arbi Barayev,[68] the infamous leader of the Special Purpose Islamic Regiment (SPIR) who was allegedly personally responsible for the deaths of some 170 people.[69] It was precisely Arbi's notoriety as a ruthless bandit and murderer that the authorities were seeking to exploit when they referred to Movsar as "Barayev," with the apparent goal of evoking resentment and condemnation by association.[70]

After Arbi was killed in June 2001 in an eight-day Russian operation in Alkhan-Khala, his body was shown on television as proof. Movsar then assumed leadership of SPIR, along with control of the main highway in Chechnya and the kidnap-for-ransom industry dominated by Barayev's group at the time. Besides Arbi, Movsar also had a famous aunt, Khava, who became the first ever Chechen suicide bomber when she drove an explosives-laden truck into a military base at Alkhan-Yurt in June 2000.[71] Yet another prominent woman from the Barayev clan was Arbi's wife, Zura, who was one of the women fighters accompanying Movsar in the Nord-Ost operation.[72]

Despite the fact that Movsar Barayev was consistently portrayed as the leader of the group, it should be noted that the operational command and negotiations were actually in the hands of a man who called himself Abu Bakar (a.k.a Ruslan Elmurzayev).[73] After the raid, Shamil Basayev, the key organizer of the attack, admitted that Barayev was only included in the commando team in September, after three other more suitable candidates were killed in separate incidents over the summer.[74] In fact, according to some accounts, Movsar, an alleged drug addict with a very short attention span, spent most of the incident sleeping in the kitchen area of the second floor lobby.[75] Elmurzayev's leadership role was evident during the crisis when he categorically overruled Barayev's consent to a journalist seeking permission to take pictures inside the auditorium.[76] Elmurzayev was resident in Moscow, and was the head of economic security and a shareholder of the Prima Bank. Several months before the attack, Elmurzayev took out two loans, for $10,000 and $30,000 respectively. This money was allegedly used to fund the attack.[77]

The composition of the Nord-Ost commando unit, which called itself the Riyadus-Salikhin Suicide Battalion (RAS)[78] was highly strategic. Nineteen out of the fifty-four armed commandos[79] were women in the age group of 16–43, many of them widows of the conflict in Chechnya. Female operatives are ideal for such high-profile operations, as they are generally considered more focused and dedicated, and thus much more result-oriented than males, who are often driven by adventurism and the machismo element. While one might expect that women would be softer on hostages because of their motherly instinct, women terrorists actually tend to be more ruthless precisely because of this instinct; once they decide that their violent actions will benefit their children and future generations, they will generally not hesitate to do what they feel is necessary for the success of the operation. This was confirmed in Moscow, where many hostages reported that the women terrorists practiced much more merciless physical and psychological treatment of hostages than most of the men. The proportion of women to men in the commando unit was of further significance. Enough women were present to form a large and powerful unit of dedicated suicide bombers, but they were still a minority, allowing the exploitation of their desire to prove their worth to their male colleagues. It is by no means a surprise that the suicide explosive belts were attached to the bodies of female rather than male terrorists, who assumed different roles. According to an Alpha unit leader who observed the terrorists throughout the incident, at least five or six of the men were highly trained and experienced professionals.[80] In addition, individual members of the terrorist team were closely interlinked through family and friendship ties, which strengthened their cohesion even more.

### Planning

The planning and organization of the Moscow operation was shockingly sophisticated, to the point that even today a wide array of conspiracy theories exists, driven by disbelief that a "terror group from the mountains" could prepare such a large-scale attack in the middle of Moscow without inside help.

According to the Chechens' own words, the preparations took two to three months and involved the recruitment of the best commandos affiliated with various armed formations operating in the Vedeno District, individuals not only capable of carrying out the operation but also willing to die in Moscow. The group then extensively trained for the operation and prepared martyr videos. In April and June 2002, small groups came to Moscow to acquaint themselves with the area.[81] No less than six weeks before the actual raid, a larger group traveled to Moscow and took up jobs as construction workers at the Central Station nightclub housed in the theater complex.[82] During those six weeks, the "workers" conducted detailed casing of the location, and reportedly stored explosives and arms in the club's back rooms.[83] On several occasions, some operatives also attended the "Nord-Ost" musical in order to familiarize themselves with the environment.[84]

The gunmen did not leave anything to chance; according to some accounts they even smuggled battle-proven weapons for the operation from Chechnya in order to minimize the risk of malfunction, possibly associated with buying new weapons in Moscow. The commando unit was well armed, carrying fifteen semi-automatic AKMS740 rifles and 3,000 cartridges, 11 Makarov pistols, 114 grenades (89 of them RGDs and the remaining 25 homemade), and even a homemade grenade launcher. The overall cost of the operation was estimated to be approximately $60,000, according to Chechens with first-hand knowledge of guerilla operations.[85]

When preparations were complete, the rest of the commandos traveled via ground transportation to Moscow from various parts of the country. For instance, Movsar Barayev traveled by train from the southern city of

Mineralniye Vody, while at least one female terrorist used a bus line from the Dagestani town of Khasavyurt. Air transportation was apparently avoided for security reasons, as anyone who flies from the North Caucasus has to go through security screening, even on arrival, and the passengers' details are run through an FSB database.[86] Basayev later claimed that only five people were involved in transporting the weapons and ammunition. Given the fact that the explosive devices in the theater were actually nonoperational, Basayev suspected that the detonators were switched at some point during the shipping.[87]

Throughout the raid itself, the terrorists were highly professional. According to the Spetsnaz, the terrorists were optimally placed around the theater, "not having a single person at an unnecessary place."[88] Every member of the commando unit had a sector to watch over, and this was uniformly practiced with great caution and discipline. The women armed with a pistol, a grenade, and a suicide belt, worked in shifts.[89] All of the key entry routes were wired with explosives, including the underground sewer passage beneath the orchestra pit, and several snipers closely monitored areas around the building. The terrorists moved from place to place within the theater via specifically complicated routes, having mined all of the intuitively more accessible pathways. Also, any outside view into the auditorium was obstructed to prevent sniper fire and reconnaissance. In the hallways, the terrorists moved in combat order, with one person covering blind areas while others passed. In addition the terrorists placed those actors of the musical costumed in military uniforms around the perimeter of the auditorium with the apparent intent of drawing fire to them in the event of an assault by security forces.[90] The Chechens also allegedly changed the position of explosives inside the theater after every release of hostages or every visit from the outside.[91] When cartons of orange juice were brought in on the third day, the terrorists made one of the Red Cross workers sample the liquid, to make sure it was not tainted with poison or a sedative.[92] And finally, according to Russian authorities, the terrorists placed several operatives outside the theater, whose task was to inform them about the events and reactions outside.[93] Overall, both preparation and execution of the attack showed a great amount of sophistication, expertise, and meticulous planning.

### Goals of the Operation

In order to analyze the potential of negotiations in resolving the incident, it is essential to assess the motivations and goals behind it. In most cases this analysis is much more complex and more nuanced than the demands proclaimed by the perpetrators would suggest, as these substantive conditions are only the reflection of a larger reality and strategic planning. There are several important components to this analysis, namely, the selection of target, timing, tactics used in the attack, as well as the overall strategic mind-set of the organization.

The selection of a theater as a target was significant for several reasons.[94] In their own words, the terrorists selected the Dubrovka theater because it was "in the center of the city and there were a lot of people there."[95] By attacking a target in the capital the terrorists intended to demonstrate that they could strike in the heart of enemy territory at any time. Also, seizing a Moscow theater during a popular performance provided a large number of middle to upper class hostages,[96] reiterating the perception among ordinary Russians that they, too, could become targets. Moreover, there was also an expressive element present in attacking a theater, which had to do with the perception that Chechen children are dying while the "heartless pleasure-seeking Russians are having fun." The theater-goers were thus seen as guilty by association, which was only strengthened by the highly patriotic content of the show. This perception of universal guilt then aided the terrorists in dehumanizing their victims. Such justification was reiterated on numerous occasions in the statements made by the terrorists to the media as well as in their discussions with hostages. For instance, when hostages expressed their sympathy for the Chechen's cause, Barayev responded: "But you don't go to rallies demanding a stop to the war! Here you are going to the theater while they are killing us there."[97]

The timing of the attack was also important. During the year leading up the incident, Russian President Vladimir Putin had made a statement declaring a Russian victory in Chechnya, and the Russian media had consistently contributed to a false sense of security by treating the issue of the war as a historical event. Such a bold attack in the capital effectively destroyed this sense of security even among average Muscovites, for whom the distant conflict in Chechnya was previously completely impersonal. From the international perspective, then, with Russia actively aligning itself with the U.S.-led "war on terror," international sympathy for the Chechen rebels had faded significantly. A high-profile incident was needed to bring Chechnya back into the spotlight.

The tactic of assuming a suicidal posture selected for the operation is significant as well. As previously mentioned, the seeming irrationality of such an operation is useful in attracting extensive media coverage. This is followed by attempts to comprehend the motivations of such an act, leading to worldwide debates about the systemic foundations of the enormous dedication and hatred demonstrated by the attackers. In the eyes of many people, the group then gains the image of committed believers willing to do anything to reach their goals, also implying that the present environment is so humiliating that death is preferable to life under such conditions.[98] This is especially true in cases where suicide attackers are women, as in Moscow. The message conveyed by this operation was also directed inward. The willingness to die for the cause has been used by

Chechen groups as evidence of their fighters' moral superiority over the Russians, who are portrayed as pleasure-seekers, essentially weak despite their dominance in numbers and military hardware. The resulting perception among many Chechens has been that due to superior determination, their final victory is inevitable.[99]

Overall, the target and tactic selection reveals the possible scope of the real goals of the operation. Barricade hostage taking is essentially an instrumental as well as an expressive act. The possession of hostages creates a "good" that hostage takers can use to trade for specific measures the group seeks to achieve. As in Budyonnovsk seven years earlier, in Nord-Ost the possession of hostages was an instrumental means for achieving the pronounced demand for the pullout of Russian forces from Chechnya. However, the *expressive* nature of Nord-Ost seems to have been even more important. Through high profile incidents such as this one, the Chechen groups tried to draw wide media attention to their cause, which then serves as a platform for conveying explicit and tacit messages. Above all, the attackers wanted to express and explain their disagreement with, and resentment for, the Russian policies in Chechnya. Second, the attack was designed to remind the world of the Chechen issue, as well as to express frustration over the inaction of the international community regarding the human rights situation in the region. Third, the apparent goal was to embarrass President Putin, who in the year leading up to the incident had announced that the war in Chechnya had been won. Nord-Ost was designed to demonstrate that the war was very much alive, and that it will affect everyone, not just the Chechens and families of the soldiers fighting in the region. Fourth, based on previous experiences, incidents such as Budyonnovsk or Kizlyar, the Chechens were sure[100] that the Russian forces would storm the theater at some point, most probably on the evening of the third day, given the recent history. Steps were therefore taken to make the assault appear as difficult as possible, in order to force the Russians to take greater risks—what might be called "homicide by cop."

In short, the terrorists' clear preferred outcome was the end of war in Chechnya and the pullout of Russian troops from the republic. If they could not achieve such an outcome, the terrorists had a fallback of forcing the Russians to kill as many hostages in the *rescue operation* as possible, while themselves dying in the attack. This hierarchy of goals was later confirmed by the mastermind of the operation, Shamil Basayev. In a statement published on the main separatist web site, Basayev acknowledged the failure of the attack in terms of forcing the Russians to pull out of Chechnya, but also praised its success in terms of "showing to the whole world that Russian leadership will without mercy slaughter its own citizens in the middle of Moscow." If this was indeed the goal, then the operation succeeded beyond expectation. The Chechens could now claim that throughout the incident their commandos had released a number of hostages as a sign of good faith, and can point to the fact that all but three of the overall 129 fatalities were victims of the *rescue operation*.

### Assessment of Volatility

From a crisis negotiation standpoint, Nord-Ost carried several signs of high volatility from the beginning. First, the incident was apparently premeditated and carefully planned; the hostage takers knew well in advance what type of situation they were getting into, and had made all the necessary mental and logistical arrangements to prepare themselves. Conventional wisdom suggests that such a premeditated incident is naturally quite difficult to negotiate due to the perpetrators' preparedness to adapt to any development, and the process is likely to be significantly longer in duration than in the case of spontaneous hostage incidents. Further, the presence of multiple hostage takers available to handle the negotiations made the situation even more unpredictable; building rapport with hostage takers is much more challenging if they are under direct pressure from their peers, and if they can effectively negate the formation of a personal relationship by simply switching representatives. Moreover, the psychological process known as "groupthink" puts the hostages in increased danger, as group hostage takers in general have the ability to be more decisive than individuals when it comes to killing hostages.

The second major volatile element of Nord-Ost was the fact that the hostage takers were well armed and heavily brutalized. Security precautions taken by the terrorists made an assault on the location extremely challenging, and the history of ruthlessness on the part of at least some members of this group made their threats of preparedness to kill hostages in cold blood quite persuasive. In addition, the fact that the terrorists at one point separated the hostages into groups by gender and nationality was very disturbing. According to hostages, several different filtration processes occurred throughout the incident, in which foreigners formed a separate group, and men and women were also grouped and placed in different parts of the theatre.[101] This filtering process not only signaled the anticipation of a tactical assault—holding hostages at different locations makes an assault more difficult, as multiple tactical teams must attack all locations simultaneously in order to limit the risk to hostages held at other locations—but also allowed for quick but "discriminate" execution of hostages, if needed. The slaying of Russian males perceived as "involved" in the war in Chechnya as potential soldiers due to conscription would have been not only psychologically easier but also less politically dangerous for the Chechens than the killing of women and children or foreign nationals. Based on past experience, such a separation of hostages has tended to be sign of bad things to come.

The third volatile element was the alleged absence of change in the terrorists' demands over time. According to the contemporary set of incident assessment criteria, in situations that are deemed as negotiable, hostage takers start bidding high but reduce their demands as the incident progresses, and as their exhaustion triggers a regression to a hierarchically lower (more basic) set of needs such as hunger, thirst, and sleep. If such a process does not occur over a growing period of time, the chances of a negotiated solution allegedly decrease considerably.[102] At the same time, the presence of multiple hostage takers prolongs this process significantly, as the hostage takers not only have the option of resting some of their crew by working in shifts, but also are able to feed off the energy and determination of their comrades. Particularly when the hostage takers widely publicize their original demands and thus publicly lock themselves into their position, it becomes more difficult to negotiate a peaceful solution, as the one thing the image-conscious and fear-dependent terrorists worry about most is the widespread perception of their weakness and failure.

But despite the fact that the hostage takers in Nord-Ost showed little willingness to give up their sole original demand—the pullout of Russian forces from Chechnya—the abstract and expressive nature of this demand provided plenty of room for negotiating. Further, the claim that no change in the terrorists' demands occurred is simply not true: the demands became more specific as the incident progressed. In fact, negotiators were unanimous in their view that the terrorists had trouble formulating their demands, and that they were unable to come up with any kind of a coherent negotiating position. This observation, while leading many observers to conclude that negotiators had no chance of success, actually represented an *encouraging* sign. The variability in specific portions of their demands provided many opportunities for negotiators to introduce further nuanced options, in order to dissect the demands and make them more manageable—a process known as "fractionization." Further, the terrorists' vagueness opened up opportunities for the introduction of new options that the terrorists might not have considered before, but ones that would satisfy some of their core interests in alternative, yet still acceptable, ways. This is especially true given the fact that over time, the terrorists' demands regressed from unrealistic toward hypothetically more achievable ones.

Finally, and perhaps most importantly, the declared desire on the part of the terrorists to die and become martyrs suggested a high level of volatility. The contemporary crisis negotiation paradigm suggests that the desire to live is a basic precondition of a negotiated settlement in barricade situations. If the hostage takers are indifferent to staying alive, it is difficult to make them focus on personal safety, and thus draw their attention away from their original demands. Also, the threat of force posed by the hostage rescue unit becomes much less powerful as a bargaining tool when survival plays no part in the hostage takers' calculation of the outcome.

Under circumstances in which the captors see it as their primary—or at least secondary—objective to kill themselves and take as many of their victims with them as possible, negotiation logically has very little chance of success. However, such situations are extremely infrequent, especially in the realm of hostage crises involving ideologically inspired perpetrators. After all, one major reason for taking hostages is to protect one's own safety during the ensuing standoff. Terrorist operations, in which the perpetrator's death is the preferred outcome, usually take the form of suicide bombings or *fidayeen* shooting attacks with no planned escape routes. In contrast, barricade operations that involve hostages are usually designed to use the captives as leverage to get something—killing them is typically not the *main* objective.[103]

Were the terrorists in Nord-Ost suicidal? It is true that their most frequent sentence was: "We are more keen on dying than you are on living," and that Basayev's fighters had carried out suicide operations in the past.[104] It is also true that many of the hostage takers spoke to the negotiators and hostages in an unusually confessional fashion, signaling a lack of expectation to survive.[105] As a result, the Chechens' suicidal posture was highly credible, and for this reason it is difficult to blame the Russian authorities for believing the threats to be genuine. However, even a genuine threat from suicidal terrorists does not, automatically, render a crisis nonnegotiable. In addition, many negotiators and some hostages have questioned the notion that *all* members of the terrorist team were destined for sacrifice.[106] For instance, on October 25, several of the hostages overheard Barayev's telephone conversation with his unidentified superior. Barayev spoke apologetically: "Yes, we made a bit of a mess here in the hall, but we'll pick it all up before we leave." After this conversation, some of the hostages were given plastic bags and were instructed to pick up trash.[107] Also, the fact that the explosive devices in the theatre were nonoperational decoys brings additional doubt into the equation. These are just two of a number of anecdotes suggesting that perhaps at least some of the terrorists did expect to survive. And while, to an outsider, such an expectation may seem completely unrealistic, one should remember that in Budyonnovsk the terrorists also assumed a very similar suicidal posture, but did eventually accept a free passage deal when favorable circumstances presented themselves.

In sum, there is no question that members of Barayev's unit were *prepared* to die during the Moscow operation, as the likelihood of such a result was very high. At the same time, it is questionable whether their death was truly designed as the operation's *preferred outcome*. There are many shades of grey between a bluff and true, unswerving suicidal intent. After all, the terrorists did pay extraordinary attention to their own security, and also kept threatening to execute ten hostages if any one of them was killed. It seems more likely that the repeated declaration of readiness to "be martyred" was a rational course of action aimed at denying the Russian threat level: the credible proclamation of the desire to die weakened the deterrent value of threats by the government to resolve the situation forcefully, strengthening the terrorists' own bargaining position.[108] Even the suicidal rhetoric, itself, adds to the incident's fear factor —a useful tool for the terrorists. For these reasons, the hostage takers' declared preparedness to die, might have made negotiations challenging, but certainly did not exclude the possibility of nonviolent resolution altogether, or at least the chance that continued negotiations would result in the freeing of more hostages, or in the public perception that the authorities were handling the situation wisely and with appropriate caution.

### Indicators of De-escalation

Besides the above-stated indicators of high volatility, positive signs hinting at the possibility of a peaceful resolution were also present as the incident progressed. The first such indicator was the apparent formation of the Stockholm Syndrome, or the mutually positive relationship between the hostages and the hostage takers. In barricade situations, the "syndrome" consists of a four-way process. The first relationship is based on the dependency of the victim on the abductor—the latter decides when the former will eat, sleep, go to the bathroom, live, or die.[109] This dynamic is strengthened by the hostage's instinct of doing everything necessary to survive. The victim's humbleness and obedience helps to reduce anger of the hostage takers, who in turn tend to reciprocate by a more humane treatment of the hostages. This reciprocation only reinforces the positive feelings on behalf of the victim. Another dependency bond is frequently formed between the hostage taker and the negotiator, who tries to project the image of someone who can hurt but desires to help.[110] The third relationship that reinforces the positive mutual feelings between the hostage and the captor is the perception of a common enemy: the tactical unit. The hostage takers feel threatened by the police for obvious reasons. The victims perceive the authorities negatively, as they feel that not enough is being done to secure their release. Moreover, the security forces represent an apparent threat to the hostages as well, due to their uncertain ability to distinguish between the hostage takers and the hostages. The shared negative relationship toward a third party makes the Stockholm Syndrome even stronger.

From political perspective, the presence of the Stockholm Syndrome is usually not welcomed, due to the fact that hostages frequently side with the terrorists' political views and make accusations against the government, sometimes even long after the incident has come to a close. However, from a crisis negotiator's point of view the syndrome's formation is seen as highly positive, since it introduces stronger psychological obstacles for the terrorists to carry out their threats of executing hostages in cold blood.

In Nord-Ost, the formation of the Stockholm Syndrome was observed as early as the second day of the incident, leading the authorities to make an absurd claim that the terrorists had a professional psychologist in their midst. But actually, in the presence of significant mutual interaction between the captors and their captives, and in the absence of the hostages' ill treatment, the formation of the Stockholm Syndrome constituted a natural development. The hostages were well fed with snacks and sweets from the theater bar,[111] and with few exceptions, were not beaten or otherwise harmed. Many of the hostages later expressed their compassion toward the Chechens by talking about their attractive appearances, sense of humor, sensitive treatment of the children, and by expressing sympathy toward the hostage takers' political and personal motives, and even by articulating grief for their eventual demise.[112]

The hostage takers were also not immune to the effects of the "syndrome." On various occasions, the terrorists would calm down the hostages, even telling them what to do during a rescue operation to avoid being killed. For instance, the terrorists moved the hostages from some parts of the auditorium, explaining that "if shooting starts outside the hall, it would be dangerous to sit on the outside edges."[113] One hostage even claims that Barayev had said that once the shooting started, the hostage takers would "hide the hostages in a safe place and protect [them] to the last bullet."[114] This positive feeling toward the hostages is also detectable in the more routine interactions that took place throughout the fifty-eight-hour standoff. For instance, in conversations with the hostages, one of the hostage takers talked "about beautiful things in [Chechnya] and that [the hostages and hostage takers could] go visit each other like guests."[115] Even in this high pressure situation in which death seemed inevitable, some of the terrorists found a strange way to comfort the hostages; by assuring them that the explosive devices were so powerful that the hostages would "not feel a thing." One of the female terrorists who held a long personal conversation with Georgy Vasiliev, even instructed him to recite the Arabic phrase "*la ilaha illallah*" at the time of his death, in a firm belief that Vasiliev's formal acceptance of Islam would grant him a place in paradise.[116] The existence of Stockholm Syndrome between the hostages and their hostage takers was undeniable.

This brings us to the second and closely associated positive sign in the crisis, and that was the absence of cold-blooded executions of *hostages*. On one hand, it is true that the gunmen in Moscow did in fact kill three people during the fifty-eight-hour ordeal, which in the minds of many decision makers might be interpreted as an indication that negotiations were simply not possible. On the other hand, however, not one of those killings was conducted in cold blood as a pressure tool; in actuality, the killings were not premeditated but rather came about out of "necessity" to maintain control in the auditorium. Secondly, none of the people deliberately killed were *hostages*; they were all individuals who voluntarily walked into the theatre during the standoff. This point is especially significant, as the absence of a past relationship between these people and the hostage takers made their execution psychologically easier, due to the absence of the Stockholm Syndrome. In addition, the terrorists' interpretation of those killed as "FSB stooges" and "spies" further contributed to their dehumanization, making the killings even easier. In sum, all of the situations in which people died required action perceived as necessary by the terrorists, who would certainly not have been able to maintain control over the crowd had they not acted. This, of course, does not acquit the terrorists of any moral and legal responsibility for the murders, but understanding the circumstances under which such killings occur is critical for accurate assessment of negotiability. While a cold-blooded execution of hostages as a negotiation tool may significantly lower the likelihood of a negotiated solution, killings under these circumstances do not necessarily have the same implications for negotiation.

The next encouraging sign in the Nord-Ost crisis was the fact that the terrorists, while making various threats tied to specific thresholds or deadlines for fulfillment of their demands, let these deadlines pass without incident. The hostage takers, at least on two occasions, did threaten to kill ten hostages per hour if their demands were not promptly met, but eventually always postponed the deadline without following through with their threats. On another occasion, the terrorists, while searching for members of the security services among the hostages, made repeated threats to kill anyone caught hiding his or her telephone or documents. When, on the second day of the standoff, the Chechens discovered that one of the hostages was a police general who had hidden his identity card, the discovery triggered considerable excitement among the terrorists, but no executions.[117]

Experience shows that once a deadline is breached, it is easier to break through future deadlines and prolong the incident. And while prolonging the incident alone does not guarantee a peaceful resolution, the failure to follow through with a threat does strengthen the chances for such an outcome, as this development is generally a sign of possible psychological or political reluctance on behalf of the hostage takers to execute hostages or, at least, a willingness to reason. Further, prolongation of the incident also provides the tactical unit with more time to study the behavioral patterns of the perpetrators and to prepare for a possible assault.

The final encouraging element in the ordeal was the periodic safe release of dozens of hostages, often without any demands or concessions attached. These releases clearly indicated the willingness of the terrorists to deal with the authorities, as well as a desire to demonstrate their "good will" to the international audience (or, at least, their sensitivity to how they are perceived). The second point was also served by frequent declaration of a preparedness to release all nationals of countries with which the Chechens had no conflict. One of the reasons why the periodic releases of hostages are a positive sign is the fact that this demonstrates the hostage takers' understanding of the principle of quid pro quo—in order to gain, they must give. Even more importantly, the early release of hostages sets a precedent for future deals and establishes a mutually acceptable "exchange rate," in the sense that it indicates what sort of concessions each side is willing to make and at what "price." This "exchange rate" may then be used as an objective criterion in further negotiations. From this perspective, the release of more than one hundred people could have paved the road to further agreements, at the end of which small groups of hostages would be freed. Moreover, the existence of multiple demands presented an opportunity for reaching numerous separate deals and procedural agreements to facilitate this process. This was happening until some of the authorities' tactics served as "momentum stoppers," by insulting the hostage takers or exhausting their patience; something we shall see again in Beslan.

## THE NEGOTIATIONS: MISSED OPPORTUNITIES

The negotiability or nonnegotiability of the Moscow theatre crisis will always be an issue of much contention, given the official portrayal of the hostage takers as indecisive suicidal maniacs, and given the unconditional and unacceptable nature of their core demand of a complete pullout of Russian troops from Chechnya. Nevertheless, the lack of a negotiation strategy—or the successful implementation of a strategy *not to negotiate*—translated into missed opportunities and probably a higher body count. This section will analyze some of the mistakes and missed opportunities of the negotiation in Nord-Ost in order to draw lessons for the future.

### Communications

The first and possibly most noncontentious blunder in the ordeal was the absence of an effective means of communication. One of the first rules of negotiation is that without communication, there can be no negotiation. Establishing an effective means of communicating is thus a basic priority. The more reliable the contact links between the parties, the lesser the chances of miscommunication and potentially catastrophic consequences. Similarly, the more direct the means of communication, the greater are the opportunities for the negotiator to establish a level of familiarity and rapport with the hostage takers, increasing his or her ability to exercise influence over the subjects' conduct, and to gather useful intelligence.

The negotiations in the Nord-Ost incident (or "contacts," as one of the negotiators has called them) were conducted mainly through face-to-face interactions and via the hostages' mobile phones. In addition, the hostage takers made several of their demands indirectly, using journalists, media interviews, hostages, prefilmed video statements, and the Kavkaz Center web site as the primary communication channels. The authorities also relied on indirect communication at times, making public announcements that carried a message for the hostage takers, with the knowledge that the people inside were following radio and television broadcasts. One of the main problems of this indirect communication strategy was its chaotic nature, which made it difficult to keep track of new developments. As mentioned earlier, in "negotiable situations," hostage takers' demands are initially highly ambitious, but, with the help of effective negotiators, should become more realistic over time. Similarly, the hostage takers' behavior is likely to undergo rapid changes as the incident progresses, starting with rage and excitement, followed by increasing frustration, stress, and then fatigue.[118] In order to observe and analyze whether these processes are taking place, the negotiation team needs to have meticulous knowledge of *all* communications with the outside, so that it can monitor details such as the changes in the suspect's tone of voice, specific vocabulary used, speech and breathing patterns, etc. In a situation where the terrorists speak to a different person each time, while also making live interviews with media outlets based in various countries, such detailed monitoring is extremely difficult.

Similarly, in this indirect communications scenario, the negotiators' inability immediately to follow up on a demand or statement made by the hostage takers is likely to result in missed opportunities. For instance, when journalists from the *Ekho Moskvy* radio station spoke to one of the terrorists over the phone, they challenged him on the issue of a pullout of Russian troops from Chechnya within a week: "You understand . . . that this would take a number of weeks?" "But we are not in a hurry," came the reply. The journalist then proceeded to plead for the release of female hostages: "Perhaps it might be possible for you to release all the women? After all, the number of men [held hostage] should be enough." The gunman responded: "The decision about who we release is to be taken by Movsar. Regarding the women? I think we will reach an agreement. But not with you."[119]

This short conversation alone, had it been led by a hostage negotiator acceptable to the terrorists, presented a list of potential opportunities. Firstly, the negotiator could have tried to take the hostage takers up on their self-described chain of authority. Since the terrorists themselves suggested that a possible decision to release hostages was to be taken by Movsar, constantly reminding them of this fact would make it more difficult for Barayev to try to shake off the responsibility for decisions by diverting to a higher authority. Similarly, the gunman's indication of an in-principle agreement with the logic of releasing all female hostages could have constantly been followed upon, while the terrorists still remembered their own words. Finally, the hostage takers' acknowledgement of the logistical problems associated with a complete pullout of 50,000 troops from Chechnya within one week, as well as the fact that this time frame was not critical to them, could immediately have been combined to negotiate the practical details of an extension of the one-week deadline. But since the above conversation did not involve an accepted negotiator, all of these opportunities, unfortunately, were missed.

This brings us to another problem of the negotiation approach applied in Nord-Ost, and that is the authorities' almost exclusive reliance on untrained proxies. In fact, there seems to have been a complete absence of a trained principal negotiator conducting the majority of discussions with the terrorists. Among the people who spoke directly to the Chechens were Russian journalist Anna Politkovskaya; famous artist Iosif Kobzon; politicians Boris Nemtsov, Irina Khakamada, Grigory Yavlinsky, Aslanbek Aslakhanov, and Yevgeni Primakov; Dr Leonid Roshal; several Red Cross representatives; and presidential plenipotentiary representative Viktor Kazantsev. Virtually all of these people were prominent political or cultural figures whose involvement was demanded directly by the hostage takers. In addition, relatives of imprisoned Chechen militants such as Luisa Ustarkhanova, Said Salim Batsiev, and several handcuffed members of Chechen gangs were also brought into the command center to try to influence Barayev over the phone.[120]

Applying the conventional crisis negotiation wisdom, there were several problems with the engagement of the above-mentioned negotiators. First, they lacked training and even basic instructions from the authorities on how to behave, what to say, what to do in certain situations, and what to avoid. In fact, the negotiators were given almost no overall guidance, and there appears to have been little interest in the negotiations and what their efforts achieved. The authorities were almost exclusively interested in the tactical intelligence gained by their presence inside the theater.[121] The commanders of the operation demonstrated alarmingly little hesitation to send the proxy figures directly to the rebels, despite the fact that face-to-face negotiations with hostage takers are generally not advisable (again, according to current conventional wisdom). This is especially true in cases where the presence of the persons doing the negotiating has been requested by the hostage takers directly, as this request may be an indication of an ulterior motive (e.g., to assassinate potential interlocutors). And while the risk to those who went inside was largely assumed to be low, given the fact that their selection by the hostage takers had likely been motivated by their favorable public stance on the issue of the war in

Chechnya, there was little reason for not attempting to conduct telephone negotiations first.

Even if the hostage takers refused this offer, the situation would have opened up a vast array of opportunities for exchange. One of the most important principles that hostage negotiators learn is "never to give anything to hostage takers without getting something back." Face-to-face negotiation with people of the terrorists' liking should have therefore been exchanged for the release of some hostages (after all, the release of a few people from among some 900 hostages was not likely to make much of a difference in the terrorists' eyes), or at least for a public guarantee of the negotiators' safety. While this may seem like a small concession, getting the hostage takers into the habit of making promises not to hurt people is a useful starting point for establishing some form of mutual trust. Alternatively, a condition could have been attached allowing the terrorists to select only one person to act as the mediator throughout the entire crisis. This would have enabled the development of rapport between this individual and the hostage takers, and would have made keeping track of events, demands, and conditions much more manageable.[122]

### Time

Another critical flaw in Nord-Ost was the Russians' understandable yet unfortunate lack of patience. On the one hand, it is comprehensible that prolonging the incident would have been difficult from a political standpoint, especially for President Putin, who had won his mandate precisely by taking a tough stance on the issue of Chechnya. Also, it is possible to understand the desire to end the suffering of the hostages, who were subjected to very challenging mental and physical conditions while sleeping between bombs and using the open orchestra pit as a toilet. On the other hand, prolonging the incident would have most likely *improved* the hostages' safety as well as the chances of a peaceful resolution, by wearing down the captors and by strengthening the Stockholm Syndrome due to the atmosphere of "shared misery." Such misery arising from unfavorable conditions for everyone inside combined with a common negative attitude toward the authorities who in the hostages' eyes seem to be doing nothing to resolve the crisis, enhances mutual empathy between the hostages and their captors.[123] This strengthens the Stockholm Syndrome, which in turn makes it psychologically more difficult for the terrorists to execute hostages.

While prolonging a hostage incident usually requires considerable effort on behalf of the negotiators, in Moscow, it was, in fact, the terrorists who strove toward this goal, as demonstrated by the fact that they requested to speak to people whose transportation to Moscow would objectively take a significant amount of time.[124] One of the terrorists confirmed this point in the aforementioned telephone interview with the Russian media, when he stated that the commando unit was "in no particular hurry." In most barricade hostage incidents, it is the authorities who attempt to prolong the incident in order to apply the standardized negotiation approach of stalling for time and wearing down the hostage takers. In Moscow, not only was the situation reversed, but the Russian leadership appears to have further enforced a self-imposed deadline on the negotiations. This was a colossal mistake—the ordeal was intense to begin with, and self-imposed deadlines only add to the pressure on everyone involved, particularly the negotiators. Even more importantly, once such a decision is made, any progress in the negotiation process is viewed by the command center with high skepticism, resulting in the de facto elimination of the chances for a peaceful settlement.

### Freeing Hostages

Another blunder in the management of Nord-Ost was the failure to take advantage of several key opportunities to achieve the release of additional hostages. For example, Abu Bakar had stated on several occasions that fifty hostages would be freed if the head of the Chechen administration, Akhmat Kadyrov, arrived in Moscow. And while Kadyrov, who had previously been sentenced to death by a Chechen separatist *Sharia* court, would likely have been executed had he actually come inside the theatre, just summoning him to Moscow and showing his presence near the siege site on television would have put more pressure on the terrorists to reciprocate in some way. This could have also facilitated a discussion about publicized safety guarantees and other possible confidence-building measures by both sides. These attempts might not have led to any concrete results, but still could have kept the communications going, which in itself constitutes a positive outcome.

At another point, the terrorists stated that they "shall be prepared to let go all hostages whose countries are not at war with Chechnya." This offered a clear logic that should have consistently been used against the terrorists until all foreign hostages were freed. This is by no means to suggest that the lives of foreign nationals were more valuable than the lives of the Russians; but since the logic for their release came from the terrorists themselves, a unique opportunity presented itself to achieve the release of seventy-six people with relative ease. In most hostage crises, it is a great challenge for the negotiator to come up with plausible logic for the release of a certain group of hostages, and then persuading the captors to accept the validity of this logic. In Nord-Ost it was the terrorists themselves who provided the logic on a silver platter, and the inability to follow up and achieve the foreigners' release is most unfortunate (though, perhaps, it made political sense from Putin's perspective; the presence of the foreigners among the hostages may have made it more difficult to kill them all, and it may have resulted in more international condemnation of the Chechen group). At the same time, the reasons behind this failure serve as a good illustration of the political realities involved in the management of the Nord-Ost incident.

Firstly, the highly distrustful terrorists insisted vigorously on handing over the foreign hostages only into the hands of the representatives of their respective countries. The reason for this becomes clear from a conversation Barayev held with one of the hostages: "We won't let you go today, because your own people would shoot you and say later that we killed you. That's what happened at Budyonnovsk. You'll leave tomorrow."[125] According to the Kazakh ambassador Altynbek Sarsenbayev, an agreement was made among the ambassadors of countries, the citizens of which were among the hostages, to "demand the release of all foreigners at once, and not to have individual countries make individual deals. Formally the terrorists agreed, but in the end, they were just buying time. Original time for the release was 12, then 2 then 8 then 10 o'clock. The same situation repeated itself the next day."[126]

The terrorists' official reason for canceling the deal was that the ambassadors arrived too late. However, the diplomats that were already present at the theatre even before the agreement was reached were not allowed to meet the terrorists, while those not already present were informed by Russian authorities that they should come only *after* the deadline of 9:00 A.M. had already passed.[127] Why would the Russians stand in the way of the offered release of all foreigners? According to some sources, the authorities insisted that the terrorists should release women and children first,[128] also rejecting the logic of separating hostages into the categories of foreigners versus Russian citizens.[129] Admittedly, there is a valid rationale behind this choice, based on the argument that the political importance of the foreigners' survival decreased the chances of the terrorists detonating their explosives, and therefore keeping them inside as hostages would provide a stabilizing influence for everyone involved. Further, from a political perspective the foreigners' status as hostages would also ensure continuous international pressure on the Chechens to end the crisis peacefully. In practice, however, the misleading public statements about the deal only served to antagonize the terrorists, and later served to raise even more doubts about the official version of events presented by the Russian Government.

### Unnecessary Provocations

Closely associated with the previous point is the next problem of unnecessary provocations, such as media censorship and manipulation, as well as careless counteroffers, which became an obstacle to the negotiation process by escalating the terrorists' aggravation. For instance, after the terrorists saw that the footage of their interview was shown on NTV in a censored version without sound, the release of a group of children already prepared to leave was cancelled.[130] In another instance, the terrorists had clearly stated in their discussions with Politkovskaya that the Russians were free to try to bargain for the release of hostages, but that the issue of the terrorists' safety should not even be brought up, as they were suicide fighters who had come to Moscow to die. To support this claim, the terrorists stated that even if all their demands were met and the hostages were then released as promised, they themselves would still stay inside and fight till death with the Russian forces.[131] Nevertheless, on the second day of the standoff, the authorities made an offer of a free passage in exchange for the lives of the hostages, which ultimately angered the terrorists and served as a pretext for rescinding other agreements nearly in place. Despite the failure of this tactic, the authorities made exactly the same mistake on day three of the standoff, with Pronichev's public promise to spare the lives of the terrorists if all hostages were released unharmed. This was either poor negotiation strategy or poor coordination on the part of the authorities. This apparently led the hostage takers to renew their threats to start killing hostages the next morning. Either by carelessness or by intent, the authorities' actions were partly responsible for the escalation of the situation.

Another possible near-mistake, albeit a hypothetical one, was the statement made by several members of the Russian Parliament, who at noon of the second day reportedly offered themselves as substitute hostages in place of the women and children. The deal was not accepted by the terrorists, who according to the official version of events reportedly stated that they would accept the MPs only as substitutes for *male* hostages, but not for women and children.[132] However, judging by the profile of hostages that had been released up to this point, as well as by conversations between the terrorists and their captives inside, this explanation for why the deal failed to materialize is not very convincing. But in any case, the negative outcome was fortunate as such a substitution would likely have done more harm than good. The introduction of new hostages would probably have disrupted the formation of the Stockholm Syndrome on the inside, and would also have raised tensions and fears unnecessarily among the responders on the outside. It is questionable, for instance, whether the authorities would still have been able to proceed so decisively with the assault had some of the most influential men in the country become potential victims. Another reason why the exchange was a misguided suggestion is the fact that substitute hostages in general tend to have an increased sense of urgency and often feel compelled to try to change the situation from the inside. This usually brings them to the terrorists' attention, which in combination with the complete absence of the Stockholm

Syndrome is likely to cause them to be the first ones selected for execution. This especially would have been a likely outcome with Russian MPs, who as top politicians, would also have undoubtedly been perceived by the hostage takers as a main guilty party in the Chechen conflict.

### Handling Demands

Another significant flaw in the operation was the manner in which the authorities handled the terrorists' demands. There seems to have been an unfortunate and excessive focus on the substantive nature of the demands, emphasizing the political unacceptability of withdrawing troops from Chechnya. The situation was then basically framed as a zero-sum game, leading many mistakenly to conclude that there was no possibility of a negotiated settlement. However, the terrorists' primary demand had many *expressive* components to which the negotiations could have been diverted: the desire for peace, the nature of Russian "mop-up" operations, acknowledgement of the humanitarian situation in Chechnya, and so on. In order to explore these expressive components, the negotiators simply should have kept asking good questions in an effort both to understand the specific (and often personal) origins of the demands and to listen for legitimate grievances that can be acknowledged with little political risk. The answers to such questions often seem obvious, but in crisis negotiations such questions need to be asked, as they provide opportunities to find "negotiable nuance," to relieve or influence the emotional state of the perpetrator, and/or to gain useful information about what might eventually be acceptable substitutes for giving into initial demands. This in turn gives the negotiator a chance to engage the spokesperson on the other side on a more personal level, by asking about his or her *personal* experience with the alleged injustices and abuse. This then provides an opportunity for the negotiator to express empathy. In ideological hostage situations, it is always very difficult to move the discussion away from ideology toward a more personal level, and this approach provides one of the best possible ways for achieving this. Forming genuine personal rapport between the negotiators on both sides is one of the critical principles upon which the crisis negotiation practice is based. Importantly, the terrorists seemed very keen to talk about both their ideological and personal grievances; as is evident from the tremendous amount of personal information they shared in conversations with some of the hostages, negotiators, and media representatives.[133] As with any conflict, those who use violence are partly motivated by the frustration of not being listened to by those in authority. The simple act of listening and demonstrating interest in the grievance (even without the intention of doing something to address it) is significant, and has the effect of reducing the level of frustration and bitterness that leads people to violent action in the first place.

Another pragmatic reason why asking good questions is important, is the fact that answers provide an insight into the hostage taker's underlying interests and motivations behind the core demands. If these interests are understood, new options that would address the terrorist's legitimate concerns, but would stop short of giving in to any of their original demands, can be introduced. And, the deeper and broader the understanding of their interests, the broader will be the scope to generate potential options. Through active listening and by introduction of new options, the hostage takers' expectations may be shaped. Also, shaping the militants' perception of having achieved some success gives them a stake in the outcome, and can prevent them from taking radical steps that would waste everything that had already been accomplished. This is why it is important in the beginning to focus on the demands that are easier to fulfill, in order to achieve some early success. And since with time the terrorists in Nord-Ost began to transform their initial demand of unconditional pullout of Russian troops from Chechnya into smaller, more specific, and more realistic options, such opportunities were clearly present. The caveat here is not to treat the terrorists like lab rats. A group of well-trained, well-prepared, and highly committed operatives engaging in an act of terrorism as complex as Nord-Ost are not likely to be as stupid as we would wish. Effective crisis negotiation is not just about trying to manipulate or outsmart the hostage takers. *Understanding* them is the key to exercising the kind of influence that might move all parties toward a better outcome.

During their talks with negotiators, the gunmen progressed to clarifying what exact actions had to be taken, and who would have to verify the initiation of these actions in order for the hostages to be freed. Their original demand seemed insurmountable. However, after several negotiators made the very logical point that a complete pullout of 50,000 troops in the seven-day period was simply physically impossible, the terrorists suggested that even the withdrawal of troops from any one district in the Republic of Chechnya would satisfy them.[134] This reduction in the ambition of the main demand was a clear indication that the processes that make hostage negotiations work were taking place, and that even extremists are capable of reason.

Further, Yavlinsky, who met with the hostage takers for an hour and a half on the night of October 24, reported that the terrorists had at this time put forward even less ambitious conditions: termination of the use of heavy weapons, namely, artillery and air force, in Chechnya starting with the next day; termination of "mop-up" operations; and a telephone conversation between Putin and separatist President Aslan Maskhadov.[135] These demands were not just logistically more feasible; they even started to approach the threshold of possible acceptability to the Kremlin. For instance, halt of artillery and air strikes as well as mop-up operations might have been granted without any danger to Moscow's overall strategy in

Chechnya.[136] Similarly, a telephone call between Maskhadov and Putin could have happened, satisfying the hostage takers' desire for high-level contact. The call could have gone badly and been quite acrimonious, but it could have been framed as a "first step" (however unsuccessful), allowing the Kremlin to save face. Given the fact that the terrorists were not on firm political ground and preferred for high level politicians to resolve the ordeal,[137] Maskhadov's direct confirmation to the terrorists that he has held talks with Putin would have likely been enough to convince them that this key demand had been satisfied, paving the way for release of additional hostages.

## CONCLUSION

One thing seems clear: the Russian authorities failed (or chose not) to fully exploit the opportunities that existed to negotiate within this crisis. For instance, the authorities refused to grant some very concrete and feasible concessions, such as bringing the requested Chechen official on-site in exchange for fifty hostages, while at the same time making allowances without gaining anything in return, as in the issue of proxy negotiators. It seems that in Nord-Ost the political realities and the desire to teach the Chechens a lesson again seemed to outweigh the concern for the lives of hostages. The Russian authorities simply had no intention of yielding to the terrorists in order to get the hostages out alive—without realizing that there might have been plenty else they could have done on the spectrum between refusing to talk and giving in to their demands. The whole approach to negotiation seems to have been little more than an effort to provide a public relations alibi, creating a perception of the exhaustion of all peaceful options in order to justify the assault. While the logic of "no negotiations with terrorists" in order to discourage future acts of terrorism may on the surface sound attractive, this case clearly demonstrates the potential cost of such thinking. As we will see in the upcoming chapter, the Kremlin's "tough" response in Nord-Ost simply did not teach Basayev that terrorism is futile; on the contrary, it only convinced him of the need to raise the stakes to strike harder and with greater efficiency in order to achieve his goals. In the end, Russia's failure even to listen to the terrorists in the Moscow theatre crisis would contribute to an even gloomier nightmare for the future.

# CHAPTER 4

# RIYADUS-SALIKHIN SUICIDE BATALLION

One of the issues that complicate the management of hostage crises involving the "new terrorists" is the fact that the contemporary protocol of crisis negotiation operates under the presumption that hostage takers are engaged in such a situation for the first time.[1] In terrorist incidents, however, the situation is frequently complicated by the existence of a past and ongoing relationship between the terrorist group and the targeted state.[2] As a result of this fact, one of the key issues that need to be factored into the processes of incident assessment and negotiation strategy selection is the terrorists' past experience in similar standoffs.

In any situation where a group holds hostages, issues demands, and threatens executions, the first thing responders must do is analyze the perpetrator's profile and motives. In the context of terrorism, knowledge of recent history will play a crucial role. Has the group taken hostages before? What were the demands? What was the outcome? If negotiation was employed, what strategies were successful? What strategies failed or proved counterproductive? Were the terrorists deceived? Did the hostage takers enforce their deadlines by executing hostages? Under what conditions? Were they suicidal? How did the crisis end? What are the lessons the terrorists are likely to have learned from the past—both from their own group's operations and from those of other groups? In addition, it is also absolutely essential to understand the context in which the present-day attack has occurred. Does it represent an escalation or a de-escalation of the group's violent campaign? What specific outcome is the group seeking? Does the killing of hostages present a viable political alternative given the group's current strategic mind-set, or is it likely to be viewed by the perpetrators as counterproductive to their political goals? What is the group's current targeting logic and what ideological angle does it use to justify the killing of innocents? These are just some of the questions that need to be answered before the designation of a suitable negotiation strategy.

Unfortunately, all too often it is the case that due to lack of experience in dealing with repeat offenders and due to the absence of in-depth training in the terrorism and negotiation fields, the responders fail to place the present hostage crisis into its broader context, limiting their worldview to a single incident. This precludes the effective use of tools like precedents, appropriate criteria, and understanding of motives, all of which are essential elements in interest-based negotiation.[3] Further, only by looking outside the box of the current incident can hostage negotiators increase the scope for inventing new options, which may satisfy some of the hostage takers' core interests and valid grievances, without necessarily giving in to their demands. And finally, given the fact that the current crisis is only a small part of a larger picture, one of the things negotiators should take into consideration is the implications of this one incident for the future. What are the lessons *we* want the terrorists to learn from the encounter? How can we use the current incident to influence the terrorists' perceptions and future conduct? And, most importantly, how can we influence the long-term trend toward a more favorable trajectory? Negotiators certainly do not want to reward bad behavior in such situations, but we also want to stress that negotiators have an obligation to *influence better behavior both within the incident and through multiple incidents over time*. When authorities miss opportunities to de-escalate within a crisis, and instead rely on clever tricks, spite, and "sending a message" to the terrorists, they often invest in a more ominous long-term trend. This is precisely what happened on the way from Moscow to Beslan.

With the goal of putting these principles into action by setting up our analysis of the attack in Beslan, this chapter will provide an operational profile of the Riyadus-Salikhin Suicide Battalion (RAS), the terrorist organization founded by Shamil Basayev in the summer of 2002, just prior to the Nord-Ost operation discussed in the previous chapter.[4] Between this date and the Beslan attack in 2004, RAS had become one of the most spectacular and lethal terrorist organizations in the world, renowned for its cunning ability to infiltrate enemy environments, and meticulously prepare and synchronize its operations. In the time period between its formation and its last attack in Beslan, RAS had perpetrated over a dozen spectacular terrorist operations, which had resulted in the deaths of more than 1,100 people and the injury of many more. Considering the fact that only 28 attacks in history[5] have killed more than 100 people, RAS' average casualty rate of nearly 100 fatalities per attack ranks the group among the most lethal terrorist organizations ever. By another comparison, the number of RAS inflicted fatalities in the first twenty-four months of its operation was over *three times higher* than the number of all Israelis who died during the same time period in terrorist attacks perpetrated by *all Palestinian militant groups combined*.[6] The purpose of this chapter is to analyze the ideological, operational, and strategic evolution of RAS that took place in the Nord-Ost aftermath, with a specific focus on the developments that carried lessons and implications vital to the management of the Beslan attack.

## HISTORY OF OPERATIONAL PROGRESSION

In order to understand the operational progression of RAS, it is imperative firstly to follow the evolution of the group's leader and operational chief, Shamil Basayev. Basayev's involvement in terrorist activity dates back to November 1991 when he and two friends hijacked a Russian TU-154 aircraft from Mineralniye Vody to Ankara, threatening to blow up the plane if Russia did not lift the state of emergency in Chechnya. Basayev's next adventure awaited in Abkhazia, where he and a group of several dozen of his Chechen fighters gained the reputation of an extremely brutal and successful fighting force. Following the December 1994 Russian invasion of Chechnya and the subsequent outbreak of the first Russian–Chechen war, Basayev was the first Chechen leader to advocate an expansion of the war to Russian territory. Then on June 14, 1995, just weeks after a Russian bomb destroyed Basayev's home in Vedeno killing several members of his family including his wife and children, Basayev launched the Budyonnovsk operation, described in detail in Chapter 2.

Budyonnovsk was significant for several reasons. Firstly, it was the first Chechen operation deliberately targeting Russian civilians. Commenting on the objectives of the siege, Basayev stated: "We wanted to show to the people in Russia that this war is very close to them, too; we wanted them to see what blood looks like, and how it is when people are dying. We wanted them to understand it, to wake up."[7] This statement is crucial, as it effectively summarizes the entire strategic logic later adopted by the RAS. The second point of significance lies in the fact that at the time of its execution, "Operation *Jihad*" was the second largest barricade hostage-taking operation in history, both by the number of attackers and the number of hostages involved. And finally, in Budyonnovsk, Basayev succeeded in the sense that Russian authorities acceded to many of his demands—a development that not only gave Basayev a high level of confidence in the effectiveness of the tactic used, but also shaped Russia's reactions to similar incidents in the future.

Following the end of the first Chechen war in which Basayev relied mainly on military means, the conflict reached its second phase in 1999 after two armed incursions of Basayev's fighters into the neighboring republic of Dagestan, and the bombings of apartment buildings that killed nearly 300 people and injured more than 550 others.[8] After the subsequent invasion of Russian forces to Chechnya, the conflict saw a radical change in the nature of the Chechen resistance, which transpired mainly by increased Islamization and the growing influence of radicals, especially

Basayev. Both of these processes were naturally reflected in the means that would be used in the fight against the Russians. In the most important development, Basayev made public statements about setting up a battalion of suicide bombers, and on June 7, 2000, the first such attack took place after Khava Barayeva (Movsar Barayev's aunt) and Luisa Magomadova drove a truck full of explosives into the temporary headquarters of an elite Special Forces (OMON) detachment in the village of Alkhan Yurt, Chechnya, killing two (or, according to Basayev, twenty-nine) soldiers.[9] In the next two years at least eight other suicide operations took place against Russian military targets in Chechnya, including a coordinated attack of five suicide truck bombers who blew up military checkpoints and a police dormitory killing thirty-three and injuring eighty-four, and an assassination of the Russian military commander of Urus-Martan.[10] In about one half of the attacks the suicide bombers were women, a phenomenon previously alien to any Islamist terrorist organization in the world.

Another turning point from the tactical perspective was the August 2002 meeting of the Military *Shura*, where Basayev proposed an attack on the "lair of the enemy in the heart of Moscow," also announcing the founding of the RAS as a new entity created specifically for this purpose.[11] It appears that at this time the RAS was meant to be a single unit for an ad hoc operation, as opposed to a permanent group. The original plan was to perpetrate four major acts of terror in Moscow "with explosions in densely populated places as part of a frightening action," which was to have culminated with the seizure of the State Duma.[12] However, following two failed bombing attempts in Moscow, Basayev modified his plan, and on October 23, 2002, hostages were taken in Nord-Ost instead.

To sum up the analysis presented in the previous chapter, Basayev's main objective for the raid was to replicate the negotiation success of Budyonnovsk. In case the negotiations failed, the next best alternative was to achieve maximum casualties among the hostages as a result of the *rescue operation* in an attempt to "show to the whole world that Russian leadership will, without mercy, slaughter its own citizens in the middle of Moscow."[13] However, Basayev appears to have grossly miscalculated the reaction of the world community to the "Nord-Ost" operation, which in the wake of 9-11 and the skillful Russian spin doctoring ended up overwhelmingly siding against the Chechens. This fact would later contribute to the immense radicalization and escalation of the RAS campaign, in which the group had apparently discarded any consideration for international public opinion. In a statement published immediately in the Nord-Ost aftermath, Basayev was quick to condemn the world for its "hypocrisy," stating that if the world had "one tenth of the sympathy [expressed for Dubrovka victims] for the Chechens, the war would have ended long ago." In addition, in a letter addressed to the heads of NATO, UN, OSCE, and EU, the "command of RAS" warned that all military, industrial, and strategic facilities on the Russian territory, to whomever they belonged, were considered as legitimate military targets.[14] Importantly, the letter also outlined a number of conditions that RAS demanded from the Russian leadership. This list is extremely significant, as it provides an extended outline of the demands later made in Beslan, and thus should have been the principle guide for negotiators to the interests and unabridged goals of the hostage takers in that incident. The conditions outlined in the letter were as follows:

1. To immediately put an end to the military operations and launch a peaceful political process with the legitimate leadership of the Chechen state to settle the Russia–Chechen relations.
2. To immediately free thousands of civilians, including hundreds of Chechen women and children. The civilians were detained by the Russian aggressors in the Chechen Republic of Ichkeria and are kept in the Russian prisons, concentration, and filtration camps.
3. To extradite to the Chechen leadership the sadistic colonel Budanov, who is a rapist and a murderer, as well as other military criminals.
4. To fully compensate to the Chechen state the moral and material damage by rebuilding the Chechen economy destroyed in the course of the two wars.
5. To unconditionally withdraw all the Russian occupying forces from the territory of the Chechen Republic of Ichkeria, leaving the ammunition, arms, and military hardware for the Chechen Armed Forces.
6. To pull the Russian troops 100 km away from the border with the Chechen Republic of Ichkeria, creating a demilitarized zone.
7. To bring to book the criminal and terrorist regime of the Kremlin and its ringleaders in an international court similar to that of the Nuremberg court.

In the aftermath of Nord-Ost, Basayev also officially resigned from all posts, duties, and obligations except for the post of *Amir* of RAS, which had now been transformed from an ad hoc unit into a permanent group focusing solely on terrorist operations against civilian targets. And finally, Basayev also made a gory proclamation: "The next time, those who come won't make any demands, won't take hostages. There will be just one main goal: annihilation of enemies and inflicting upon the enemy the maximum possible damage."[15] In the next twenty-four months, he would live up to this promise.

The RAS struck again on December 27, 2002, when a twin suicide truck bombing destroyed the offices of the pro-Russian Chechen Government in Grozny, the most heavily protected target in Chechnya.[16] The attack leveled the building killing over 80 people and wounding 210, but failed to kill the intended target, Akhmad Kadyrov—the same man whom the terrorists in Nord-Ost demanded to come to Moscow to negotiate.

In the next five months after the Grozny carnage, Basayev took his time preparing for "Operation Boomerang," a massive terrorist offensive designed to create an atmosphere of perpetual terror leading up to the Chechen presidential election of October 2003.[17] On May 12, 2003, three suicide bombers drove a truck bomb made of agricultural nitro, cement, and aluminum powder into the headquarters of the Federal Security Service (FSB) in the town of Znamenskoye. The blast, equivalent to 1.5 tons of TNT, destroyed the second most heavily protected building in the region killing at least 60 and injuring over 300 people. The results could have been a lot worse, but the truck could not fully reach the building due to a barrier that had been installed just two days before the incident.[18] According to some sources, the attack occurred in the light of the March referendum initiative in which 90 percent of Chechen voters approved a new constitution confirming Chechnya's status as an internal Russian republic; others have suggested a link between Znamenskoye and the al Qaida affiliated bombings in Riyadh and Casablanca, which occurred during the same week. According to investigators, however, the targeting of Znamenskoye had a more specific objective than simply killing a lot of people. The main purpose allegedly was to eliminate Mayerbek Khusiyev, the man in charge of the investigation of three crimes perpetrated against family members of former Chechen leader Doku Zavgayev, and the destruction of all evidences related to the investigation.[19]

Then, only two days after Znamenskoye, at least eighteen people were killed and forty-three injured when a female suicide bomber dressed as a journalist detonated a bomb hidden in a video camera during a religious festival in Ilaskhan-Yurt. The ultimate target was again Kadyrov, who once more managed to escape unhurt. Both the Znamenskoye and the Ilaskhan-Yurt operations are significant in that they demonstrated RAS' indiscriminate nature, documented by the group's willingness to produce a high number of casualties even in operations where the objective was the assassination of a single individual. In many ways, these two attacks were a sign of things to come.

On June 5, 2003, a woman dressed in a white overcoat killed eighteen people when she detonated her explosive belt while trying to board a bus carrying Russian airmen to their base in Mozdok, North Ossetia. Only two weeks later, a man and a woman driving a suicide truck attacked the MVD multistory police building in Grozny, but failed to penetrate the inner perimeter. The explosion that occurred 300 feet from its target still managed to kill six and injure thirty-six more.[20] Then on July 5, 2003, the focus of "Operation Boomerang" shifted to soft targets in the heart of Russia, as two female suicide bombers detonated their explosive belts killing fourteen and injuring sixty others at the open-air rock festival at Moscow's Tushino airfield. The casualty levels again could have been higher but one of the detonators malfunctioned, failing to detonate the main charge and killing only the bomber. Five days later another bomber, Zarema Muzhakoyeva, was arrested after intentionally failing to detonate her explosive near the Mon-Café restaurant in the heart of Moscow. A police officer died while trying to defuse the device.

Muzhakoyeva's arrest was significant, as it provided a fascinating insight into the internal links within RAS that would later become crucial in relation to the attack in Beslan. Muzhakoyeva revealed that she was supposed to be the original bomber during the first Mozdok attack, but fell ill and was unable to participate. She was then sent to Moscow with the two women that later detonated themselves in the Tushino rock concert. Muzhakoyeva's interrogation following her arrest led to the apprehension of Rustam Ganiev, who was accused of recruiting and training suicide bombers, and whose two sisters, Aishat and Khadizhat, were among the nineteen female terrorists in Nord-Ost. Ganiev also had very close links to a number of the Beslan terrorists. For instance, the one person who was arrested along with Ganiev was Mayrbek Shaybekhanov, who would, however, under mysterious circumstances later be freed,[21] and who, in September 2004, died in the storming of the Beslan school along with his wife, who allegedly served as one of the female suicide bombers.[22] Another Beslan terrorist with close links to Muzhakoyeva and Ganiev was Khanpashi Kulayev, who coincidentally was also supposed to be sitting in jail at the time of the Beslan attack.[23] According to Muzhakoyeva's testimony, she and Khanpashi not only belonged to the same division, but also "practically lived together" though officially never married.[24] Similarly, one of the Beslan leaders—Vladimir Khodov—was not unknown to authorities, having previously been wanted for the February 2, 2004, bombing in the center of Vladikavkaz, in which three police cadets died.[25] Although a wanted man, Khodov freely moved around, and even visited his home village of Elkhotovo in Ossetia several times.

Despite Ganiev's arrest "Operation Boomerang" continued, returning back to Mozdok on August 1, 2003, where two suicide bombers drove an explosive-laden truck into the 58th army military hospital, killing fifty and injuring dozens.[26] Another suicide-truck-bombing-attempt took place in the neighboring republic of Ingushetia on September 15, 2003, but the 600-pound-truck bomb detonated 16 feet short of the newly constructed FSB building in Magas, killing "only" three people.[27] The masterminds of the attack were the self-described "Ingush Chief of Staff" of RAS Ali Taziyev (a.k.a. Magomed Yevlovev), and Ruslan Khuchbarov (a.k.a. Colonel)—the same men who trained suicide bombers for the operations in Nord-Ost and Mozdok, and who would later become the key leaders of the raids in Nazran and Beslan, respectively.[28]

In October 2003, Akhmat Kadyrov defended his presidential seat by a suspiciously comfortable margin, having received 81.1 percent of the popular vote on a turnout of 83.46 percent.[29] The Kremlin immediately used this outcome as clear evidence of the success of the government's policy in Chechnya, while skeptics countered by pointing to the many irregularities associated with the election. To the surprise of many, RAS remained quiet. Then on December 5, a suicide bomber, with grenades strapped to his legs and carrying a backpack shrapnel bomb made of 66 pounds of TNT, was detonated by remote control onboard a commuter train in the Stavropol region in southern Russia, killing 44 people and wounding 150 others.[30] Four days later, 6 people were killed and another 14 wounded in a suicide bombing outside Moscow's National Hotel—an attack the apparent target of which was the Russian Duma, the same building the terrorists allegedly originally wanted to seize in place of the Dubrovka theatre. In late December, Basayev claimed responsibility for both attacks, saying that the "successful bombings were planned military operations in response to Russian aggression, carried out by fighters of [RAS] brigade."[31] Basayev also denied Russian claims that the attacks were meant to disrupt the Russian parliamentary elections. In total, the RAS had killed over 300 civilians in 2003 alone.

The year 2004 would end up being even bloodier. On February 6, RAS was suspected of carrying out what appeared to be a suicide bombing in the crowded Moscow subway, which killed forty-one people.[32] Then on May 9, 2004, RAS launched an operation that will be remembered as one of the most sophisticated terrorist assassinations in history—the killing of President Kadyrov during the public Victory Day parade at the Dynamo Stadium in Grozny. Having failed to kill Kadyrov in twelve previous attempts, the RAS had formed a special forty-member team, which managed to infiltrate the stadium four weeks before the event disguised as a construction team responsible for the repair of the Boxing Ring Hall located just beneath the VIP box. The team successfully planted two bombs in the ceiling of the boxing hall, and placed another trotil-hexane bomb packed inside an artillery shell into the concrete structure near the VIP section. Anticipating that the security services would be jamming remote control signals, the terrorists wired a detonation cord under a thin layer of plaster for some 100 meters from the VIP section where an activation switch was later attached to detonate the bomb. Further, the RAS team also planted three insurance bombs, each with its unique mode of detonation in order to circumvent any possible countermeasures.[33] As a result, the RAS succeeded in killing Kadyrov along with twenty-three other people, including the head of Chechnya's state council, the chief of state security, and the finance minister, despite the stringent security arrangements at the parade which involved the use of metal detectors, dogs trained to detect explosives, and remote signal jammers.[34]

In an e-mail statement claiming responsibility for the attack, Basayev also threatened that RAS was ready to launch a series of special operations that would be "very painful for the Putin regime and [would] take

[Russia] by surprise."[35] Basayev delivered on June 21, when he personally commanded more than 200 of his fighters in the attack on the former Ingushetian capital of Nazran.[36] The attackers wore local police uniforms and set up roadblocks at which they stopped and killed the real police officers who raced to reinforce their colleagues. Nearly 100 people, including several ministers, died before the fighters withdrew and disappeared. Importantly, at least seven of the Beslan hostage takers participated in the operation, including the key leader of the attack, Ruslan Khuchbarov. In addition, thirty-one of the attackers who were captured during the raid later became an object of the Beslan negotiations. And finally, it has now been reliably established that among the weapons found in the possession of the terrorists in Beslan, seven Kalashnikov assault rifles and three pistols had been stolen from the MVD armory in Nazran that was raided during the attack.

Throughout the month of July, a number of additional incidents related to the Nazran raid and Beslan took place in Ingushetia. These included the death of deputy police chief of Malgobek and the deputy head of the Malgobek criminal police in a shootout with suspected terrorists on the city's outskirts; the discovery of a large stockpile of weapons from Nazran in the woods near Sagopshi; and two shootouts near the same village, in which one militant was killed and another escaped.[37] Little did anyone know that in the forest on the hill overlooking Sagopshi and Psedakh was a training camp in which the Beslan team was preparing for the operation, and that the man who escaped from the shootout was Musa Tsechoev, whose body would later be found among the thirty-one corpses of Beslan terrorists.[38]

Following the Nazran raid, a similar operation also took place in Grozny on 21 August, resulting in at least twenty-two fatalities.[39] Then only three days later RAS launched its "week of terror." On August 24, 2004, two female suicide bombers detonated hexogen bombs onboard two domestic flights originating at Moscow's Domodedovo Airport, killing all eighty-nine passengers and crew. This was the first time since 1970 that two aircrafts were coordinately bombed in midcourse flight,[40] and only the third historical incident in which suicide bombers were used to attack aircrafts.[41] The planners apparently studied their targets well, as suggested by the small amount of explosives used and the fact that both women sat by the window just nine rows from the tail, which is generally considered to be the most vulnerable part of the plane.[42] Then on August 31, another female suicide bomber detonated herself at the entrance to a Moscow subway station, killing ten other people. This attack occurred only two days after another round of Chechen presidential elections, in which another Kremlin-backed candidate became Kadyrov's successor. And finally, September 1, 2004, was the date of operation "Nord-Vest," in which terrorists took more than 1,200 hostages on the first day of school in Beslan, North Ossetia, demanding the complete Russian military withdrawal from Chechnya.[43]

## IDEOLOGY AND STRATEGY

Due to its originality with regards to employing large-scale suicidal hostage-taking operations, the systemic use of female suicide bombers, past involvement in radiological terrorism, indiscriminate targeting logic, extreme lethality, the use of suicide bombers on airplanes, RAS falls into the category of the most spectacular terrorist organizations of all time.

There are several important lessons and implications of the operational chronology presented above with regards to management of hostage incidents carried out by RAS. The first such lesson has to do with the dynamically evolving nature of the group's ideology and strategy. Ideology is important as it is an organization's motivational foundation that frames the worldview of its members and thus also provides a sense of collective identity. Ideology is also instrumental in identifying the enemy, while also providing the necessary explanation and justification for its targeting. Moreover, it is again the ideology of a group which determines its core objectives and the strategy for how and by what means these objectives are to be achieved. And finally, ideology is a critical component in determining a group's ambitions, as well as the overall perception of urgency for armed action in order to fulfill those aspirations. In short, terrorists seek to inflict real harm on their enemies while at the same time trying to attract sympathy for their cause among a broader audience. Exactly how groups strike the balance between harm and sympathy depends on the nature of the group's ideology. Understanding the group's core beliefs is thus critical to successful management of any ideologically inspired hostage incident.

The ideology of RAS, in most basic terms, could be described as a combination of separatist ethno-nationalism and radical, militant Islamism. To a great extent it is this religious dimension that distinguishes RAS and its affiliate groups from the more secular elements of the Chechen resistance, which emphasize the national liberation aspect of the struggle against Russia. In Chechnya, Basayev and his associates are commonly referred to as Wahhabis or the "bearded ones," a label that does not by any means bear a positive connotation, given the fact that many of the Wahhabi elements have had a history of violently enforcing contributions for the *jihad* from the local population.[44] This may be one of the reasons why Basayev repeatedly denied being a Wahhabi: "None of us are Wahhabis," he claimed.[45]

Historically, Basayev's ideological progression is rather inconsistent, considering that in the past he had fought on the Russian-supported Abkhazian side in the separatist campaign against Georgia, and had even personally protected Russian President Yeltsin with two grenades in his hand during the Communist Party coup attempt of August 1991 in Moscow. Belonging to the traditional Naqshbandi Sufi order, Basayev had shown little interest in radical Islam, until he "learned that he was leading a *jihad* from Russian NTV television," as one Moscow-based "Wahhabi" preacher had sarcastically commented.[46] In order to understand Basayev's ideological and strategic mind-set, it is particularly useful to focus on his various influences and role models such as Ernesto "Che" Guevara, whose poster Basayev kept on the wall of his dorm room while he was studying at the Land Tenure Engineers Institute in Moscow, and from whom Basayev learned the basics of guerilla strategy.[47] An even stronger influence was Imam Shamil, the historical Chechen figure, who between 1830–1859 led the forefathers of today's Chechens in a bloody struggle against Tsarist Russia, later establishing the first Islamic state in the Caucasus. Basayev took great pride in being named after Imam Shamil, and his incursions into Dagestan and Ingushetia demonstrated the desire to reestablish Shamil's Islamic state ranging from "the Black to the Caspian seas." Another clear influence in terms of ideology was Samir Saleh Abdullah Al-Suwailem a.k.a. Omar Ibn-al-Khattab, the Saudi *mujahid* and Afghan veteran alongside whom Basayev had fought in Nagorno-Karabakh and Chechnya for almost a decade. Under Khattab's influence, Basayev's thinking gradually became integrated into the global *jihadi* agenda, as demonstrated by the 1999 invasion of Dagestan with the proclaimed goal of "freeing [the province] of Zionist influences."[48] And while the RAS has always carefully defined its war as one of national liberation, amid the growing disenchantment with the lack of overt international sympathy for the Chechen cause after Nord-Ost, the group rapidly claimed solidarity with the global *jihadi* agenda even more.

Like ideology, Basayev's strategy had also been an evolving phenomenon. For almost a decade Basayev had argued that time was on the Chechen side, anticipating that the longer the Russian occupation of Chechnya persisted, the greater pressure at both the domestic and international level would be created to end the war. A strong component of this strategy was the emphasis on casualties, summed up in Basayev's observation that "[the Russians] can't handle heavy troop losses. They know that if it happens, the Russian people will eventually rise up against the war."[49] However, Basayev's patience with the inaction of the international community seems to have run out over time, and Basayev decided to make one last desperate attempt to capture international sympathy with the hostage-taking operation in Nord-Ost. Following a miserable failure in this regard, Basayev's strategy changed radically. Firstly, there was a shift toward an increased emphasis on terrorism, as opposed to guerilla operations, and the RAS was established as a permanent group dedicated specifically to this purpose. This shift revealed the increasingly apocalyptic nature of Basayev's campaign, both in terms of intensity and targeting. In this regard, Basayev's long-existing strategic emphasis on attrition remained constant, but had gradually shifted from military to civilian targets, leading all the way up to the deliberate targeting of schoolchildren in Beslan, with the goal of provoking a large-scale war in the entire Caucasus. Secondly, suicide operations against civilian targets, especially ones utilizing female suicide bombers, became Basayev's principal weapon of choice in the Nord-Ost aftermath. The RAS had adopted the classical underdog explanation for this action stating: "We have no warplanes, so we will be blowing ourselves up in Russian cities."[50] Suicide bombings thus became not only the way of producing a maximum amount of casualties; they also represented the ultimate form of protest against the current conditions, especially when the bombers were women.

Basayev's obsession with sacrifice dated back a long way, as did his imagination and touch for capturing attention of the international audience. As far back as Budyonnovsk, Basayev remarked: "We don't care when we die. What is important is how [we die]."[51] In other words, for an individual fighting in Chechnya death is only a matter of time; but a cleverly "staged" demise can have extra benefits. Basayev, known for his cunning touch for propaganda, was quick to exploit this issue. For instance, in the video recorded right before her death, the first Chechen suicide bomber Khava Barayeva pleaded to Chechen men to "not take the women's role by staying at home."[52] This type of a message not only served to provoke Chechen men into action; the "black widow" phenomenon also sent a message of absolute desperation to the international media as well as to potential donors in Gulf countries. Given the enormous propaganda benefits of such a message, it is not surprising that female suicide bombers were quickly adopted in other countries such as Palestine, Uzbekistan, Iraq, and Jordan.

In his own words, Basayev had described the RAS strategy as "the worse, the better," arguing that "difficulty is followed by ease, and the harder it is for [the Chechens] today, the faster this relief will come, the faster victory will come. [The Chechens] are laying naked bare nerves, and forcing the whole world to remember that there is still a war in Chechnya, although Putin lies and claims there is none."[53] This statement also reveals another core element of RAS strategy: the deliberate embarrassment of Russian leadership through the effective use of counterpropaganda, the goal of which was to prove that the Russians were distorting the facts about the status of the war in Chechnya. It was with this specific purpose in mind that Basayev organized high-stakes hostage crises in the Russian territory such as Nord-Ost or Beslan. The principal goal was not only forcing the Russian leadership to choose from among highly unattractive options, but more importantly these incidents were launched with the fallback strategy of producing a high level of casualties for the purpose of subsequently pointing the finger at Russian leadership for incompetence and cruelty.

Similarly, Basayev also relied on planting as many seeds of doubt as possible in the minds of the Russian population with regard to the possibility of Russian government's *direct* complicity in the attacks. Both in Nord-Ost and Beslan, the terrorists made a deliberate effort to expose the police corruption that allowed them to attack their target. For instance, one of the terrorists in Moscow took money from his pocket and proclaimed in front of the hostages: "This is all that's left. I had to give the rest to cops on the way—some of them fifty, some a hundred rubles."[54] Similarly in Beslan, one of the leaders told the hostages: "Nobody cares about you. Your police sold you out for $20,000."[55] The terrorists' desire to feed the doubts and conspiracy theories was also documented by the recorded message that they left behind in the school, which apparently also referred to the question of how the terrorists (frogs) made it to Beslan (puddle):

> There's a small puddle. There's nothing here, no lakes, no rivers. No sources of water at all. Just trees, leaves, animals, and that puddle. One question really interests me: Where did the frogs come from?

The government's dismissive reactions to any criticism, media censorship, frequent contradictions among "official" versions of events, and seeming lack of accountability in the wake of both hostage crises played into the hands of RAS and their goal of undermining government authority in the eyes of its own citizens. It also does not help that the only police officer who actually tried to stop the terrorists on their way to Beslan, received less than a hero's welcome—the fact that he was not killed was enough for the local police to accuse him of being an accomplice and, apparently, to torture him during interrogation.[56]

## TARGETING LOGIC

Besides strategy, another area the understanding of which is absolutely crucial for successful management of terrorist hostage crises is the perpetrators' targeting logic; in other words, the ideological and psychological mechanisms used to justify the targeting of innocents. As early as the group's formation in the summer of 2002, Basayev sent a message to the Russian civilians declaring them a legitimate target: "To us you are unarmed military men, because those who by majority approve the genocide of the Chechen people cannot be peaceful civilians. According to Sharia law, mere verbal approval of war puts peaceful citizens in the ranks of the enemy. You are just unarmed enemy."[57] In retrospect, this statement was a clear indication of a growing lack of discrimination in RAS targeting, which was further clarified by Basayev in the Nord-Ost aftermath: "It is the enemy who sets the limits to our actions, and we are free to resort to the methods and actions that the enemy first employed against us. We are ready, and want to wage war according to international law ... but we do not want to be the only side to espouse those tactics."[58] This type of logic has consistently been repeated in RAS statements which claimed and justified other terrorist attacks, including the deaths of children in Beslan. After this particular incident Basayev used an explanation that appears to have been copied directly from Osama bin Laden's 2002 "Letter to the American People," in which bin Laden argues that all Americans who pay taxes effectively fund attacks against Muslims, and are thus legitimate targets.[59] Almost identically, Basayev now argued that "peaceful people are those that don't pay taxes for this war, people who don't participate, and who speak against this war."[60] Even more radical and dehumanizing were his proclamations of January 2005 when he referred to the struggle against Russia as a "war between the descendents of monkeys—about whom your Darwin said [sic]—and the descendents of Adam. That is today's war, between good and evil ... This is the war of the descendants of Adam and Eve to put the animals in their place."[61] This statement clearly demonstrated the growing dehumanization of the Russian civil population in the eyes of the RAS. Following the perception of betrayal by the international community and the associated decline in the perceived value of setting limits to its own methods and targets, in order not to alienate the West, RAS embarked on a trail of truly indiscriminate high-casualty violence.

In short, RAS' targeting logic made no distinction between Russian civilians and military personnel since it was based unconditionally on the traditional "Koranic" rule of reciprocity, which could be summed up in the following quote of Ibn al Khattab: "Allah orders us to fight the unbelievers as they fight us." This reciprocity, which Basayev sometimes equated to the Newton's law—for every action, there is an equal but opposite reaction—is a critically important axiom in negotiating hostage crises involving the "new terrorists." As we saw in Nord-Ost, the traditional tactic of pointing to the innocence of women and children hostages was quickly rebuffed by the argument that since Russian soldiers did not recognize the innocence of Chechen women and children, the terrorists did not feel compelled to do so either. While this explanation sounds rather cold-blooded, it reiterated that the terrorists did follow a consistent pattern in logic, and that their actions were from this perspective quite rational. In the future, one of the key challenges for negotiators will be to find ways of using this principle of unconditional reciprocity to their advantage. This issue will be explored in greater detail in Chapter 6.

CONCLUSION

When the news of the seizure of hostages in School No. 1 in Beslan became public, it was immediately obvious that the attack carried all the signs of an operation masterminded by Shamil Basayev. A large heavily armed team of militants dressed in camouflage, two to four women wearing suicide belts, the use of mines and booby traps to secure the site, the strategic positioning of snipers, and overall signs of meticulous preparation—the situation did not look good. At the same time, this early identification of the likely culprit provided an opportunity to assess the situation based on Basayev's previous hostage incidents, with a key focus on past demands, readiness to execute hostages, history of enforcing deadlines, past negotiation strategies of both sides, and the final settlements.[62]

Based on the operational profile presented in this chapter, there are several important implications that stem from the analysis of the hostage takers' behavior during past hostage incidents, as well as from the overall shifting mind-set of Basayev's strategy. In all past hostage crises, the operations had been extremely daring and well planned, all involved an unusually high number of ready-to-die commandos, some of whom were women. In all previous cases, strong family and friendship ties existed among the hostage takers' team members, strengthening their cohesion. In addition, in all cases there was a strategic deployment of snipers, mines, and booby traps to secure the site, which along with the exceptionally large number of hostages and hostage takers made the launching of low-casualty rescue operations practically impossible. Further, in each case, the terrorists demonstrated considerable tactical improvement over the previous incidents, learning from their own mistakes as well as from the Russian operational procedures. All of the past operations presented the demand for an unconditional pullout of Russian forces from Chechnya. In all cases, the hostage takers presented their own death as an inevitable part of their mission, but after several days the perpetrators chose to live and evacuate the location if a suitable opportunity presented itself. In all of the previous cases, there was a willingness not only to negotiate, but also to release hostages independently or in exchange for certain concessions. In all of these cases, the terrorists let deadlines pass, and only in Budyonnovsk were there pressure executions of hostages.[63]

The initial analysis of these facts about past incidents seemed to suggest that negotiation would be a viable option for the management of the Beslan crisis. At the same time, in light of RAS' evaporating concern for international sympathy in combination with the likely perception of the defeat in Nord-Ost as a product of an excessively "soft" approach, it was probable that Beslan would employ a "harder" approach featuring more severe treatment of the hostages and a stricter enforcement of deadlines via executions. In addition, the terrorists had learned about their susceptibility to the use of incapacitating gases in the rescue operation, thereby taking preemptive steps to eliminate this vulnerability. As a part of this effort to obstruct any chances of a successful rescue assault, Basayev also attempted to up the ante by the deliberate targeting of a large group of schoolchildren. The logic was straightforward: public opinion would be strongly against endangering the children's lives in a rescue operation, thereby decreasing its appeal, and consequently, also diminishing the likelihood of its occurrence. And if the storming did in fact take place, the political consequences for the Russian leadership, despite the most effective spin doctoring, would be devastating. Basayev understood the pattern in Russian responses to hostage crises, and knew that despite the increased stakes the Russians would still eventually assault the location. He understood that the authorities would probably stall for time in order to create a perception of exhaustion of all peaceful options while using the time to gather intelligence for an assault. Based on a previous pattern, Basayev could predict the Russian response to the slightest detail, including the likely timing of the assault. In addition, Basayev had also learned not to trust Russian promises after postsettlement assault on Raduyev in Kizlyar and the diversionary phone call made by general Kazantsev in order to facilitate the storming of the theatre in Nord-Ost.[64] As a result of this escalatory learning curve, the settlement (whether peaceful or violent) of the Beslan school crisis would inevitably be even more difficult than any other crisis in the past.

Overall, based on the initial incident analysis it was immediately clear that Beslan would be incredibly challenging but not impossible to resolve via the process of crisis negotiation. At the same time, to anyone familiar with Russia's political realities it was sadly obvious that a bloody rescue operation would eventually put an end to the siege, and that this would most likely happen on the third day of the crisis.[65] The terrorists knew this, too. According to hostage Regina Kusraeva, on the first day one of the hostage takers told the hostages, "Judging by past experience, we suspect that there will be an assault. If the lights go out, everybody lay on the floor, but don't run; they'll kill you."[66]

# CHAPTER 5

## BESLAN

### DAY 1

On September 1, 2004, around 8:00 A.M., a group of terrorists set off from their camp located in the woods near the village of Psedakh in the Malgobek district of the republic of Ingushetia.[1] Just after 9:00 A.M., they arrived at the School No.1 in Beslan, and with swift action took over 1,200 people hostage. Originally, the attackers divided the hostages into classrooms, later gradually summoning them into the gymnasium and deploying 127 homemade explosive devices around the school building. In the gym itself, devices were placed in basketball hoops, hung on a string running through the middle of the gym, and pasted to the walls.[2] Some of the male hostages were immediately selected out of the crowd and forced to hang up bombs and to barricade windows in the hallways and classrooms. An hour into the siege, the terrorists announced their plans and set the ground rules, among them the order for everyone to speak only in Russian. One of the fathers, Ruslan Betrozov, got up and translated the terrorist speech into Ossetian,[3] and tried to calm everyone down. When he was finished, a terrorist came up to him and asked: "Have you said everything you wanted to say?" the man nodded and was then shot to death in front of his two sons.

The terrorists were highly organized. There were about seven guards inside the gym at any given time, and they were working in shifts. The only two doorways to the gymnasium were guarded by two female suicide bombers whose role also included the supervision of small groups of hostages on their way to the bathroom. Other terrorists were dispersed in classrooms and the cafeteria, with the main leaders spending most of their time in the library and the second floor teachers' room, where televisions and the remote detonation mechanism for the daisy chain of explosive devices were also located.

The initial response to the incident consisted of a brief shootout of armed parents with the hostage takers. As soon as the terrorists warned that they would kill ten hostages for every single one of them killed, the shooting stopped. An hour and a half after the takeover, soldiers and policemen finally started arriving at the scene. This is amazing considering the fact that the main police station is located a mere 200 meters from the school. It was later reported that the late arrival of policemen on the scene was caused by the fact that the duty officer with the key to the weapons locker could not be located for a full forty minutes.[4] The operational command center was set up nearby in the Technical School No. 8. and was headed by the president of North Ossetia, Alexander Dzasokhov. Several hours after the takeover, two deputy directors of the Federal Security Service of the Russian Federation (FSB)—Vladimir Pronichev and Vladimir Anisimov—arrived from Moscow along with several other officials and set up another headquarters.

At this time, it has been reported, the terrorists began calling from the windows for the release of some of the attackers arrested in the June raid on Nazran, Ingushetia. However, this demand does not figure anywhere in the official record of the negotiations. The initial telephone contact was reportedly handled by a local FSB negotiator, Vitalii Zangionov.[5] He spoke to a man who on the inside was know as Ali, but for the negotiations used the name "Sheikhu." In the initial conversation, the negotiator focused on the issue of providing medical help for the injured, and an offer for the terrorists to get access to the media.[6] This met with a mocking response from Ali: "Why would I need a doctor—I'm not ill. Why would I need journalists? I did not come here to shoot a movie."

In this initial conversation, Ali also demanded Aslanbek Aslakhanov, Putin's special advisor on Chechnya, to come to Beslan for negotiations. In an apparent attempt to stall for time, the negotiator raised the issue that Aslakhanov was in Moscow, to which Ali responded: "Airplanes don't fly in Moscow or what?" He was subsequently offered something else, to which he answered, "I don't decide these things. I'm just the press secretary. Let me check with the amir."[7]

From the very start, it was clear that the terrorists were instructed by their leadership to speak only to high-level officials. According to hostages that sat close to Ali, he spoke with someone on the phone ending a conversation by saying: "I will only talk to the president." His phone rang again in 15–20 minutes. "President?" "No, his aide." Ali interrupted the talk at once.[8] Also, efforts to engage Mufti Ruslan Valgatov—religious leader of North Ossetia's Muslim minority—were refused, and he was threatened to be killed if he tried to approach the school. In the meantime, the authorities compiled their first list of hostages, and publicly announced that there were only 120 of them.

Around this time, Dr Larisa Mamitova was treating two of the hostage takers who were injured in the initial takeover by one of the fathers, who shot them with his pistol. During this interaction, Mamitova carefully asked her patients about their intentions and goals, and was told that the objective was peace for Chechnya and the justification for the involvement of women and children in this attack was based on the fact that Chechen women and children were also suffering. Mamitova offered her help in communicating with the authorities, and was summoned to the school's library to meet with the leader of the group, Ruslan Khuchbarov (a.k.a. "Polkovnik"). He pointed to a chair next to him and started fishing his pockets. First taking out a drawing of the plan of the school, and then putting it back in, Polkovnik finally found a piece of paper with prelisted telephone numbers. He gave Mamitova another piece of paper and started dictating a message:

> 8-928-738-33-374 (telephone number)
> We demand for negotiations President of the Republic Dzhosokhov, Zaizikov, president of Ingushetia, Roshal, children's doctor. If they kill any one of us, we will shoot 50 people to pieces. If they injure any one of us, we will kill 20 people. If they kill 5 of us, we will blow up everything. If they turn off the light, even for a minute, we will shoot to pieces 10 people.

Mamitova was then placed under a sniper's crosshairs and sent outside to hand over the note. Shortly thereafter, Alsanbek Aslachanov, Putin's advisor on Chechnya, called the school. According to his own account, he said: "I'm getting ready to leave. There are things for us to discuss. Are you ready to talk to me?" He was greeted with an angry reply: "Why do you lie all the time? We have over 1,200 people here, 70 percent of them children. People have been killed already and you are talking about 'things to discuss?' If you go on like this we will start shooting them and then you'll see how serious things are."[9]

From early on, the terrorists selected out two groups of men and led them outside the gym. One group had the task of barricading windows, while the other was forced to kneel in the corridor with hands behind their heads facing the wall. The first group never returned. Once their job was finished, they were led to a classroom on the second floor, lined up against the wall and shot. Their bodies were thrown out of the window.

As the incident progressed, tensions started to grow even higher. In the afternoon, the hostages overheard an argument between the terrorists and their leader, in which particularly the female attackers expressed their displeasure with holding children hostage. Around four o'clock in the afternoon one of the suicide bombers detonated, killing five or six of the men lined up in the hallway and injuring many more. The cause of the detonation is still a point of contention. According to one version, the woman was detonated remotely by Polkovnik because of her disobedience. But, since the bomber detonated in a doorway, also killing the other suicide bomber and another terrorist in the process, it seems more likely that the detonation was an accident.[10] The dead hostages were carried upstairs and the injured were ordered to join them. Once in the classroom, a terrorist sprayed all the injured men with gunfire, and their dead bodies were later thrown out of the window. At this point, the number of dead hostages already reached twenty-one.

In the meantime, negotiations continued as Mikhail Gutseriev—the former speaker of the Russian State Duma and president of the Rusneft oil company—called the school, claiming to have been empowered to lead the negotiations by Putin himself. After an attempt to speak Ingush, Gutseriev was rebuffed and instructed to speak only in Russian. His suggestion for a Muslim cleric to enter into negotiations was allegedly rejected, as was the offer to exchange the children for the release of the thirty-one terrorists arrested in the Nazran raid.[11] According to the now former president of Ossetia, Alexander Dzasokhov, a deal had almost been made, but at the last moment the terrorists backed out. When Gutseriev asked about specific demands, Sheikhu suggested that they be handed over in writing. In this context, the name of Ruslan Aushev, former Ingushetian president and a highly respected figure in the Caucasus, reportedly came up for the first time.[12]

After 7:00 P.M., another man demanded by the terrorists for negotiations, Dr Leonid Roshal, claims to have called the school. Never requested by the authorities, he flew to Beslan on his own initiative after being informed of the situation by journalists. Once he reached the school, Roshal called the terrorists expressing his readiness to enter with water and medicines. "If you come closer than 30 meters, you'll get a bullet" came the reply. In a strictly one-sided discussion, the threat was made that hostages would be executed in case the phone was turned off, or if it was on but there was no answer when the terrorists called, or if soldiers were spotted outside, or if the lights were turned off. Sheikhu further instructed Roshal that he could only enter the school with the other three men demanded earlier; if he approached alone he would be shot.

## DAY 2

In the early morning of 2 September, Mamitova overheard a radio broadcast reporting that only 354 hostages were held inside the school, and that the telephone number provided by the terrorists was nonoperational. She asked to see Polkovnik and informed him of the report. "No one needs you so no one calls. They are still reporting that you are 354 people in total. Perhaps we should kill the rest of you," was the reply. He also added, "How can the phone not be working when I am still talking to people on this?" Nonetheless, he took another handset and called the first phone. The call did not go through. Mamitova then suggested sending another note with a new telephone number. Polkovnik tore a piece of paper from a notebook and handed it over to Mamitova. "Write again," he said and dictated some other telephone numbers. In the middle of dictating, he became angry, took the piece of paper from her, and threw it out. He gave her another one and dictated again: "Our nerves are at a breaking point . . . "

In the morning of the second day, the authorities attempted a bold move by summoning Luisa Kodzoyeva—the wife of one of the alleged terrorists—to the school, to try to convince her husband to release the children. Perhaps more importantly, the authorities were sending a message that the terrorists' family members could also be found and punished. In a videotape made by the authorities, a part of which was later shown on television, Luisa stated: "If you are there, let the children go. Help the children; after all, you have five of your own." However, the first sentence, in her statement was not aired: "Iznaur, I know that you're not there . . . They forced me."[13] There was no response.[14]

Inside the school, the terrorists were becoming increasingly angry and frustrated, mainly due to the repeated government claims made in the media that the number of hostages was 354, and that the hostage takers had not presented any demands. The hostage takers saw this as a deliberate attempt to obstruct negotiations, and to justify the launching of an armed assault on the school. The downplaying of the number of hostages was then supposed to aid the authorities in covering up the number of the victims of the rescue. Infuriated, around noon of the second day, the terrorists called a "dry strike" and stopped giving the hostages water. From this point on, the hostages really started to suffer from the lack of food, water, and deteriorating conditions inside. Throughout the rest of the crisis, some of the hostages would drink their own urine in a futile attempt to extinguish their thirst.

Just before 2:00 P.M., the terrorists' mood suddenly changed and they became visibly happy, hugging each other "as if they had just met after a long time." From the top floor they announced that a "big person" was coming in for the negotiations. Near the bathroom where all the nursing mothers were relocated with their babies on the first day, a terrorist offered a hint: "If they let him come in, maybe we will let the breast-fed children out."[15] This "big person" turned out to be Ruslan Aushev, Afghan war general and former Ingush president. From Khodov's comment, it seems that the terrorists were not sure until the last moment whether he would be let through. Aushev asked to see the hostages, and then was led to the window in the second floor from which he was shown the corpses of the twenty-one dead men executed on the first day. Afterward, Aushev and Polkovnik held a discussion in the teachers' room. They spoke about evacuating the infant children and collecting the bodies of those men who were shot on the first day.[16] At the end of the meeting, Aushev was handed a handwritten note dated August 30, 2004, addressed to "President Putin from Allah's slave Shamil Basayev." He was asked to read the message out loud to make sure everything was clear:[17]

> Vladimir Putin, you were not the one to start the war, but you could be the one to end it, that is if you find the courage and resolve to act like de Gaulle. We are offering you peace on a mutually beneficial basis in line with the principle "independence for security." We can guarantee that if you withdraw the troops and recognize Chechen independence, then: We will not strike any political, military or economic deals with anyone against Russia; We will not have any foreign military bases even temporary ones, we will not support or finance groups fighting the Russian Federation, we will join the Commonwealth of Independent States, we will stay in the ruble zone, we could sign the Collective Security Treaty, although we would prefer the status of a neutral state; we can guarantee that all of Russia's Muslims will refrain from armed methods of struggle against the Russian Federation, at least for 10–15 years, on condition that freedom of religion be respected ... The Chechen nation is involved in the national liberation struggle for its Freedom and Independence and for its preservation. It is not fighting to humiliate Russia or destroy it. As a free nation, we are interested in a strong neighbor. We are offering you peace and the choice is yours.

The terrorists set a deadline for the Kremlin to respond by the morning of 4 September.[18] Aushev promised to hand over the letter, and asked for the release of kids. "You also have kids, don't you?" he said.[19] Khuchbarov agreed, and the nursing mothers were released along with one baby each, some of them having to leave their other children behind. After leaving the school with the twenty-six released hostages, Aushev immediately transmitted the text of the letter to the Kremlin with an urgent plea for negotiations. In addition, a list of specific demands was also handed over in writing. These demands were never made public, but available evidence suggests that the list corresponded to the one later provided by Basayev himself:

- We demand that the war in Chechnya be stopped immediately and that the withdrawal of forces be carried out;
- We insist that Putin immediately resigns from his post as president of the Russian Federation; and
- We insist that all hostages, be it children or adults, go on hunger strike in support of our demands.

Also, the following conditions were reportedly set:

- We will give water to everyone provided Putin immediately stops the war, sends all his troops to the barracks and begins the withdrawal of his troops;
- We will give food to everyone provided Putin begins the withdrawal of his troops in reality;

- We will release children under ten as soon as they start withdrawing the troops from mountainous areas;

- We will set others free after they complete the withdrawal of the troops; and

- If Putin submits a letter of resignation, we will release all the children and go back to Chechnya with others.


In the evening of the second day, Aslakhanov called the school again. The conversation was very strict and to the point. He was informed that he could come to Beslan to negotiate only if he had the authority to do so granted by Putin. Aslakhanov answered affirmatively and pointed out: "Some demands are unrealistic and you know it. Some we will fulfill. I'll talk to the president." Sheikhu replied: "If you do, then see you tomorrow at 3:00 P.M., we'll hold an official meeting." According to his own account, Aslakhanov then spoke to President Putin, who allegedly stated that "the children's lives must be saved at all costs. Agree to everything. But the first two demands cannot be met."[20] This is an extremely interesting point. If Aslakhanov did indeed talk about the possibility of satisfying some of the terrorists' demands, it clearly contradicts the official claim that no demands were made. Similarly, Putin's comment about the unacceptability of the "first two demands" confirms their existence. It is not clear, however, what the President meant by "agree to everything;" if the first two demands—withdrawing of troops from Chechnya and his own resignation—were unacceptable, then there was nothing else to agree to but the demand that hostages go on a hunger strike. So while the statement "agree to everything but the first two demands" by itself may be interpreted as evidence of the Russian leadership's willingness to offer almost any concession in order to save the lives of the hostages, in the context of the actual list of demands it translated into agreeing to absolutely nothing.

Another interesting point is the discrepancy between the claims of the officials in terms of the course of the negotiations, and the desperate reactions of the terrorists inside. For instance, while Aslakhanov's statement above may seem like rapid negotiations were going on, inside the school the terrorists complained to the hostages that nobody wants to speak with them. For instance, Polkovnik even sought out Mamitova and told her that if there were any members of parliament or other politicians that she knew, she should call them. Mamitova replied that she did not know anyone, but pleaded to try calling her colleague at the emergency room, perhaps she could be of help. After being allowed to call and explaining the conditions inside, she offered the distrustful woman on the other side of the line to come to the school and see for herself. Polkovnik set a deadline of ten minutes and offered a guarantee of safety, but no one ever appeared. Mamitova then remembered hearing from someone in the gym that the children of the North Ossetian Parliament speaker Mamsurov were also among the hostages. Through Lydia Tsaliyeva, the school's headmaster, the kids were identified and summoned to the teachers' room. Before they left the gym, Ali took aside the boy, hugged him, and kissed him on the head. "Don't worry. Nothing bad is going to happen to you. We just need you to help us jumpstart the negotiations. Talk with your daddy and tell him what's going on."[21]

When Mamitova and the children finally managed to get through to Mamsurov, he replied: "The government has ordered me to leave my parental emotions at home." Mamitova then pleaded for Mamsurov to contact Ossetian president Dzasokhov and to ask him to call the school within ten minutes. Mamsurov agreed. The time passed without anyone calling. Visibly upset, Polkovnik then turned on the TV, where the government media were still reporting that there were only 354 hostages, and where Dr Roshal was claiming that kids were not in immediate danger, and that they could survive eight to nine days without water. The TV station also said that Aushev led out twenty-six mothers and children. Polkovnik exploded: "We let out just a couple of people and you're already claiming twenty-six! And then you'll say forty more, seventy more! We're not going to let out a single person any more!" Polkovnik then sent Mamitova and the kids back to the gym. "Go, nobody needs you."[22]

On the evening of September 2, Ali came into the gym visibly distressed. When asked by Larisa Kudzieva what had happened, he replied: "I don't want to lift my foot off the trigger,[23] but I'm forced to do it. They don't want to talk. The answer is no. They told me that Russia will never talk to terrorists. That the problem does not exist." When she asked what that meant, Ali replied: "I don't know what that means. They told me I have a day and a half to sort it out." Kudzieva countered: "That can't be. Maybe you misunderstood." "No, I understood. I understood everything."[24]

The authorities have a different story. According to official sources, Roshal called the terrorists in the evening of the second day and offered them free passage. The offer was allegedly bluntly refused. And yet, officials apparently cleared the way for the terrorists to leave by ordering a group of policemen to move their post back and not to interfere with any passing terrorists. According to one of these policemen, later, two terrorists walked out of the building and surveyed the countryside, and then they shouted "*Allahu Akbar*," shot into the air and retreated back to the school.[25]

In the command centre, several ideas were allegedly being discussed, including the signing of a fake decree about pulling troops from Chechnya, but the idea was quickly abandoned as it was assumed that the terrorists would need to see more evidence of a pullout on TV, which would be a point of no return.[26] In the evening of the second day, Aushev suggested to engage Aslan Maskhadov, the last elected President of the separatist government for negotiations. Maskhadov had publicly condemned the attack and this gave a glimpse of hope. On the other hand, the Kremlin had tried to implicate Maskhadov in previous acts of terrorism, and providing him an opportunity to appear as a savior by engaging him in this crucial role, was hardly going to be acceptable to the Kremlin. Nevertheless, both Dzasokhov and Aushev contacted Maskhadov's envoy Zakayev in London.[27] The reply was that Maskhadov was ready to assume the negotiating role, but asked for a guarantee that he would be provided unhindered access to the school and that the Russians would not kill him. By midnight, at the civilian segment of the local crisis staff, an agreement was allegedly drafted, with key components oscillating around negotiations between Russian leaders and Maskhadov, a plan for Chechen autonomy, and a gradual troop withdrawal.[28]

## DAY 3

The morning of September 3 brought some optimistic news: Maskhadov had sent a message through Zakayev confirming that he was ready to fly to Beslan to negotiate. The local authorities responded by announcing that they needed only two hours to organize his safe passage and travel arrangements.[29] Around noon, Ossetian presidential spokesman Lev Dzugayev told the journalists: "Important new faces are about to enter the negotiation process, they will arrive soon." In addition, he also announced that this step had the full support of the Kremlin, and that an agreement had also been made with the terrorists to collect the bodies of the hostages killed on the first day. Only an hour after this announcement the storming started, leading some sources to speculate that the explosions that triggered the mayhem were no accident, and that their purpose was to deny Maskhadov the chance to come in and save the day.[30] The federal authorities in turn, categorically denied Maskhadov's willingness to come to Beslan to negotiate.[31] Further, after Beslan they accused him of actually planning the attack and put a $10 million bounty on his head.[32]

The small glimpse of optimism that was present outside following Dzugayev's announcement, however, was not shared by the people inside the gym. Conditions were rapidly deteriorating, with at least two of the kids already reaching the verge of death due to dehydration. The overall feeling shared by everyone in the school was that something must happen soon, as the hostages were becoming increasingly uncontrollable, and the terrorists knew that based on past experience an assault would be starting before long. Some hostages noticed that the number of terrorists had gotten smaller overnight, with some specific individuals nowhere to be seen on the third day.[33] The desperation of the remaining terrorists was evident. They were acting increasingly aggressive, became even less responsive to hostages' anxious pleas for water, and their anger grew with their inability to quiet the hostages down.

Just before 1:00 P.M., Mamitova was told that a lorry would be coming to collect the bodies of the dead hostages. Polkovnik told her to stand by the window, and to let the people in the lorry know about the situation of the kids. He wanted her to let them know that the kids were feeling very bad and that for three days the terrorists had not killed anyone. At 1:02 P.M., the lorry approached and several shots were fired. Almost simultaneously, the first explosion inside the school ensued, followed by a large explosion exactly twenty-two seconds later. Shortly thereafter, all hell broke lose. According to the court testimony of Nur-Pasha Kulayev, the sole captured terrorist, Polkovnik ran into the gym following the first two explosions and screamed that a sniper had shot and killed the operative who had his foot placed on the book that was rigged as a detonator to the bombs. At the same time he was speaking on his mobile and yelled. "What have you done, you want to storm? Do you know how many children there are? You lied to us. You bear responsibility for everything." Gutseriev on the other side: "But there's no assault!" Polovnik replied: "That's it. We're blowing up." After that he smashed the phone and ordered to shoot everyone. "It doesn't matter; they will take pity on no one."[34] By this point the firefight had become irreversible. At 6:13 P.M., there was one last contact with the hostage takers. "It's all your fault. Say 'hi' to Putin!" Around 2:00 A.M., more than twelve hours since the initial explosions, the last shots were fired.

## INCIDENT ASSESSMENT

This portion of the chapter will analyze the potential of negotiations in resolving the incident. Firstly, the motivations and strategic calculus of the attackers will be examined. What were they trying to achieve? What was the desired outcome? What was their best alternative to a negotiated agreement (BATNA)? Without understanding these questions, it is impossible to design an appropriate negotiation strategy. Secondly, traditional analytical framework for assessing the negotiability of hostage incidents will again be used to identify the negative indicators of volatility, as well as the comparatively positive indicators of de-escalation that were present. And finally, this section will analyze the successes and missed opportunities in the handling of the Beslan incident in order to draw lessons for the resolution of similar crises in the future.

### Goals of the Attack

As has been made clear in the pervious chapter, in order to understand the terrorists' calculation behind launching the Beslan operation, we must examine several aspects, namely, the selection of target, tactic used, and overall strategy. The target was indeed striking, and it was clearly designed to raise the stakes. In Nord-Ost, the Russian leadership resorted to storming a theater full of hostages in the middle of Moscow and politically survived this decision despite 129 civilian casualties. From RAS' strategic perspective, taking hundreds of schoolchildren hostage would introduce even greater decision-making dilemmas and greater public pressure not to storm the school, leaving the Kremlin with few options but to negotiate. According to Basayev's own words, Moscow or St. Petersburg would have been even more attractive locations for such an operation, and he allegedly even considered attacking two locations at once. However, due to operational and financial limitations, a target substitution had to be made. Ossetia then provided an ideal substitute because, according to Basayev, "it is Russia's fort post in the North Caucasus, and all bad that comes to [Chechens] comes from the territory of Ossetia, with the silent consent of its population."[35] The selection of Beslan in particular made sense, as the School No.1 is one of the largest in the region to which even the Ossetian elite sends its children.[36]

The tactic that was used in the attacks was also striking. As in previous incidents, there was the idea of taking hostages as a means to create a "good," which could then be used to "trade" for political concessions. As mentioned earlier, taking a large number of children hostage significantly raised the stakes. Fortifying the location, placing a large number of explosive devices throughout the school, booby-trapping possible entrances and monitoring them with remote control surveillance cameras,[37] deployment of snipers in strategic positions, use of gas masks and sentry dogs in order to prevent the use of anesthetic gas, and other protective measures taken, were designed to overtly minimize the perceived chances of success of a rescue operation. Few hostage crises in history have presented the response teams with such formidable tactical and political challenges.

The apparently suicidal tactic selected for the operation was significant as well. Firstly, the repeated expression of determination to die during the incident was aimed at denying the counterpart threat level: the proclamation of the desire to die weakens the deterrent value of threats by the government to resolve the situation forcefully.[38] Secondly, the suicidal and ruthless nature of the attack was designed to emphasize the uncompromising dedication of the RAS fighters to their cause, sending a strong message to the Russian population that since the Chechens were not afraid of death, the only way to stop their bloody campaign was to give in to their demands. This message was designed to capitalize on the panic that had been instilled throughout the hearts of the civilian population in Russia following Nord-Ost and the high level of attrition in the "Operation Boomerang." Thirdly, the seeming irrationality of suicidal operations is useful in attracting extensive media coverage, which triggers popular attempts to comprehend the motivations of such an act, leading to world-wide debates about the systemic foundations of the enormous dedication and hatred demonstrated by the attackers. In the eyes of many people, the group then gains the image of committed believers willing to do any-thing to reach their goals, also implying that the present status quo of their constituency is so humiliating and so unacceptable that death is prefer-able to life under such conditions. As mentioned earlier, this is especially true in cases where the suicide attackers include women, as has frequently been the case in Chechen operations. This was apparently the element that the terrorists were trying to capitalize on in Beslan as well, as on numer-ous occasions they would engage the hostages with questions like: "You know why our women sacrifice themselves like that?" or "Do you think our women blow themselves up because they like it?" In addition, it is also clear that featuring images of female suicide bombers in their video footage from the site was particularly important for public relations pur-poses; after the original two bombers died on the first day, one of the ter-rorists approached hostage Larisa Kudzieva with an offer to release her children if she agreed to put on the *hijab* and a suicide belt.[39]

Overall, the goals of the operation were multiple. Basayev's success in Budyonnovsk had convinced him that large-scale hostage takings can be instrumentally successful in forcing the Russians to the negotiating table. At the same time, he also learned from past incidents that the Russian leadership can always be expected to launch a rescue operation—typically around the end of the third day of the crisis—and that these actions pro-duce on average more than 130 deaths.

In light of these experiences Basayev's explanation of the goals of Beslan was logical: "We came there not to kill people but to stop the war, and if it works out that way, to force the Russian leadership to kill its own civilians, if only through this to force the lying and vain world to understand what is really going on, to lay bare our wound and pain, because people don't see what is happening in Chechnya. They see it only when huge actions like this one occur on the territory of Russia itself."[40] From a negotiation perspective, this logic is highly disturbing, as Basayev was able to convert a barricade hostage scenario that under normal circumstances is not so fa-vorable to the hostage takers, into a situation where, by his own definition, at least, he could not lose. The logic was simple: If the Russians satisfy the demands, Basayev wins. If the Russians storm the building and a large number of hostages die, he also wins. Finally, the desire—or at least the acceptability—of dying a martyr's death on behalf of hostage takers then erased any possible downsides in his own mind.

There was yet another strategic goal that would be fulfilled in Beslan regardless of the outcome of the incident: the provocation of violent re-taliations by the predominantly Orthodox Christian Ossetians against the Muslim Ingush minority in the province.[41] These were then supposed to provide a spark for a large-scale Christian–Muslim confrontation in the entire Caucasus, not only taking the pressure off Chechnya, but also creating a nightmare scenario for Moscow.[42] In light of this purpose, and in consideration of Basayev's long-term strategic goal of expanding the Chechen conflict throughout the region, attacking Ossetia with a team featuring a majority of Ingush attackers was a logical strategic choice, since more than 600 people had already died in ethnic clashes between both groups in 1992.[43] The resurrection of such historical violent conflicts may only need a small spark. Although official versions deny this, an armed group of Ossetians heading to Ingushetia to avenge Beslan was actually stopped by the federal troops at the Nazran checkpoint shortly after the incident.[44] Since the siege in Beslan, the tensions between the two ethnic groups have followed an escalatory pattern.

Besides understanding the strategic calculus of the masterminds of the operation, it is also important to examine the profiles and backgrounds of the executors, as they are essentially the ones who will make the very final decision in terms of executing hostages, dying, surrendering or taking up an offer of free passage. And, although ideological hostage incidents typically feature little independent decision making on behalf of the executors, based on the analysis of Basayev's claim of responsibility, it seems that in case of Beslan this element was present, as the demand to release the imprisoned attackers from the Nazran raid appears to have been the executors' own initiative.[45] Understanding the personality and group dynamics of the hostage-taking team inside the school is therefore another important component to designing a suitable negotiation strategy.

This chapter is not the appropriate place to provide the life saga of each of the Beslan terrorists, which by itself presents enough material for a separate book. As a result, only a basic overview can be provided. The official number of terrorists was thirty-two—two of them women—although hostages claim the actual number to have been much higher, possibly 50–70.[46] Published reports and interviews with investigators, hostages, and the terrorists' family members reveal the following scope. Some of the terrorists had a long history of fighting in the separatist struggle; others were violent criminals who escaped punishment in the lawless regions of Chechnya or Ingushetia, only to later join the rebels. Some were fanatical Islamists, others seem to have been driven by more personal grievances and revenge, and one was an Orthodox Christian who converted to Islam under the influence of his brother. Most of the terrorists had some family members either killed or kidnapped and tortured by the Russians in Chechnya and Ingushetia. Some had a history of conducting terrorist attacks against civilians; others had previously only killed soldiers. Their roles in the crisis were apparently different: while some attackers were clearly destined for sacrifice, others were almost certainly meant to survive. Some held important positions in Basayev's RAS and participated in the planning of the operation, others were only marginal players who didn't even have advance knowledge of their target. This fact even resulted in a serious argument among the terrorists about the idea of taking children hostage.[47] This overall diversity of background, prior experience, rank, division of labor, and differing fates bring an important element into the analysis of negotiation options and strategies. Did the schisms inside the group perhaps provide an opportunity for the negotiators to drive a wedge between the hostage takers?

### Assessment of Volatility

From the perspective of the traditional crisis negotiation framework, it was clear from the beginning that Beslan would be incredibly challenging to resolve. In fact, as mentioned in the introduction, traditional analytical checklists would place Beslan into the category of nonnegotiable incidents requiring a tactical resolution. However, upon closer inspection it becomes apparent that there were a number of dynamics present in the crisis that rendered the commonly used generic incident assessment checklists obsolete. This section will identify the traditional indicators of volatility as well as some of the shortcomings of their mechanical application.

The first volatile factor was represented by the fact that the incident was obviously premeditated and carefully planned. As mentioned earlier, such deliberate hostage crises are naturally more difficult to negotiate, and the process is likely to be significantly longer in duration than in the case of spontaneous hostage incidents, such as surprise police intervention during a bank robbery or a domestic violence situation. Quite simply, if the hostage takers are mentally and physically prepared to be in the given situation, the less likely they are to start second-guessing their decision to take hostages. This, however, does not mean that we should automatically conclude that this shift would not take place. It only means that changing the terrorists' expectations and resolve will need much more time than is the case in most other hostage incidents. Further, while the Beslan terrorists did bring with them vitamin supplements and rations for at least three days, not everyone was comfortable with the idea of taking children hostage. This provided some window of opportunity for planting a seed of doubt in the minds of at least some terrorists. Of course, they also had direct communication with off-site leaders and shared several family and social bonds that might have made it difficult.

Secondly, the presence of multiple perpetrators available to handle the negotiations made the situation even more unpredictable: building rapport with hostage takers is much more challenging if they are under direct pressure from their peers and if they can effectively negate the formation of a personal relationship with the negotiator by simply switching representatives. This was also the case in Beslan, where the negotiations were handled by at least two different terrorists. Further, they also cleverly employed the "deferment of authority" principle, in which the person who speaks is never the one who can make the final decision. This is one of the principles that is routinely employed by police–hostage negotiation teams, and which is designed to allow the negotiator never fully to commit to any deals, without consulting his superior. The negotiator can then deny an agreement previously reached without losing face by pointing to the decision maker as the one responsible for the change of heart. This makes negotiations more difficult than when the decision maker is confronted directly.

Another, volatile element of the crisis was the fact that the hostage takers were well armed and heavily brutalized. Security precautions taken by the militants made an assault on the location without a significant loss of life virtually impossible, and the history of ruthlessness on the part of a number of the terrorists in this group made their claims of preparedness to kill the hostages in cold blood quite persuasive. Further, the fact that hostages died in the initial takeover was also a highly negative development, as deaths of hostages in the early stages usually complicate subsequent negotiation efforts because, in the eyes of the law, the hostage takers would have reached a "point of no return." Negotiations, of course, are much easier before any hostages are killed, as this could be used to facilitate the surrender or free passage in the final stages of an incident "before things get more serious." Further, the commanders of hostage response teams become less amendable to pursuing negotiation once hostages have been killed, and there are greater legal and public opinion obstacles to granting the terrorists free passage.

Another worrying factor right in the beginning of the incident was the fact that the stronger male hostages were separated out of the group and transferred to another location. This filtering process not only signaled the anticipation of a tactical assault—holding hostages at different locations makes an assault more difficult, as multiple tactical teams must attack all locations simultaneously in order to limit the risk to hostages held at other locations—but also allowed for a quick "discriminate" execution of hostages if it became necessary to pressurize the authorities. The slaying of the males, who were perceived not only as dangerous to the hostage takers due to their muscular build but also as morally "involved" in the violence in Chechnya and Ingushetia, would have been psychologically easier and also less politically dangerous for the terrorists than killing women and children. Tragically, this proved to be the case during the afternoon of the first day, when the terrorists did in fact execute several men in cold blood. Later, additional people died in the suicide blast, and the ones injured were also finished off and thrown out of the window. This extremely bold measure, rarely seen in historical hostage crises, constitutes one of the most important dilemmas for the future. The current modus operandi of crisis response teams goes by the rule that until hostages start dying, negotiations take priority. Once hostages start being executed in cold blood, the last resort option of a full-scale rescue operation is employed. But as discussed earlier, in cases like Beslan, the rescue operation has only a miniscule probability of success. Is it better to risk more deaths resulting from the rescue, or to continue negotiations? Does the execution of several hostages really constitute a sign of absolute nonnegotiability? Because of the historical rarity of such a development, there are no statistics to tell us for sure. Similarly, could the absence of executions of women and children be interpreted as a positive sign of possible restraint in terms of *indiscriminate executions* on behalf of the terrorists? What does the absence of executions on the second and third day tell us about the prospects of successes of an eventual negotiated settlement? Again, these questions are not by any means meant to suggest a moral relativity of the issue, or to imply that lives of male hostages are less precious than that of women and children. But on utilitarian grounds, decision makers need to ask themselves: Which approach can result in the deaths of fewer people? Storming of the location or further negotiations? All of these questions need to be analyzed, and the premises upon which the current hostage rescue "playbooks" rest, need to be reevaluated—at least in cases involving "new terrorism."

The third possible volatile element was the absence of change in the terrorists' demands over time. In "negotiable incidents," hostage takers typically start bidding high but reduce their demands as the incident progresses and as their exhaustion triggers a regression to a hierarchically lower set of needs such as hunger, thirst, and sleep. If such a process does not occur over a growing period of time, the contemporary paradigm suggests that the chances of bargaining decrease considerably.[48] However, this paradigm is again based on past experience in nonterrorist hostage incidents where ideology is not involved, and where many of the demands made are not thought out beforehand. In such cases, it is not surprising that hostage takers modify their demands over time. With terrorist hostage takers, who have received a clear set of demands from their leaders and who lock themselves in their position by stating their demands publicly, this process cannot be expected to occur on the same timeline as nonterrorist incidents, as the one thing the image-conscious terrorists fear the most is the perception of failure. Also, the presence of multiple hostage takers in cases like Beslan prolongs this process significantly, as the hostage takers not only have the option of resting some of their crew by working in shifts, but also are able to feed from the energy, determination, and mutual support structure of their colleagues. As a result of these factors, in combination with the lack of sufficient experience and data on terrorist hostage takings à la Beslan, we simply do not know if and when a change in the hostage takers' demand can be expected to occur. Implicitly we should not tie ourselves down to specific time horizons and limit our options based on this indictor alone.

Another potentially volatile element was the alleged use of drugs on behalf of the hostage takers. In general, the presence of psychotropic substances makes the situation less predictable, sometimes giving the hostage takers the "courage" to resort to more radical measures than they normally would. This is one of the reasons why providing drugs or alcohol to hostage takers is considered as a "nonnegotiable demand." Following the autopsies of the dead Beslan terrorists, investigators claimed that tests revealed that twenty-one of the thirty-one gunmen had heroin or morphine in their bloodstreams. Another six allegedly used light drugs ranging from codeine to marijuana.[49] According to local prosecutor Nikolai Shepel, tests even revealed levels exceeding lethal doses of heroin and morphine in most of the thirty-two terrorists, suggesting that they were drug addicts. Alexander Torshin, who headed the federal investigative committee, even claimed that the terrorists used some kind of a "new generation drug" that allowed them to continue fighting despite being badly wounded and presumably in great pain.[50] However, all of these allegations were strongly disputed by the hostages, as well as the North Ossetian parliamentary commission which in its report stated that "no traces of strong narcotics were found in the bodies of the hostage takers." In Beslan, the assertion about "drug addicts" has long been dismissed as Moscow's attempt to cover up the failure of the authorities to negotiate.[51] Fascinatingly, even the Beslan terrorists could predict this development; in one of the conversations with Larissa Mamitova, Polkovnik asked whether she saw any drug addicts among his men. When she shook her head, he replied. "Remember my words, they will call us drug addicts . . . "[52] Another similarly manipulated tale was the story of the terrorists raping young girls inside the school. It all apparently started by a rumor coming from a boy that heard from a hostage that some girls were taken to another room and then a scream could be heard. As the story passed from source to source, it snowballed into a version in which the laughing terrorists raped young girls with bayonets, while capturing the act on video.[53] However, actual hostages, even those who have absolutely every reason to hate the terrorists for killing their children vigorously deny the rape story. On the contrary, they claim that whenever girls revealed any skin in an attempt to relieve the immense heat that formed in the gym, they were ordered by the gunmen to cover up immediately. Similarly, Khodov, when asked by one of the hostages whether he was going to rape her, replied defensively: "We did not come here for this. We don't need it. There's a greater reward for us with *Allah*. The other stuff is simply not interesting to us."[54]

This is not to say that the behavior of the terrorists toward the hostages was not unusually brutal. After the terrorists stopped giving the hostages water on the second day, some of the hostages resorted to drinking their own urine in an attempt to relieve the immense heat of the packed gym. Despite numerous pleas from the hostages, this policy was never changed. Further, at least some of the terrorists clearly demonstrated that they had no psychological obstacles to killing hostages. One of the men who died on the first day from injuries suffered during the initial takeover, was taken away before his death and shot through the knees and his skull was broken into pieces with rifle butts.[55] Some of the terrorists even psychologically tormented the children. For instance, they placed boxes of chocolate in everyone's view to tempt the hungry kids, but simultaneously telling them: "Who even touches it will be shot."[56] In addition, Khodov would occasionally beat some of the older boys with his riffle butt.[57] And while there were no executions of women and children, the overall behavior of some of the terrorists did not suggest the formation of Stockholm Syndrome (the mutually positive relationship between the hostages and their captors) that was so prevalent in Nord-Ost. Again, in this regard as well, there was no uniformity among the members of the team. Hostages agree that only about five or six terrorists behaved especially cruelly, while many others were remembered as "normal," "decent," or even "kind" and "nice." Many of the terrorists secretly gave the hostages water and chocolate, or at least looked the other way when they saw some of the hostages violating the ground rules. One of them almost paid for this with his own life; when he offered a bottle of water to Marina Khubayeva, another terrorist walked up and shouted at him: "Do you want a bullet in your head?"[58] At least two of the terrorists apparently even guarded the kids from the hail of bullets in the final storm risking their own lives in the process. Several others, on the other hand, shot at the backs of the children running away.[59] The unfortunate fact was that despite their numerical inferiority, the hostage takers that were the most brutal such as Khodov and Khuchbarov, were the leaders of the group. The absence of psychological barriers to killing hostages on the part of these men in charge made the situation extremely volatile.

Finally, and perhaps most importantly, the terrorists' repeatedly declared desire to die and become martyrs suggested a high level of volatility. One of the identified preconditions of negotiability of barricade hostage incidents is the desire on behalf of the hostage taker to live—in its absence, the threat of force posed by the hostage rescue unit becomes much less powerful as a bargaining tool. Contrary to popular opinion, the terrorists in Beslan were indeed concerned about their safety.[60] One of the themes that kept being repeated during the crisis was the threat to kill fifty hostages for every terrorist killed, and twenty hostages for every terrorist injured. Throughout the conversations with hostages, it also became apparent that some of the terrorists did expect to survive. For instance, at one point, Khodov who was injured on his right arm, was told by Dr Larissa Mamitova that he needed to see a doctor as soon as the crisis ended, as he was in danger of developing gangrene. Khodov then asked specifically what type of doctor he should see, suggesting that in his case the question of survival was still open-ended.[61] During the same conversation, Khodov also changed his behavior to become very unfriendly once Mamitova told him that she worked in the village of Elkhotovo. It wasn't known to her at the time that Elkhotovo was Khodov's home village, where his mother still lived and worked, coincidentally also in the medical field.[62] One plausible explanation for the change in behavior toward Mamitova could be fear of being identified, something that would not matter to a terrorist who had already discarded the possibility of survival.[63] In short, while there is no question that members of Polkovnik's unit were *prepared* to die during the Beslan operation, it is again questionable whether their death was truly designed as the operation's only *preferred outcome*. The key challenge of the negotiation process was to come up with a solution that would be more attractive to the terrorists than their own demise and the deaths of the hostages. For this reason, the declared preparedness to die on behalf of the terrorists might have made negotiations extremely difficult, but certainly did not exclude the possibility of a negotiated resolution altogether.

### Indicators of De-escalation

Besides the above-stated indicators of high volatility, signs of de-escalation[64] were also present as the incident progressed. Unfortunately, compared to the indicators of volatility, these have been very few in number. One possibly positive indicator was the fact that the attackers let several deadlines pass, and that they failed to follow through with some of their threats. Experience shows that once a deadline is breached, it is easier to break through future deadlines and to prolong the incident. And while the prolongation of the incident by itself does not automatically guarantee a peaceful resolution, it does strengthen the chances for such an outcome. At the very least, it provides the tactical unit with more time to study the behavioral patterns of the perpetrators and to prepare for an assault. In that sense, the Beslan terrorists' failure to follow up some of their threats with action constituted a positive development. For instance, since the very first day, the terrorists were concerned about the authorities turning off the lights or shutting off communications, so they threatened to kill twenty hostages if the mobile phone signal was jammed, if it was on but no one answered their call, or if the lights were shut off. Late in the first day, the cell phone number Polkovnik passed outside for communications was in fact turned off, but no executions followed. On the second night of the crisis, lights were shut off during a thunderstorm but no hostages were killed. And while these facts constitute positive signs that are only minor, in crises like Beslan where there are almost no good news, they provide at least a glimmer of hope.

Another encouraging element of the crisis was the release of the nursing mothers with their babies following Aushev's intervention on the second day. This move demonstrated the willingness of the terrorists to make agreements and to release hostages. Fascinatingly, it was not so difficult for Aushev to convince the terrorists to release the nursing mothers. He simply agreed to convey the terrorists' demands to Putin, and asked for the kids to be released.[65] This suggests that the principle of quid pro quo was clearly understood by the terrorists. In addition, it also appears that they were in fact prepared to release more people if the negotiations made some headway. According to hostages, on the first day the terrorists compiled a list of all kids under the legal school age, presumably to provide quick reference to the hostages to be released in future deals. And since a precedent for the release of a small number of hostages had already been set, it could have been used to pave the road to further small agreements at the end of which other small groups of hostages would be freed. Moreover, the terrorists had multiple demands, which presented an opportunity to dissect the discussion in the negotiation into many small pieces and small procedural agreements to facilitate this process.

### Negotiations: Missed Opportunities

As in the case of Nord-Ost, the negotiability or nonnegotiability of the Beslan crisis will always be an issue of much contention. Throughout the crisis, the federal authorities kept denying the existence of any demands whatsoever, implying that there was nothing that could have been done to save the lives of the hostages but to storm the location. How could one possibly negotiate with a group of suicidal drug addicts that has no demands? Further, according to the head of the investigative group of North Caucasus directorate of the Russian Prosecutor-General's office, "Proof exists that the terrorists who seized the school in Beslan did not intend to negotiate with anybody."[66]

However, these statements are dubious. The terrorists did come to Beslan to achieve certain political objectives. They presented a clear but difficult-to-meet set of demands. Throughout the crisis the terrorists were eager to speak to the authorities, but according to hostages, no one would talk to them.[67] At every moment they waited for someone to get in touch with them telling the hostages: "Be quiet, we can't hear the cell phone. If they call, maybe things will get better for you."[68] Some of the terrorists also told the hostages: "We will not kill anyone, we have a plan. If it is fulfilled you will go home." Yes, it is true that the terrorists also kept repeating that they came to Beslan to die, that they would blow up the school, that the hostages are "not needed by anyone," that "no one will leave alive," and that the hostages would be "killed by their own." But this does not change the fact that it is beyond reasonable doubt that the

terrorists' primary objective was to achieve a specific set of political concessions. In addition, not only did the attackers put forward a clear set
of conditions and demands, they also specifically stated what they were
willing to offer in exchange. Yes, their stated demands were by themselves
extremely difficult to grant, both logistically and politically. However, the
fact that their proposal included multiple demands and specific conditions
provided much room for discussions without necessarily giving in.

With regard to the key demand to end the war in Chechnya, the main
problem was the mistaken focus of the authorities on the *substantive* nature of the demand and on the political unacceptability of fulfilling it. The
situation was basically seen as a zero sum game, leading many mistakenly
to conclude that there was no possibility of a negotiated resolution, or at
least that it was not worth negotiating any number of smaller deals that
may have resulted in more lives saved. However, the main focus should
have been placed not on the instrumental, but rather on the *expressive* nature of that demand; to ask more questions about them and to engage the
hostage takers in useful conversation about what drove them to this desperate act. As discussed in Chapter 3, this in turn gives the negotiator an
opportunity to engage the spokesperson on the other side on a more personal level, as a part of a genuine effort to understand, as well as to build
rapport. Another reason why asking more questions is important, is the
fact that answers can provide an insight into the hostage taker's underlying interests and emotional state. Also, shaping the militants' perception
of having achieved some success, gives them a stake in the outcome, and
can prevent them from taking radical steps that would waste everything
that had already been accomplished. This is why it is important in the beginning to focus on the demands that are easier to fulfill and to create as
many opportunities as possible for exchanges—even of just information.
Specifically, the demand about the release of the hostage taker's imprisoned comrades from the Nazran raid provided hope, as this was something that could feasibly have been discussed. According to Aslakhanov,
trading these prisoners for children hostages was, in principle, acceptable
to President Putin as well.[69]

Beslan was, of course, an extremely challenging situation with huge
stakes, executed hostages, extremely well-prepared terrorists who seemed
to be holding all the cards and who had an obvious knowledge of the
hostage negotiation playbook. However, this by itself was not a sufficient reason to give up on negotiations—or the possibility of a negotiated settlement—altogether. The art of active listening (the single most
important skill for any negotiator) is useful in trying to "unpack" the terrorists' demands into as many smaller "pieces" as possible, which would
then be discussed in more detail. For instance, the demand of the president issuing an edict that would end the war in Chechnya. The negotiators should have focused on asking about the language of the text. For

example, would the Russian word "Chechnya" or the Chechen separatist term "Ichkeria" be used? What else was to be included? Simply a commitment to a withdrawal of troops? Does that mean just the army or all *federal* troops? Which district should be evacuated first? Is there an understanding of the logistical issues involved in such a massive operation? What sort of guarantees are the terrorists prepared to offer, to prove that they will keep their promise and release the hostages once the pullout is completed? What gestures of good faith were they ready to offer? Perhaps providing water to the children? Or even releasing kids under seven years of age, the list of which the terrorist collected on the first day with apparent intent to release them in future agreements? In the event that the hostage takers demands are satisfied, what assurances can Basayev provide regarding the fulfillment of the promises made in the letter to Putin, such as the "guarantee that all of Russia's Muslims will refrain from armed methods of struggle against the Russian Federation, at least for 10–15 years"? Moving the conversation to detail and working toward clarity is essential for a number of reasons; not just stalling for time or looking for some way to outsmart the hostage takers, but also to find as many opportunities as possible to move the situation in a favorable direction (e.g., identifying possible points of agreement that might result in the release of some hostages, or in de-escalation of the crisis). In addition, it is essential here to remember that negotiation is not just about reaching "deals" and making quid pro quo exchanges; it is also about *exercising influence over the thinking, behavior, and decision making* of others. Any information gained in conversation—and the very act of *having* the conversation itself—may present such opportunities at any time.

These are just some examples of the issues that could have been raised and negotiated in order to engage the terrorists in dialogue. On day two, it was clear that the top priority of the negotiations had to be the improvement of the conditions inside the school to enhance the survivability of hostages. Levels of dehydration among the hostages were reaching dangerous levels; indeed some children had already started dying. The authorities should have worked step by step to offer deals to facilitate, at a minimum, the provision of water, and then work toward prolonging the incident in an attempt to wear out the hostage takers. The terrorists only stopped giving water to the hostages on the second day, after the officials repeated their claim that there were only 354 people held in the gym. It seems possible, if not probable, that simply admitting the actual number of hostages could have been 'exchanged' for water for the hostages.

Another opportunity was presented by the demand for the four negotiators specified by the terrorists to come to Beslan. Individually, they were unacceptable—the terrorists wanted to face Dzasokhov, Zaizikov, Aslakhanov, and Roshal all at the same time. According to the testimony of the sole surviving terrorist, Polkovnik offered to release 150 people for each negotiator. When asked whether these men would be executed, Polkovnik made a guarantee for their safety.[70] Importantly, Polkovnik had previously made the same guarantee for Aushev and had kept his word. The situation of the other four men was less predictable, to be sure. Basayev had previously issued a *fatwa* calling for Zaizikov's execution, and criticized and condemned Roshal for the statements he made after Nord-Ost. Dzasokhov and Aslakhanov were obvious targets by their official representative identity alone. All of these facts suggest that they would likely have been killed if they entered the school. Nevertheless, just summoning all of them to Beslan, and showing their presence near the siege site on television would put more pressure on the terrorists to reciprocate in some way. It could also have facilitated discussions about possible confidence-building measures by both sides. These attempts might not have led to any breakthroughs (which are never guaranteed), but they might have created useful opportunities to influence the situation and/or to save lives.

Overall, the biggest mistake in Beslan was the failure of the authorities even to communicate with the terrorists. True, the political reality cannot be overlooked. President Putin had won his first presidency largely because of his tough stance on Chechnya; he could scarcely afford being seen to give in to any of the terrorists' demands. Allowing Maskhadov to enter the negotiations, and perhaps even succeed, would also have been a huge political blow to Putin. Nevertheless, an unpublicized, small-scale, behind-the-scenes negotiation effort could have worked to contribute toward saving the lives of hostages while at the same time limiting the negative impact associated with the public perception of a terrorist victory. Not to mention, a simple willingness to listen would have presented an opportunity for the Kremlin to demonstrate that Putin was not as unreasonable as RAS claimed, increasing the chances for some success in negotiations.

In the end, it would not be worth arguing that the incident in Beslan could have been resolved without the loss of life. Doubtless the chances of negotiating a complete surrender or a free passage for the terrorists were very slight, especially given the Russian Government's recent track record of deceiving militants with false promises of safety in similar situations in the past. Yet, even if the incident was bound to end in bloodshed, maximum effort should have been made to get as many hostages out of the school as possible via negotiations. Not only did the federal authorities fail to do this, they essentially failed to even try. Even more disturbingly, the official reactions and statements on television, such as the clearly deliberate downplaying of the number of hostages inside, exacerbated the crisis. As in past hostage crises in Russia, the Kremlin seems to have had only one goal in mind—to discredit the separatist leadership and to "teach Basayev a lesson." Negotiation was ignored as a possible crisis management tool, again assuming only the unfortunate role of a public relations alibi.

### Operational Management

Perhaps, even more pressing and disturbing than the failure of the authorities to negotiate is the bleak picture surrounding the storming of the school, and the contradictory statements made by various officials with regard to the negotiation efforts. This section will focus on some of the discrepancies and problems associated with operational management. Although not directly related to negotiation, a critical evaluation of the causes of the tragic results of the Beslan siege is a key component of a thorough analysis of the incident.

From the beginning, the response management of the Beslan siege was highly disorganized. The incident was handled by at least six different command centers with little cooperation among them. The chaotic nature of the setup was underlined by the number of agencies that were present at the site, including the elite Alfa and Vympel units, Military Intelligence troops (TRU), Interior Army (BB), Local FSB division, Center of Special Purpose (USNRSB), local police, Army Secret Police (GROU), Special Purpose Detachment of Militsiya (OMON), Rapid Deployment Special Troops (SOBR), and regular Russian Army (technical support: tanks, transporters, etc.).[71] All of these had their own chain of command, and mutual communication among them was limited. Two principal perimeters existed, with the external perimeter set up by the 58th Army about three hours into the attack. The Army was later joined by some local policemen who took up positions on their own initiative without any specific orders or instructions. In the inner perimeter, there were a number of different operational teams and local civilians with guns. This presented a major problem, as this perimeter was too close to the school, and there were frequent exchanges of sniper fire with the terrorists. On the second day, the terrorists even fired a rocket-propelled grenade (RPG) at a car to force the armed men outside to keep their distance. In addition, the gunmen reportedly tried to provoke divisions between the federal and Ossetian officials in the operational headquarters by trying to convince the locals that they should form a human shield around the school to prevent storming.[72] The armed locals took this idea even further. With vivid images of the 129 dead hostages in the Moscow theatre crisis in mind, some threatened to shoot the federal troops themselves if they started storming the school. Yet throughout the incident, these local volunteers were never disarmed and neutralized. This added a high level of emotional instability to the already difficult situation. Further, the double perimeter was simply not made secure enough, despite the large number of troops present. For instance, Russian journalist Madina Shavlokhova—who arrived several hours into the crisis—accidentally found herself right in the school's courtyard without running into a single police or Army barrier.[73]

In short, the entire setup of the operation was highly chaotic. There was no consensus on who was in charge; too many bodies were without sufficient communication systems and coordination; and armed civilians were not controlled in any way. The operational scene was a disaster waiting to happen. Thus it is hardly surprising that the origin of the explosion that triggered the storming has been the subject of such intense speculation. No less than fourteen different versions of what allegedly caused the initial explosion have been uncovered thus far. Perhaps four of them are plausible, but in each case, there are many other pieces of evidence that do not seem to fit. The two versions with the highest level of plausibility include an accidental detonation of the first bomb and the "sniper theory." The former is essentially the official version, which claims that one of the bombs, attached to a basketball hoop by adhesive tape, detonated accidentally after it slipped off the hoop. The scorching temperatures in the gym are thought to have softened the adhesive holding it in place. The second explosion, which occurred twenty-two seconds later, was then allegedly triggered deliberately by the terrorists, believing they were being stormed. However, this version is not wholly viable for several reasons. First, it was not the bomb in the hoop that exploded initially, rather it was the one hanging on a string connecting the two hoops. Second, according to hostages, the bomb exploded in the air, implying it was triggered by something other than the impact with the floor. Third, according to Andrei Gagloyev, the commander of the Engineering Troops of the 58th Army, "such explosive devices cannot be triggered by hitting the floor."[74] Fourth, the explosion happened at the very same moment a lorry pulled up to collect the bodies of the twenty-one men killed earlier indicating a possible connection between these two events.

The sniper theory received much publicity after Kulayev's testimony. He claimed the detonation occurred as a result of a sniper killing the terrorist whose foot rested on the detonation pedal to prevent the electrical circuit from closing. But in Beslan, it was Fatima Dudiyeva's account, the local policewoman who later became a hostage, which first mentioned the sniper theory. Moments before detonation, she was sitting next to the window stretching her back and reaching her arms up. At that moment she "heard a sound like a stone being thrown through the window. And then there was pain." She looked at her right hand and it was bleeding out of a hole in her palm.[75] Shortly, thereafter, there was an explosion. Ala Ramonova, another hostage, confirms this: "Right before the first explosion, something flew into the gym with a whistling sound, and the terrorist standing on the switch clutched his side and fell over."[76] The Federal Commission in Moscow was extremely quick to discredit this story. The head of the Commission, Alexander Torshin explained that the gym windows were coated with a special plastic called "Lexan," which makes them opaque. Consequently, it would have been impossible for a sniper to see anything going on inside. "Besides," said Torshin, "this terrorist [with the foot on the switch] was standing in a 'dead-zone,' meaning he could not have been in the line of fire. Terrorists are not idiots."[77] However, even if Lexan was used to coat the glass, as early as day one, the terrorists purposely broke top sections of each window for fear the authorities would use gas, as in the case of Nord Ost, thus effectively removing the supposed obstacle to visibility. In addition, from the upper floors and the roof of one of the two five-storey apartment buildings near the school, where snipers were positioned, it is not only possible to see inside the gym through the top parts of the windows, but to target the terrorist in a clear line of fire. In addition, the fact that the blast took place as the lorry pulled up to collect the bodies might suggest a level of coordination, as the distraction provided a good opportunity to strike. Overall, while the cause of the initial explosions is still uncertain, there is mounting evidence indicating that the tragic events were in fact triggered by actions from the outside.[78]

Another point of acute controversy relates to the sequence of events after the initial storming of the school. From the outset of the crisis, FSB First Deputy Director Vladimir Pronichev spoke categorically against any military scenario, claiming that as a matter of principle, the FSB did not develop any plans to attack the school.[79] This was, of course, nonsense. The necessity of having a rescue operation plan in place as an option of last resort should the hostage takers start killing hostages is a fundamental component of any response to a hostage situation.

According to witnesses, tanks and armored vehicles pulled up to the school on the evening of day two.[80] These were later used not only as a cover for the advancing Spetsnaz troops, but were also used to fire tank shells at the school during the later stages of the rescue operation. According to a testimony given by Sergeant Godovalov, the commander of one of the T-72 tanks in question, the tank fired on the school on the orders of an Alpha officer, part of the elite antiterrorist unit. According to the testimony, the tank "fired four times at a spot where one of the terrorists was believed to be located, and was then moved to another area, where, again on the Alpha officer's orders, it fired three 'anti-personnel rounds' at three outermost windows on the school's second floor."[81] Whether the tank fire took place while hostages were still at the gym is a point of much contention. For instance, Andrei Gagloyev, the commander of the Engineering Troops of the 58th Army, testified at the Kulayev trial that the tanks fired when the gym no longer contained any hostages.[82] However, first deputy chairman of the parliament of North Ossetia, Izrail Totoonti, disagrees. He claims that he first heard the tanks fire at about 2:00 P.M.: "That was before we began bringing hostages out of the school."[83] Totoonti's version is in concert with the testimonies of hostages, and therefore, this issue remains a source of intense anger among Beslan residents, who lost family members or friends in the siege.

Tanks were not the only unsuitable equipment used during this hostage rescue operation. Even more controversial was the use of Shmel flamethrowers. The Beslan Mothers Committee claims that in 218 of the 331 fatalities, burns were established as the cause of death.[84] The issue of Shmels first arose after Beslan residents found several launchers and passed them over for investigation. Originally, the authorities denied using these weapons, claiming that they belonged to the terrorists. However, two of the used launchers were found on the roof of an adjacent building, suggesting they were used to fire upon the school. This is consistent with hostage testimonies, which claim that even after the initial explosions, there was only a small fire inside the gym. At the same time, melting plastic was dripping on them from the ceiling, long before any fire was visible from the inside. Eventually, an aide to the Vladikavkaz garrison military prosecutor, identified as Major Justice Eminov, confirmed that Shmel flamethrowers were used. He stated that they might have "possibly killed hostages or caused them bodily harm of varying degrees of severity."[85] It did not help that the fire trucks arriving at the scene ran out of water almost immediately.

Notwithstanding the myriad complexities and obstacles encountered by the rescuers, the rescue operation was, overall, a blunder. Perhaps most alarming was the use of tanks and flamethrowers to fire at the school while it apparently still contained hostages, which suggests that the lives of hostages were, once again, considered secondary to the punishment and elimination of the terrorists. What's more, the heavy-handedness of the Russian authorities actually played into Basayev's strategy.

## CONCLUSION

In the aftermath of Beslan, Basayev, unsurprisingly, placed all the blame on Moscow, declaring that he regretted that "so many children died at the hands of the Russians," though did not regret the seizure of the school itself.[86] But unlike in Nord-Ost, he did not make any attempt to plead for international sympathy; rather, he threatened to attack "citizens of states whose leaders support Putin's Chechen policy," and proclaimed that "we would sooner set this world on fire than refuse to fight for our freedom and independence!"[87] In another interview conducted in January 2005, Basayev confirmed his intention to launch more "Beslan-style" operations in the future.[88]

On July 10, 2006, Basayev was killed in the Ingush village of Ekhazhevo. He was riding in one of the cars escorting a truck filled with 220 pounds of explosives in preparation for an attack, when the truck exploded.[89] Since then, the Chechen separatist movement has suffered many setbacks.

However, Basayev did leave behind a network of so-called "Caucasian Front" militants, which now operate in Dagestan, Chechnya, Ingushetia, North Ossetia, Kabardino-Balkaria, Karachaevo-Cherkessia, Adygea, Stavropol, and Krasnodar. So far, the Caucasian Front has upheld its strategy of focusing mainly on guerilla operations and avoiding civilian targets. So far . . .

More disturbingly, current developments suggest that similar operations may also be carried out by other groups outside of Russia. Basayev is now an icon within international *jihadi* circles, and other groups around the world have taken note of his signature tactic. In the aforementioned tenth issue of al Qaida's online manual *al Battar*, as discussed in Chapter 2, the late Abdul Aziz al Muqrin offers detailed instructions on carrying out barricade hostage operations, making numerous references to the tactics used in "Shamil's operation in Moscow."[90] Given the growing importance of online manuals as operational blueprints for the newly formed independent *jihadi* cells around the world, the threat of "new terrorist" barricade hostage crises is likely to grow in the future.

# CHAPTER 6

## NEGOTIATING WITH THE "NEW TERRORISTS"

In the introduction to this book, negotiation has been defined not just as the act of making deals or bargaining, but as the deliberate proccess of exercising influence over someone else's thinking, behavior, or decision making. One of the most important keys to exercising influence effectively is understanding one's counterpart. This is for several reasons, among them the fact that we do not think, behave, and make decisions based on objective truth; rather we act according to *our perceptions*—which are, by definition, subjective. Secondly, we are each persuaded by different things, and to differing degrees. Influence is not a "one-size-fits-all" proposition. Therefore, if we want to maximize our ability to influence any particular individual, we must make an effort to understand what will be most persuasive *to him/her*. In the area of responding to terrorist threats, this has been one of our greatest limitations, as our assessment of the characteristics of our enemies is frequently based simply on the projection of our own fears and biases, as opposed to an actual understanding of their motivations and strategic mind-sets. The widespread use of the term "terrorist" alone, expresses an understandable revulsion and disagreement with the other party's beliefs and methods, but all too often leads to the refusal even to attempt to understand the terrorists' motives; driven by the fear that such a process in itself constitutes a violation of our core values and allegiances. This comes as a result of one of the biggest obstacles we have to effective negotiation; confusing *empathy* with *sympathy*, and adopting the unquestioned assumption that *understanding* someone is seen as too close to *agreeing* with him/her. As a result there is a common tendency automatically to attribute to the terrorists all the worst possible characteristics and to simplistically explain their motivation as "evil nature" or "hate of our freedoms," while completely ignoring the validity of some of their grievances and the conditions and personal perceptions which drove them to their extreme behavior. Such a misguided assessment, while perhaps useful in generating political support at the domestic level, does not bring us any closer to accurately assessing the terrorists' motivations, resulting in the crafting of counterstrategies that not only have little hope of success, but sometimes even directly contribute to fulfilling the terrorists' strategic plan.

Nowhere is this phenomenon of projected attribution of motive more prevalent than in the common portrayal of the "new terrorists" as irrational fanatics who do not seek to benefit an "earthly" constituency and whose violent actions are a self-serving mission to fulfill their twisted interpretation of God's will. Common responses to the idea of using negotiation as a potential tool for a peaceful resolution of barricade hostage crises involving such actors include claims that religion is nonnegotiable, and that since the "new terrorists" do not use violence as a means to an end but rather as an end in itself, the baseline for exercising influence via rational communication is assumed not to exist. However, it has been this very assumption on *our part* that has represented the greatest obstacle to a negotiated settlement.

A good crisis negotiator makes a clear distinction between the *human being* who, for some reason, has chosen to engage in an act of terrorism and the *act itself*. As we have seen in the case studies surveyed throughout this book, when terrorists embark on a mission to take hostages in a barricade setting they do so with specific—and rational—purposes in mind. With the exception of acts such as the 9-11 operation (a hostage taking used only as a means to take control of the aircraft with the sole purpose of using it as a guided missile), these purposes consist of attempts to achieve the fulfillment of rational instrumental demands, such as specific political concessions, pullout of enemy troops, or release of comrades from prison. In fact, no terrorist *barricade* hostage crisis in history has *ever* been conducted with the primary aim of killing the hostages. Terrorist operations that were designed to serve this purpose have taken the form of suicidal killing sprees à la Khobar, bombings, artillery and small arms attacks, and even attacks with chemical and biological agents, but so far have never come in the form of taking hostages with the purpose of killing them all in front of an audience. This is not to suggest that such a scenario is inconceivable or even improbable.[1] But what this does suggest is that when terrorists deliberately take hostages in a barricade setting, they do so with the expectation that they can achieve more by using the hostages as a tool than by killing them directly. In fact, the sole act of deliberate capture of hostages in the barricade scenario is in itself an expression of confidence on behalf of the terrorists that negotiating terms are possible. If that is the case, then why should *we* assume otherwise?

"But what about their uncompromising religious ideology?" would be the common rebuttal. Actually, an exhaustive historical survey of global terrorist incidents suggests that this rational approach to barricade hostage taking holds true for *all* terrorist groups, regardless of the specifics of their belief system. On the one hand, it is true that a group's ideology does have some predictive value with regard to the perceived strategic utility of launching barricade hostage incidents in the first place. For instance, a nationalist-separatist group that seeks to attract international support for its bid for autonomy is likely to be attracted to barricade hostage crises or skyjackings, because of their ability to attract worldwide attention without necessarily committing the potentially politically damaging act of murder. In contrast, apocalyptic terrorists are much less likely candidates for the launching of such instrumental tactics, because these become ineffectual with regard to their overall strategic objective of "destroying the world in order to save it." But while this analysis of a group's ideology provides us with an insight into the likely perpetrators of barricade incidents, history has shown us that when a group does in fact embark on such a mission, the decision is based on a rational, instrumental calculus—regardless of how "irrational" the group's ideology may seem to us. Even Aum Shinrikyo's sole hostage-taking incident,[2] the 1995 hijacking of Nippon Airways flight 857,[3] was motivated by a rational demand for the release of the cult's guru from prison—despite the fact that Aum's ideology was based on a "cosmically scientific" mix of prophetic cultic practices that was difficult for most people to comprehend. The implication here is that even "religious" terrorists have employed a highly *coherent* approach to barricade hostage taking. Contrary to popular expectation, the "new terrorist" hostage takers are not delusional fanatics who claim to speak directly to God and who lack the capability to engage in rational conversation; they are highly politically aware, understand the principle of quid pro quo, and have a set of goals and expectations with regard to the outcome of the standoff. In essence, the "new terrorists" in general are effectively very similar to their secular counterparts: they are individuals who fail to see alternative perspectives on the issues for which they are fighting, and who empathize with—or attempt to embody—the victimization of their own people, while exercising minimal empathy for their victims. Both the "old" and the "new" terrorists see their violent activity as an essentially altruistic act of self-defense. It is still the perception of humiliation, victimization, and injustice that drives the so-called "religious terrorist," rather than a perceived command from God. The use of holy rhetoric by most groups commonly labeled "religious" serves much more as a uniting and morale-boosting tool than as a justification for acts of unrestrained violence. That is not to say that for many terrorists, religion does not represent a tremendous legitimizing force and that it does not inspire the perception of enormous gratification and empowerment. But the terrorists are still primarily motivated by grievances that are very real. The fact that ideological support mechanisms have in recent decades shifted from secular to religious does not necessarily mean that the nature of core terrorist motivations and beliefs has changed, or that religion has become the primary *motivating* factor for acts of political violence. As a result, the common assumption that it is impossible to negotiate barricade hostage crises with the "new terrorists" because of the "absolute nature" of their ideology is fundamentally flawed.

To sum up, virtually all states that are victims of a terrorist campaign insist on projecting their opponents as irrational fanatics. This is quite logical, as such labeling can have a delegitimizing effect on the terrorists' cause—someone who sees himself as fighting on God's orders is popularly perceived as an irrational zealot, with whom no compromise is deemed possible. Rather, this "worshiper of evil" is seen as an exceptionally dangerous creature which uses claims of a just grievance only as a misleading cover, and who can only be stopped by merciless elimination. But while this strategy of promoting the opponent's image as one of an irrational religious fanatic may in some cases be successful in generating domestic political support, it carries with it the danger of failing to recognize the actual grievances that motivate the terrorist. In the context of barricade hostage crises, this will lead to the automatic dismissal of the "new terrorists" as irrational and essentially will rule out even the mere possibility of negotiation. But as we have seen in the case studies discussed in this book, such a dismissal is likely to have tragic consequences. The key point to emphasize here is that, especially in cases involving the "new terrorists," who in addition to achieving their main objectives have prepared the fallback of rendering a rescue operation as costly as possible, there is nothing to be lost by talking with the hostage takers. On the contrary, in situations where a tactical resolution would simply be too detrimental to present a viable alternative, there is absolutely nothing to be gained by the assumption that the "new terrorists" cannot be negotiated with. In such cases the a priori dismissal of negotiations as an option would probably lead to tragic results. Further, the negative outcome of such a course of action would extend further than single hostage incidents—it would also contribute directly to the trend of rising lethality of the "new terrorism," as terrorist groups mirror governments' uncompromising rhetoric by being more uncompromising themselves and raising the stakes each time. In this sense, all those who have eschewed negotiation and taken a "tough," exclusively tactical stand have contributed to the rise of the "new terrorism" as well. We are not suggesting that the answer is to be "soft" on terrorists, nor to make unwise concessions; but rather, to use influence more effectively to change the game, whenever possible, and to realize that—as we approach each incident—we are incentivizing future behavior by the same and other groups. And, if our strategies contribute to a trend of higher stakes, more hostages, greater lethality, and lesser willingness to negotiate, then we are fighting the wrong war because we are the ones who have more to lose.

## DEVIATING FROM CONVENTIONAL GUIDELINES

The above finding about the terrorists' inherently rational approach to barricade hostage incidents is partially consistent with the aforementioned consensus within the crisis negotiation community that the "current set of negotiation strategies and tactics available to law enforcement provides viable alternatives from which to choose, whatever the motivation for the taking of hostages"[4] or that "political orientation of our adversities might have changed, but our time-proven stabilizing effective negotiation tactics have not."[5] Some of what is on the current menu still holds, yet many of the assumptions on which some of the traditional guidelines and checklists are based no longer apply in cases of "new terrorism." In other words, in negotiations with the "new terrorists" the same principles of negotiation such as active listening, focusing on understanding interests and alternatives, generating options, and the use of criteria are all still relevant. That being said, we need to be aware of the well-recognized danger of applying a one-size-fits-all approach to managing hostage crises. As illustrated abundantly throughout this book in situations involving the "new terrorists," many caveats and unexpected developments are likely to take place, requiring improvisation and deviations from the protocols established in the traditional crisis negotiation "playbook," given the fact that many of the conditions which have long been believed necessary in order to negotiate (and many of the indicators of so-called "nonnegotiability") are no longer relevant or affordable. Therefore, in principle what works in negotiation still applies—even in negotiations with the "new terrorists." But the metrics we use in order to determine the "negotiability" of an incident and the indicators we use to measure our progress, and many of the assumptions on which these are based, must change. A mechanical application of the crisis negotiation manual, built mainly on the lessons drawn from nonideological incidents involving individuals without a premeditated plan, is likely to yield undesirable outcomes.

Unfortunately, there is a common tendency in law enforcement and military organizations to resist change, and to resort to the rigid application of rules and procedures.[6] One of the critical aspects of negotiation is thinking out of the box and generating new options. Unfortunately, the all-too-common treatment of the general crisis negotiation guidelines collectively as the "bible" runs the risk of developing another "box," outside of which crisis commanders do not dare to step. And while the need for creativity and improvisation is recognized by the admission that "not all situations lend themselves to standard procedures"[7] and that "negotiation is not an exact science," deviation from prescribed guidelines is essentially discouraged by constant reminders that these guidelines have been built on experiences of generations of negotiators,[8] or alternatively, by pointing out the possible risk of legal repercussions associated with deviation from standard procedures.[9] In addition, the fact that crisis negotiators routinely experience success in more familiar, common types of incidents by following the step-by-step approach prescribed in the manuals only strengthens the dependence on them. In combination with the inherent tendency quickly to diagnose and compartmentalize the hostage takers into neat and distinct categories in order to bring at least some certainty into a chaotic situation,[10] this creates an environment in which creativity and improvisation are unwelcome distractions. And while this frequently rigid approach of "do's" and "don'ts" may be effective in routine situations for which abundant experience exists, the historical rarity of incidents involving the "new terrorists" will make the necessity of deviations from standard incident assessment checklists a near-certainty. For this reason negotiators will need to learn critically to reevaluate many of the fundamental assumptions upon which they routinely rely. These assumptions are found, primarily, in the guidelines listed in Figures 1.1 and 1.2 of this book, and some of our more common assumptions about how we measure success in barricade hostage scenarios.

## CHANGE OF EXPECTATIONS AND NONNEGOTIABLE DEMANDS

One of the inevitable adjustments that we will have to make is to change our expectations with regard to what constitutes a successful outcome. In the contemporary setting the negotiators' main objective is to get everyone out alive, including the hostage takers. In incidents encountered by law-enforcement officers on day-to-day basis, this is a reasonable expectation, and crisis negotiation teams certainly have the track record to warrant such an ambition.[11] In incidents involving the "new terrorists" however, such an outcome is highly improbable and crisis managers need to understand this, in order to avoid panic and the rejection or abandonment of negotiations in case of any unexpected developments. And while we have argued that one of the biggest obstacles to negotiation in general is the a priori assumption that something cannot be achieved, an unrealistic expectation of a perfect outcome can be just as debilitating. For instance, if the survival of everyone inside constitutes the incident command's only definition of a successful outcome or the only basis for continuing negotiations, then executions of hostages will come as a shock that will likely lead to a knee-jerk reaction and a complete reassessment of negotiability. So while responders certainly should not give up on the desire to save as many people as possible, they should prepare themselves for the likelihood of violence while still pursuing negotiation.

Another area where definitions of a successful outcome will need to be changed is the fate of the hostage takers. In standard situations the ambition is to achieve the immediate apprehension of the suspect. In most manuals the question of providing free passage to the hostage taker is a priori ruled out as a "nonnegotiable demand,"[12] while in others it is suggested that hostage takers' demand to provide transportation is an item that can be discussed, even if the authorities have no intention to provide it.[13] Either way, the idea of letting a criminal move locations or "get away" is, understandably, unacceptable to law-enforcement agencies—whose job it is, in part, to catch criminals. This mind-set is also transparent in the explanation used to justify the unacceptability of another "nonnegotiable demand," the release of individuals from prison. Here the manuals have consistently argued that such an exchange is nonnegotiable, because "nothing is gained for the police, only the hostage takers come out ahead."[14] But we should realize that in cases involving terrorists who have planned the operation and involve teams of individuals willingly participating in the operation, we are placed in some difficult dilemmas. The most important one to think about is how we balance the conflicting objectives of saving the lives of hostages and bringing criminals to justice. When dealing with the "new terrorists," we may need to think of achieving these objectives separately—possibly even at different times and in different places.

The a priori ruling out of certain demands is often not helpful. The general idea should be to be flexible in the area of demands, as there is nothing to be gained by dismissing a demand immediately as "nonnegotiable." Rather than seeing the choice as "negotiate or not" or as "agree or deny" any particular request, we must use anything the hostage takers say as a basis for good questions in an attempt to understand motives and to gain information. While providing the hostage takers with a nuclear weapon in exchange for a hostage is probably not a good idea, any demand that is put forward by the hostage taker carries tacit massages and provides clues to the hostage taker's interests. For this reason, any demand put forward by the hostage takers should be discussed, and the negotiator must always be looking for ways to exercise influence.

## FREE PASSAGE

Hereby lies another important lesson of the case studies presented in this book. All too frequently is it the case that the issue of free passage is first brought up in the form of an offer from the authorities. This is a serious error, as one of the cardinal rules of crisis negotiation is that negotiators should avoid asking the subject for demands. The meticulously planned nature of "new terrorist" incidents, as well as the involvement of hostage takers who assume an overtly suicidal posture, is likely to make such an offer counterproductive. Firstly, the terrorists are likely to be offended by the public questioning of their commitment to martyrdom or by the invitation to "run." Secondly, it is foolish to expect hostage takers to accept such an offer, if they themselves did not initiate the discussion. A preferable course of action is to prolong the incident in order to change the hostage takers' expectations and to leave it up to the terrorists to initiate debates about their safety. This does not mean that the negotiator always wants to avoid drawing the terrorists' attention to their personal safety, but this needs to be done through active listening and subtle communication, as part of an exchange or a conversation about bringing the incident to a negotiated conclusion. Quite simply, unless it is the terrorists who initiate the demand for free passage, negotiators should avoid raising the issue. Another problem of many of the case studies surveyed in this book has been the initiation of the free passage conversation way too early into the incident, while the hostage takers were still highly energetic and perceived their position to be one of complete control. Such a step is more likely to be seen as a tactical provocation than as a serious offer. Further, we have seen that in some cases such an early offer was indeed more of a demonstration of the rejection of negotiations, than a serious attempt to achieve a peaceful outcome. In Nord-Ost or Beslan for instance, the offer for a free passage seemed to have served the sole purpose of building an alibi later to justify a rescue operation by providing proof that all options on the negotiation front had been exhausted. While in these cases the motive may have been political, we should realize that such a tendency is actually not uncommon. But we should remind ourselves that crisis negotiation is a highly dynamic process in which more important than the rejection of an offer itself, are the circumstances and timing in which this development occurs. According to research conducted by the German elite counterterrorism unit *Grenzschutzgruppe-9* (GSG-9), most barricade situations begin with the hostage taker experiencing rage and making the decision to take hostages. This stage is later substituted by excitement, as the hostage taker is getting accustomed to the perceived position of absolute power. When the suspect discovers that not everything is going according to his or her initial plan, he or she becomes increasingly frustrated. Frustration then increases the already high level of stress, resulting in a more "rational" approach to the situation. At this point, the level of the captor's adrenalin drops and he or she begins to feel the signs of fatigue, which later turn into exhaustion.[15] While "standard" barricade situations that serve as the experience pool from which lessons for the negotiation manuals are drawn last on average roughly ten hours,[16] in absolute terms ranging from one to forty hours,[17] in planned incidents involving multiple attackers working in shifts, it may take weeks before the change in expectation begins to occur. So while on day one the "new terrorists" will only be offended by a discussion about their personal safety, in week five they may well assume a different position; especially if there has been some movement on issues associated with their core interests. For this reason, the issue of free passage should be held until later, and negotiators should wait for the terrorists to raise it first (without, of course, setting a deadline for such a request to be made). Negotiators must change their expectations with regard to the timing of changes in hostage takers' behavior. Because our experience in dealing with "new terrorist" hostage takers is extremely limited, we have too little data on which to base our expectations. After all the longest modern barricade hostage crisis[18] at the Japanese Ambassador's residence in Lima, Peru lasted 126 days (from December 17, 1996 to April 22, 1997), and even then was cut short prematurely by a very lucky rescue operation.[19]

The lack of demand for a free passage over a comparatively longer period of time is no reason to panic, and should not serve as a pretext to the dismissal of negotiations as an option. On the contrary, in cases showing signs of meticulous planning, the hostage takers' insistence on free passage early into the incident may provide an indicator of *volatility*, due to possible presence of an ulterior motive, such as the use of a hijacked plane as a guided missile or a possible ambush of pursuers. But even in cases involving hijacked aircraft, providing a free passage may be possible. This would include mainly initial discussions and assurances from the terrorists that their plan is to use the plane solely for transportation, and not to use it as a weapon. In light of 9-11 such a discussion would be necessary. The second step then would be to negotiate a flight path to the terrorists' stated destination that would circumvent any population centers as well as an escort of the plane by fighter jets with the understanding that if the aircraft deviates from the agreed flight plan, the jets would be forced to shoot it down before it reaches a populated area or potential strategic target. If the terrorists are really interested in obtaining free passage, such an arrangement might be considered acceptable.

## ASSESSMENT OF NEGOTIABILITY

As discussed in Chapter 1, one of the shortcomings of the traditional crisis negotiation manuals is the fact that many of the diagnostic tools used to assess negotiability of an incident show a limited applicability to cases involving the "new terrorists." On the one hand, most of the indicators used to measure negotiation progress, such as reduction in subject's expectations, decrease in threatening behavior, humanization of hostages over time, and the passing of deadlines without incident, would still apply. On the other hand, the same cannot be said of the indicators of volatility. Most of these indicators tend to be inherent in incidents involving terrorists such as premeditation, history of violence, prior confrontations, presence of excessive weapons or explosives, isolation or dehumanization of hostages, insistence on a particular person to be brought to the scene, violence even after negotiations had started, or the presence of multiple hostage takers.[20] And yet, many terrorist incidents have either been resolved via negotiation or negotiators achieved significant gains at times during such incidents, which raises the question of how reliable the indicators of volatility really are with regard to their use in determining the "negotiability" of terrorist barricade hostage crises.

Conventional wisdom suggests that negotiations are likely to be more successful in cases where the hostage situation is a product of desperation, than in premeditated incidents. In nonterrorist cases, such situations are typically associated with criminal activity or domestic violence, where the hostage taker is essentially not determined to kill in the first place, and where his or her main objective in the standoff is to minimize the consequences of past behavior; thus providing strong incentives not to harm the hostages. This lack of readiness to carry out threats, as well as the hostage takers' dependency on cooperation with the authorities in order to fulfill the core objective, works in the negotiator's favor, by creating an environment in which the risk to hostages is low. The hostage taker often willingly engages in bargaining to get the best possible terms, and the negotiator operates from a position of strength, backed up by the threat of force and the warning that any violent acts by the hostage taker will only get him into more trouble.

Given the crisis negotiators' environment in such cases in which the spontaneous nature of the incident and the expectations of the hostage taker give the negotiator more leverage, it is not surprising that incidents showing signs of prior planning are then assessed as volatile.[21] A premeditated siege will obviously be more difficult to negotiate due to the perpetrators' likely ability to negate many of the levers on which the current crisis negotiation approach relies, and due to their preparedness to foresee and adjust to possible contingencies. But as we have seen throughout the case studies presented in this book, in terrorist cases, the planned nature of an incident may actually have a *stabilizing* effect with regard to the level of threat posed by the terrorists to the hostages' safety. The "new terrorists" tend to kill their hostages mainly in situations where they experienced obstacles to their initial plan or in cases where they have been pushed too far into a corner and then use threats to the hostages as levers of influence back on the negotiators. Especially if the terrorists are not on a hostage-taking mission but rather on a killing spree in which they take hostages as a reaction to unexpected developments, their "killing mindset" makes such a situation more volatile than a planned and highly organized hostage-taking operation, in which the terrorists are less likely to be thrown off guard and panic. Planning makes sudden violence against the hostages less likely. Further, as we have discussed earlier, the planned nature of a terrorist barricade hostage crisis is likely to be associated with a particular strategy and set of goals, which will likely mean a more rational, calculated approach to negotiations. So unlike in day-to-day crises where premeditation is considered an indicator of volatility, in terrorist incidents it is rather the inadequate preparation on behalf of the terrorists who have taken hostages on their way on a suicide mission that we should be worried about. In short, well-prepared terrorists with a thoughtful plan make for a more difficult, but less volatile negotiation.

## EXECUTIONS OF HOSTAGES

Perhaps the most crucial indicator of volatility currently used to determine "negotiability" of a barricade hostage incident is the act of executing hostages. Experience shows that the vast majority of hostage casualties in barricade incidents occur in the opening moments of the siege, when the hostage takers are aroused and highly nervous as they are trying to establish control over the panicking crowd. In only very few instances do the hostage takers initiate executions later in the incident. As discussed in Chapter 1, the conventional theory holds that executions of hostages outside of the initial stages of a siege "provide evidence of [the hostage takers'] depraved mind." Based on the rationale that captors are psychopaths who will kill again, hostage executions commonly lead incident commanders routinely to conclude that negotiations have no chance of success, and the center of gravity, therefore, shifts toward a tactical resolution.[22] However, in the context of the "new terrorism" in which the opponent has the capacity to make any assault or rescue operation as costly as possible, such a decision will likely have catastrophic consequences. Based on the utilitarian principle of saving as many lives as possible, instead of giving up on negotiations, we must rather continue to look for ways to exercise influence and de-escalate the situation. The decision to abandon negotiations should never be made out of frustration, and should never be purely a reaction to a calculated violent provocation. Too often, government officials and police and military personnel see negotiation as a luxury that they can no longer afford when things get "serious." The "new terrorists" know that cops and soldiers (and, especially, their commanders) think this way, and their frequent strategy (or at least their backup plan) is to bait them and provoke a mutually disastrous tactical response.

Significantly, the case studies discussed in this book have demonstrated that in the context of terrorism, the killing of hostages throughout an incident does not by itself represent a reason to abandon negotiations. In addition, with the possible exception of Rezaq Omar Ali Muhammed, the executioner in the Egypt Air Flight 648 hijacking, there is no evidence of any psychological abnormality among the population of terrorist hostage takers. This makes the argument upon which the execution of hostages is frequently used as evidence of "nonnegotiability" invalid. Rather than the act of execution itself, it is the understanding of the logic used for the victims' selection and the circumstances in which these killings occur, that become vital to the analysis of whether the terrorists are indeed prepared to kill *all* of their hostages indiscriminately or whether they are baiting the authorities.

Ample evidence exists to support this claim. In Budyonnovsk, for instance, Basayev executed eleven hostages, all of them either military pilots or other men in uniform that had already been injured during the initial takeover. In light of Basayev's vow to kill every Russian pilot he ever encountered, these killings did not constitute the strategic "execution of hostages" to pressurize the government, but rather "just punishment" of people Basayev perceived as guilty for the bombing of his house in which eleven members of his family were killed. No matter how much we may disagree with this logic, Basayev's willingness to kill these specific hostages in this incident did not necessarily translate into the resolve also to kill civilians. On the contrary, Basayev stated: "We do not intend to kill any hostages. We shot employees of the [Russian] government ... [because] snipers killed or wounded our comrades. There is absolutely no intent to kill [the hostages]. We will not shoot women and children—we're not maniacs."[23] Similarly, the three people killed by the terrorists in Nord-Ost were all perceived as "FSB stooges" and "spies" who came from the outside in order to disrupt the terrorists' control over the crowd. Again, this did not necessarily translate into the readiness to execute civilian hostages in cold blood, and indeed, the terrorists did not resort to killing hostages even when they knew the rescue operation was in progress. In Beslan the terrorists executed Ruslan Betrozov, after he translated the terrorist speech for everyone in the gym into Ossetian, thereby breaking the ground rules forbidding anyone from speaking other languages than Russian. Most of the twenty-one men killed throughout the incident died in the accidental blast of one of the female suicide bombers, or were injured and later finished off. Again, the killing of a male already injured does not necessarily translate into the strategic or psychological readiness to execute women and children in cold blood. True, on the first day the terrorists also killed several of the men who were tasked with barricading the windows, but it is likely that the hostage takers killed them in order to neutralize a potential tactical threat. In sum, in the cases involving RAS, hostages were, of course, put in harm's way, and some were killed for particular reasons, but none was killed indiscriminately.

There are only a few other cases in history where terrorists demonstrated a willingness to execute hostages in order to create pressure on the government to concede to their demands. Due to the historical rarity of such occurrences and their importance to incident assessment, all of these cases can briefly be recounted here. The first such incident was the 1970 hijacking of British DC-10 airliner from Dubai to Tunisia by the Palestinian Rejectionist Front, in which a drunken German passenger was selected for execution after he deliberately insulted the hijackers by mockingly making homosexual advances toward them.[24] Significantly, despite this execution, the negotiations continued and the crisis was eventually resolved without further bloodshed. Next was the 1975 hijacking of a passenger train in the Netherlands by the South Maluccan Independence Movement, on the second day of which the terrorists selected one of the passengers, Gerard Wanders, for execution in order to prove their seriousness. Wanders was allowed to pass a farewell message to his family. Fascinatingly, after hearing his highly personal and emotional confession, the terrorists were not able to kill Wanders, and selected a substitute whom they killed on the spot. In this case, as well, the unfortunate passenger was described by other hostages as a "troublemaker," whom "nobody missed when he was gone."[25] Despite the killing, the crisis again ended in a negotiated settlement. Another incident in which the executed hostage directly contributed to his own death was the famous Prince's Gate incident of 1980, in which six gunmen from the separatist Khuzestan region in Iran took over the Iranian embassy in London. During this incident embassy employee Abass Levasani repeatedly mocked the terrorists by vociferously praising their archenemy, Ayatollah Khomeini. When he was threatened, Levasani exposed his chest and challenged the gunmen to kill him, stating that he wanted to become a martyr. On the sixth day of the crisis the terrorists accommodated him and threw his body into the street.[26] Similarly, Abu Abbas, the lead hijacker of the *Achille Lauro* cruise ship in 1985, justified the killing of Leon Klinghoffer, the sixty-nine-year-old wheelchair-bound man, by saying that "[Klinghoffer] created troubles. He was handicapped but he was inciting and provoking the other passengers. So the decision was made to kill him."[27] During the same year, U.S. Navy diver Robert Dean Stethem was beaten and executed by the Hizballah hijackers of TWA Flight 847, who wanted to ensure that their demands would be taken seriously.[28] Some accounts suggested that Stethem was selected for execution because of a mistranslation of his occupation into German, which allegedly might have driven the terrorists to believe that he was somehow associated with the Marines in Beirut.[29] Further, the investigators also believe that Stethem may have been selected for execution due to his strong physical build, which may have caused him to be perceived by the terrorists as a threat.[30]

Slightly different are the aforementioned cases of Egypt Air 648, Pan Am 73, or the Air France 8969, in which it seemed to have been solely the victims' nationality that sealed their fate. This was also the case of the 1984 hijacking of Kuwaiti Airlines Flight 221 to Teheran, which began with the terrorists demanding all Americans and Kuwaitis on board to identify themselves, and after locating four Americans, they were brought into the first-class cabin and beaten. U.S. Agency for International Development (USAID) employee Charles Hegna was the first to be executed, followed by his boss, William Stanford, who was killed after he apparently tripped when walking back to his seat after making a plea over a megaphone.[31]

The two remaining Americans were beaten and tortured, but survived. Interestingly, while engaging in these extreme actions, the terrorists concurrently demonstrated a willingness to release women and children, and instead of resorting to additional killings, they staged them by pretending to have shot two Kuwaitis—pouring ketchup on their bodies before inviting journalists to visit the plane and take photos.[32] This action again underlines the fact that terrorists' willingness to execute certain hostages does not necessarily translate into a willingness to kill *all* captives indiscriminately.

In virtually every instance in which terrorists engaged in executions of their captives during a barricade hostage crisis, there was a clearly identifiable motive behind the terrorists' selection of their victims. The traditional incident assessment tools described earlier are based on the premise that the hostages have no value to the hostage taker except for the audience the incident will create.[33] There is also the related assumption that once a hostage taker has killed, he will inevitably do so again. While this may be true for criminal incidents commonly encountered by police crisis negotiation teams, an exhaustive survey of historical cases has demonstrated that, in the context of terrorism, these assumptions clearly do not hold.

The main reason for why that is the case lies in the fact that a terrorist hostage taking is a highly expressive act, in which hostages become more than instruments for attracting attention or an insurance policy against a violent resolution. They are sometimes pawns in a game of cat-and-mouse with a government, or bait in a planned "homicide-by-cop," where the authorities are provoked into a deadly assault for which the government will be at least partly blamed. Hostages are also often perceived as representatives of their respective nationalities, religions, or ethnicities; stripping them of their neutral status in the eyes of the hostage takers and instead making them targets upon which the terrorists project their grievances and channel their anger and frustration. In other cases, highly aggressive conduct or threatening behavior of some hostages toward their captors is also likely to make them targets. Because of this disparate status among hostages in terrorist incidents, the high level of threat to some groups of captives does not necessarily translate into the same amount of risk to the others. And while we again must emphasize that, from a moral and legal perspective, the circumstances under which the terrorists murdered their innocent victims make no difference, in order to accurately assess the negotiability of an incident in which a hostage has been killed, the decision makers must consider the "discriminatory" criteria used by the terrorists to select their victims and the specific circumstances under which they are killed. From this diagnostic perspective, the knowledge of these exact circumstances has the potential not only to help differentiate the level of threat posed to the safety of individual hostages inside, but also to determine the terrorists' preparedness to execute hostages on a truly *indiscriminate* basis or in larger numbers. The responders need to assess whether there is any particular logic to explain why the hostages that have already been killed might have been chosen. If there is some rational explanation (however offensive or unjustified), experience suggests that this should not constitute an insurmountable barrier to negotiation. Further, in the event that a selection pattern other than aggressive behavior is identified, negotiation strategy can be adjusted accordingly in order to prioritize the negotiated release of hostages either focusing on those at the highest risk of being executed or on those most likely to be released. If successful, this move could potentially reduce the chances of further executions or, alternatively, create the chance to save some lives. Judging by the instruction to execute strong males in the beginning of a barricade incident prescribed in *jihadi* Internet manuals on hostage taking, negotiators may want to find an effective argument to persuade hostage takers to release all the able-bodied *men* first, in order to remove the potential threat—without having to murder them, as opposed to following the traditional priority for evacuation of women and children first. This could serve a few purposes which might be agreeable to some hostage takers; they will be at less internal, tactical risk, while they will maintain the most effective deterrent to an assault (the children and women), while, at the same time saving some hostages and, possibly, making the situation inside less tense with the internal physical threat removed.

Overall, there is no doubt that the killing of hostages in barricade incidents substantially complicates subsequent negotiation efforts. On the other hand, ample evidence exists suggesting that death of hostages throughout *terrorist* hostage-taking incidents does not automatically create an insurmountable barrier to negotiated agreement. How should negotiators proceed in cases where executions have taken place? In essence, the primary task should be to discourage executions as something that will not speed up the authorities' compliance, but will only make it less likely. Before any executions occur, negotiators should talk through the logical steps with the hostage takers, explaining that if we do not give in to a particular demand under the *threat* of execution, then how could we later give in to the same demand *after* a hostage (or hostages) has been "murdered." Clearing up the progression of coercion and decision making upfront can, in some cases, make for less uncertainty later. If hostages are indeed executed, negotiators should inquire about the feelings on the other side, asking about the perception of accomplishment ("How do you feel now?"; "Do you feel like you have accomplished anything?"). One of the things decision-makers should avoid is panic and knee-jerk reactions.[34] Negotiators should explain that the killed hostages would have died in vain if the authorities concede to the terrorist demands under such circumstances, which makes the immediate fulfillment of the concession only more difficult. At the same time negotiators should avoid rewarding "bad behavior" by heeding the pressure created by the executions and immediately fulfilling the demand. Rather, whenever possible, the negotiators must offer an alternative *process* that will show more promise for the hostage taker than a series of coercive executions that only dig a deeper hole. It is critical to try to do this early on. All too often, negotiators find themselves already well into a process that they can no longer influence.

As we have seen throughout this book, executions of hostages at deadlines are extremely rare. One of the reasons for this is the fact that deadlines for fulfillment of specific demands are typically arbitrary, with little intrinsic meaning attached.[35] As a result, these deadlines can be broken if the authorities show a sign of at least some movement on the issue, while simultaneously providing a plausible explanation for why the demand cannot be met in the time given. As we have seen in the case studies presented, executions at deadlines took place when the terrorists reached the conclusion that the authorities were not negotiating in good faith, not negotiating at all, or even insulting the hostage takers. In most cases, this perception was accurate. The key lesson here is that in cases where the authorities communicate in good faith (whether or not they actually concede to demands), there is less danger to the lives of hostages.

## SUICIDAL POSTURE

Another highly volatile scenario for negotiators is the management of hostage crises involving subjects who assume a suicidal posture. This becomes even more dangerous in cases involving the "new terrorists," who besides being suicidal, simultaneously pose a high level of threat to the hostages, and whose objectives are more far-reaching than simply committing "suicide-by-cop." In the minds of most people, the hostage taker's desire to survive serves as a prerequisite without which negotiations are allegedly not possible. This argument is based on Maslow's hierarchy of needs, and assumes that since the desire to live is stronger than any other need, in its absence there is nothing for the negotiators to offer.[36] Implicitly, hostage crises involving perpetrators who proclaim that "[they] are more keen on dying than [we] are on living" (as Barayev did in Nord-Ost), are likely to be popularly preceived as "nonnegotiable" from the outset.

Here lies another weakness of the "old school" manuals with regard to their applicability to terrorist incidents or more specifically, with regard to the mechanical application of this criterion for purposes of incident analysis. It must be emphasized that even in cases where the hostage takers assume a highly suicidal posture, it is essential to make the distinction between the *willingness* to die and the unwavering *intention* to die. Most terrorists are willing to die for their cause; but only a few see their death as the preferred outcome in a particular incident. According to Corsi's statistical analysis of incidents recorded in the ITERATE dataset, terrorists engaging in barricade hostage crises were suicidal in only 1 percent of the cases, while in 94 percent of incidents they were willing to give up their lives, but preferred not to.[37] This implies that even when terrorists repeatedly express their determination to die during a standoff, this claim alone should not be assumed an insurmountable barrier to negotiations. And even though the likelihood of encountering suicidal hostage takers is much higher in the context of the "new terrorism" than in Corsi's sample, declarations of readiness to "be martyred" still should be treated as a rational course of action aimed at improving the terrorists' negotiating position by denying the authorities threat level. The proclamation of the desire to die weakens the deterrent value of any threats by the government to resolve the situation forcefully.[38] Clearly, in the context of "new terrorism," the validity of viewing the desire to live as a universal baseline condition for negotiability of an incident requires a significant reevaluation.

As previously argued by Slatkin, even though the terrorists may have a desire to become martyrs, "it should not be assumed that they are ready or willing to die on *that day* [emphasis in original]."[39] In addition, while we have emphasized the necessity of knowledge of the perpetrator's operational trajectory as a precondition of negotiation strategy selection, we must also be careful to assess the given situation based on the tactic used in the individual attack, and not necessarily project other tactics favored by the group onto the barricade scenario. In other words, just as a criminal hostage taker's lack of a history of violence does not automatically preclude the possibility of him killing the hostages, the fact that a given terrorist group has previously embarked on a bloody suicide bombing campaign does not necessarily mean that a barricade hostage scenario perpetrated by this group will inevitably result in the killing of all hostages in a suicidal act. Moreover, as we have seen on the example of failed Moscow suicide bomber Zarema Muzhakoyeva as well as on a number of other examples from Turkey or Palestine, even bombers sent on a suicide bombing mission can sometimes experience a change of heart. If even operatives on missions that ostensibly guarantee certain death can change their minds, then why assume that hostage takers engaging in an operation that has an open-ended outcome cannot be similarly influenced? And even if the desire to become martyrs may be unshakable, why assume that there is nothing to be gained by negotiating the conditions under which that happens and whose lives are taken along with the "martyrs'"?

In most cases, the outcome of dying a martyr's death represents the terrorists' fallback, or "plan 'B'." This means that as long as negotiators can maintain the perception that there is a chance of achieving something more attractive than this baseline position, negotiations are possible. In the era of "new terrorism," the terrorists' alternatives have been strengthened considerably by the proliferation of the culture of martyrdom, which makes death much less unappealing. At the same time, if martyrdom were more attractive than the possibility of a negotiated settlement, the hostage takers would likely embark on a suicide bombing mission rather than hostage taking, and they would demonstrate less concern for their own safety.

As we have seen throughout the case studies presented in this book, even the "new terrorists" prioritize a negotiated agreement over martyrdom. In such situations, the hostage takers are unlikely to blow themselves up as long as an alternative of another outcome exists, or as long as they believe governments may actually fulfill their demands. Even if that is not the case, negotiators should still ask themselves what they can do to maximize influence—even hostage takers who prefer to die have additional interests that can be explored, and about which something might reasonably be done. For instance, the handing over of the terrorists' bodies to their families, or even offers of burial in accordance with the respective religious and cultural traditions are likely to be negotiable issues. And even if the hostage takers decide to die *"on that day,"* an opportunity may still exist to trade for an "honorable" final shootout among combatants on both sides as suggested by the terrorists in Nord-Ost, which may be more politically attractive to the perpetrators than a vision of an indiscriminate slaughter of children.

## USE OF INTERMEDIARIES

Besides indicators of progress and volatility, crisis negotiators also rely heavily on experiences from past incidents in the form of "do's" and "don'ts."[40] Some of the "don'ts" have already been discussed in the section commenting on the a priori dismissal of some demands made by hostage takers as "nonnegotiables." Along similar lines, another practice that traditionally falls into the category of "don'ts" is the idea of using third-party intermediaries as negotiators, under the rationale that intermediaries lack specialized training, are out of the negotiation team's direct control, and may have a past relationship with the subject that can be destabilizing.[41] However, in situations involving the "new terrorists," where police negotiators are unlikely to be viewed as trustworthy counterparties (due to their affiliation), it may very well be the case that third-party intermediaries are sometimes preferable. Further, as we have seen throughout this book, with the exception of cases involving ulterior motive such as the aforementioned Air France or Pan Am hijackings, the "new terrorists" tend to demand particular figures to serve as negotiators. In most cases, they can be expected to ask for someone whose general views on their grievance they are familiar with, and for people that have the authority to make decisions. Very rarely have terrorists accepted an offer to provide an intermediary such as a well-known religious authority, presumably out of fear of being manipulated or simply because the idea came from the authorities. Nevertheless, the incidents cited in this book support the view that it is more important to consider the "who, why, when, and how" an intermediary might be used, as opposed to whether or not they should be used at all.[42]

It is difficult for the police even to consider allowing intermediaries in most crisis negotiations for two reasons, in particular. Firstly, the police see it as their job to handle or resolve such situations (which it is), but they therefore also tend to think that they—and only they—are the best people for the job (which is not always the case). Secondly, of course, there are legal liability issues involved with putting civilians at risk (or allowing them to put themselves at risk) in such a dangerous situation. In some cases, however, these must be seen as obstacles to be overcome, rather than accepted as reasons for not allowing intermediaries to participate. One of the main reasons is that the dynamic between terrorists and the authorities is almost always one of mutual animosity in which neither side can back down, or make concessions to the other. Introducing a third party can change that confrontational dynamic into one in which a credible third party may make suggestions that both sides might consider without having to cede credit for it to an enemy.

The involvement of well-known figures such as journalists, politicians, celebrities, academics, or private negotiation professionals, whose perspective on the issue at hand is seen as neutral or sympathetic by the hostage takers, is often a good idea, when managed skillfully. After all, in negotiation, one's currency is influence. Logic would suggest that in situations where the authorities' main source of influence over the hostage takers (the ability to coerce them with threats) is minimized through preparation, tactical countermeasures, independent channels of communication, and the ability to work in shifts, a useful next step would be securing new sources of influence—one of which is an intermediary that has a different relationship to the hostage takers and a higher level of credibility with them. Though the practice is generally discouraged, for this category of intermediaries, it is sometimes possible to hold face-to-face negotiations,[43] provided that this opportunity is used to obtain some concession from the terrorists such as the release of some hostages, or at least for a public guarantee of the intermediary's safety. While this may seem like a small concession, getting the hostage takers into the habit of making promises not to hurt people is a useful starting point for establishing a better process than the mutual coercion that is likely to result in violence if left to fate. Alternatively, a condition could be attached allowing the terrorists to select only one person to act as mediator throughout the entire crisis, in order to allow for the development of rapport between this individual and the hostage takers, to establish credibility and consistency in process, and to make keeping track of events, demands, and changes in mood more feasible.

Another guideline in the "don'ts" category is the rule that "the boss does not negotiate," under the logic that such an action would disrupt one of the key "tricks" in the crisis negotiation toolbox—the deferment of authority or a version of the "good cop, bad cop" routine. One of the keys to gaining strategic advantage in a hostage crisis is achieving the perceived position of an intermediary between the authorities and the hostage takers, which allows the negotiator to stall for time by pointing to the difficulty of locating a key decision maker, or some other objective obstacle to meeting the terrorists' deadline. Further, the negotiators' lack of decision-making authority also allows them, in theory, to disassociate themselves from any official refusal to comply, while empathetically validating the reasonable component of the demand and promising to keep trying to convince the authorities in favor of its fulfillment. This tactic is useful in stalling for time, decreasing the hostage takers' expectations, and creating a bond between the negotiator and the suspects when the perpetrators are naïve and not well prepared. But, unfortunately for us, the "new terrorists" have studied this game, they have read the manuals, and they are no longer likely to fall for these tricks.

The "new terrorists'" knowledge of the crisis negotiation manual will likely trigger future attempts to counter the deferment of authority tactic by demanding a top decision maker personally to enter the negotiations. Such a demand should be deflected, if possible, but if the likelihood of hostages being executed in order to force compliance is high, the engagement of a decision maker in some form may actually be beneficial,[44] particularly the appointment of a senior representative of the decision maker to conduct negotiations. Firstly, the involvement of political decision makers alone would provide terrorists with some level of perceived success, thereby perhaps discouraging radical steps that would waste this accomplishment. In addition, having one of the enemy's leaders actively listen to their grievances and validate some of their frustrations would contradict many of the terrorists' demonized perceptions, perhaps casting doubts upon the view that violent escalation of the struggle—and bringing innocents into it—are the only possible ways to achieve the desired outcome.

Further, negotiators with decision-making authority have the potential to help the terrorists make their demands more reasonable, by pointing out the need to be able to survive politically in order to insure their implementation. If, in the aftermath of a negotiated agreement, the decision maker were to lose his or her position, it would likely hinder or negate the realization of the negotiated agreement by his or her successor. This line of reasoning is likely to be persuasive with an intelligent hostage taker, and just having this conversation has the potential to de-escalate the situation. Take, for instance, the Beslan crisis, in which the terrorists' two principal demands were the unconditional pullout of Russian troops from Chechnya and President Putin's resignation from office. Had one of Putin's senior aides personally made a phone call to the terrorists, listened to their grievances, and used the argument that any agreement to end the war in Chechnya would require Putin to stay in power in order to prevent his decision from being overturned immediately, this would likely have led to some progress such as the release of dozens of hostages, the dropping of the demand for Putin's resignation, and the hostage takers' surprised realization that the Kremlin can be engaged in a rational dialogue. This progress, while likely not having brought the incident to an end, certainly would have had a chance to move it toward a better outcome than the one that eventually came to be. What is painful to realize is that such progress was achievable simply by listening and without granting the terrorists a single *substantive* concession. Certainly, there was a range of options that could have been discussed about a possible statement on the humanitarian situation in Chechnya, or a pledge to consider prosecuting any clear-cut cases of war crimes associated with the well-known "mop-up" operations in Chechnya.

The final important issue associated with the terrorists' demands for specific intermediaries has to do with the demand to bring to the scene specific individuals that are likely to be killed. As in the case of other "don'ts," in this instance as well there is little to be gained by an a priori categorical denial of such a demand. Instead, negotiators should inquire about the terrorists' motivations for the involvement of the given individuals and should voice concerns about their safety. If the hostage takers validate this concern by explaining why they believe that specific person should die, the discussion should focus back on grievances and validation of what is not unreasonable about these grievances. It might then be possible to negotiate the exact terms and limits of their appearance; perhaps allowing direct communication without sending the requested person off to be killed, or arranging that the requested person meet instead with a member of the terror group not on-site, under safer conditions (e.g., supervision of the authorities).

## SHIFTING CENTRE OF GRAVITY

One of the issues that have been highlighted in Chapter 1 has been the dramatic influence of the proliferation of modern communication technologies on the dynamics of future barricade hostage crises. Firstly, the terrorists' immediate ability to consult with their leadership via mobile phone will deprive the negotiators of much of the influence they typically strive to gain by disrupting the hostage takers' chain of authority, and thus forcing the perpetrators to make their own decisions in isolation from their leadership. And while terrorist hostage takers of the past had often embarked on operations with minimal instructions from their leaders, thus frequently finding themselves in a position of having to make decisions on their own, today's technological reality that gives the terrorists immediate access to their superiors has radically altered the situation. Since the leaders, unlike the hostage takers, will not be confined to the location under a constant threat of immediate forceful resolution, the processes that form the baseline foundation of the contemporary practice of crisis negotiation will not take place, making the task of lowering the terrorists' expectations much more difficult.

One result of these developments is the shift of the centre of gravity in negotiations from the hostage takers located on scene of the hostage crisis to decision makers situated in a separate location. This phenomenon, reminiscent of the dynamics present in the kidnapping scenario, was observed for the first time in Nord-Ost, during the final stages of which the terrorists declared: "We have freed everyone we could free. What happens now depends on Russia's leadership, on what agreement it can reach with our senior representatives." As is apparent from this statement, the terrorists applied the same deferment of authority tactic prescribed in the crisis negotiation manuals to create an advantageous negotiating position, or, at least, to minimize risk. It follows that besides the need to influence the behavior of the hostage takers inside who have direct impact on the safety of the hostages, negotiators in future barricade incidents will need to be aware of the fact that the key to successfully negotiating an end to the crisis may be to influence the leaders who are not located at the scene. This will require a significant change of mind-set as well as a change in strategy.

In the first instance, negotiation teams will need to reevaluate their dependency on containment as a precondition to success in negotiation efforts. The contemporary paradigm holds that in order to be effective in negotiations, the authorities must speak from a position of strength, and containment of the hostage takers as well as the threat of a violent resolution is a crucial part of the equation.[45] However, in the "new terrorist" environment this dynamic is likely to be countered by the measures outlined earlier, negating many of the tactics that make the success rate of barricade hostage negotiations so impressive. But while this decreasing effectiveness of available tools is likely to complicate future negotiation efforts, the need to adjust to this new reality may actually present an opportunity in disguise. The traditional crisis negotiation practice relies too heavily on negotiation "tricks" and on circumventing and ignoring the real issues by the deflection of focus toward instrumental demands, or by introducing issues pertaining to primary needs.[46] This is one of the reasons why the terrorists' knowledge of the manual complicates the lives of crisis negotiators so severely—exposing "tricks" usually makes them ineffective. If we learn to place more emphasis on negotiation fundamentals as opposed to manipulation of the subject, the terrorists' knowledge of our approach is likely to support (as opposed to hinder) the negotiators' efforts. In other words, if the terrorists learn that crisis negotiation is more about genuine intention to deal with the real issues as opposed to deception and tricks, this knowledge is likely to reduce the level of volatility and enhance negotiators' credibility, thereby decreasing tensions and facilitating conduct of negotiations in future incidents[47]—a development we would likely prefer to the current trend of rising stakes, increased lethality, higher numbers of hostages and hostage takers, and lesser willingness to engage in dialogue.

In addition, the reality of the "new terrorism" underlines the ever-decreasing effectiveness of deception to outsmart hostage takers in order to bring an end to barricade hostage crises. Despite the existence of legal precedents in many countries determining that promises made to hostage takers during hostage negotiations are not legally binding contracts,[48] and despite statistical analyses suggesting that bluffing, even if detected, does not necessarily reduce the likelihood of a negotiated solution,[49] deceiving the hostage takers is a short-sighted approach that is likely to have negative consequences for future incidents. Firstly, the wide media coverage barricade situations receive can make bluffing costly in the long run, as public familiarity with deceptive police tactics will make establishing credibility in future hostage negotiations much more challenging. Secondly, the proliferation of advanced communication technologies makes the terrorists' independent verification of official versions of events much easier, thus increasing the likelihood that any deceptive tactics will be detected, even during the incident. And finally, lying to the hostage takers will only reinforce the terrorists' perception of the evil and untrustworthy nature of their adversary, leading not only to the escalation of tactics but also increased recruitment opportunities through propaganda. As we have seen in Nord-Ost and Beslan in particular, one of the most important moments of escalation came with media censorship and apparently deliberate release of inaccurate information about the number of hostages and the denial of the existence of terrorist demands. It follows that given the "new terrorists'" increased ability to detect deception and effectively disseminate their own version of events, ensuring the accuracy of official statements and media reporting will be essential to the credibility of the government—a critical component of any successful negotiation efforts.

## ROLE OF ACTIVE LISTENING

One of the negotiator's main tasks is to deal with the question of demands. As we have seen throughout the case studies analyzed in this book, hostage crises involving the "new terrorists" are likely to present us with demands that will be very difficult to fulfill, such as the complete cessation of military hostilities in a war, termination of material or diplomatic support of particular governments, or the resignation of a country's leader. But before we jump to the assumption that incidents featuring such demands will be impossible to negotiate, we must remind ourselves that all such demands have both *instrumental* and *expressive* values.[50] In other words, each substantive demand also constitutes an expression of a certain type of emotion or a psychological need. It is especially the expressive value of the demand that the negotiator should concentrate on and seek to understand, as this provides insight into the captor's underlying interests. The negotiator then should engage the hostage takers in dialogue whenever possible, and work with them to find alternative ways to satisfy the legitimate interests that can be identified, sometimes by acknowledging the validity of the terrorists' grievances. And, in some cases, such interests can be satisfied, at least to some degree, simply by listening empathetically.

In order to explore this expressive component, the negotiators need to keep asking good questions in an attempt to understand as much as possible. Even when the answers to the questions may be obvious, it is still useful to ask in order to provide the terrorists with an opportunity clearly to state their grievances and vent their anger. This in turn gives the negotiator a chance to engage the other side on a more personal level, by asking about his or her *personal* experience with the alleged injustices and abuse. This then provides an opportunity for the negotiator to express empathy. In ideological hostage situations, it is always very difficult to move the discussion away from ideological language toward a more personal level, and this approach provides one of the possible ways for achieving this outcome. While there is some risk in triggering volatile emotions by engaging in dialogue about the hostage takers' personal experiences (especially with violent conflict), forming personal rapport between the negotiators on both sides is one of the critical principles upon which the crisis negotiation practice is based.

Another reason why asking questions is important, is the fact that answers provide insight into the hostage takers' underlying interests behind their core demands. If these interests are understood, new options that would address the terrorist's root motivations and concerns, but would stop short of unwise concessions, can be introduced. Through active listening and the generation of multiple possibilities by introduction of new options, the hostage takers' may be willing to alter their course of action. A big part of the negotiator's effort will be to use active listening skills to uncover and validate whatever is reasonable about the demands and/or grievances, in order to influence the hostage takers to make their demands more reasonable.

Another area where active listening will be essential is the justification used by the terrorists to validate their actions. And while the initial explanation is likely to be cloaked in ideological or religious rhetoric, the negotiator will again have to use active listening skills to penetrate this ideological veil. For instance, a common justification used by Islamist terrorists is the Koranic reference to self-defense and equity of means along the lines of: "Allah orders us to fight the unbelievers as they fight us."[51] This "Newton's Law" based on unconditional reciprocity will be used to rebuff any moral appeal to release hostages, based on the argument that since Muslim women and children are also being killed in the conflict, the targeting of women and children in the hostage operation is also justified. Instead of pushing back and arguing about the difference between "collateral damage" and deliberate targeting of civilians, negotiators should encourage the hostage takers to speak about the grievances and suffering of the people on whose behalf they see themselves as fighting. By active listening, expression of empathy and validation of the moral unacceptability of civilian deaths, the negotiator has a greater chance of influencing the hostage takers eventually to accept the logic for why women and children should be released in future deals.

Another set of tools that will be particularly useful are persuasive criteria, especially ones that are seen as objectively independent of the will of either side. If negotiators on both sides can agree on the validity of a certain criterion beforehand, its application to a particular issue becomes more effective. For instance, a typical mechanism for justifying the targeting of civilians is Osama bin Laden's 2002 "Letter to the American People," in which bin Laden argues that all Americans who pay taxes effectively fund attacks against Muslims, and are thus legitimate targets.[52] Another variation is the terrorists' likely argument that the people held hostage are responsible for electing their own government and are thus also accountable for its actions. Instead of resisting this logic, negotiators should learn to use it to their advantage by holding the hostage takers accountable to their own logic. For example, after listening closely and asking clarifying questions about the specifics of the hostage takers' judgment, the issue of tax payment or voting rights should be raised. Without necessarily validating the logic, negotiators should ask about its applicability to the hostages that are under the legal voting age. What is the responsibility of a fourteen-year old that cannot legally vote and does not pay taxes for the actions of his government? Doesn't a strong argument exist for the release of hostages that do not fit the terrorists' own criteria of guilt? The more negotiators listen, the more likely they are to learn about interests, alternatives, and persuasive criteria. The more negotiators know about them, the more chance we have of being persuasive when it counts.

# EPILOGUE

The game is changing. The "new terrorists" are intelligent, well prepared, tactically savvy, heavily armed, willing to die, and they have read the manuals. And, if you think like a cop, they will know your next move. When confronted with hostage barricade scenarios at the hands of the "new terrorists," many of the fundamental principles of crisis negotiation still apply, but many of the old rules—and the obsolete assumptions on which they are based—no longer hold. The best way to approach a fluid, challenging crisis situation involving a capable adversary is not by the rigid application of the traditional checklist. Instead, we offer a few additional guidelines:

- Always keep in mind that negotiation is not just about reaching "deals" and making quid pro quo exchanges; it is also about *exercising influence over the thinking, behavior, and decision making* of others. Any information gained in conversation—and the very act of *having* the conversation itself—may present such opportunities at any time.

- Be (and remain) self-diagnostic: understand your own biases and constantly question your assumptions about the hostage takers, their motives, and their willingness to negotiate (keeping in mind that there is a big difference between self-*diagnosis* and self-*doubt*). Do not cling to conclusions out of frustration or disgust, or you will miss important clues and opportunities.

- Do not negotiate with the "terrorist," negotiate with the *rational human being who, for some set of reasons, has chosen—or felt forced into—an extreme, violent course of action.*

- Use an active listening approach to the negotiations, not just a bargaining approach; focus at least as much on asking good questions, learning, and understanding grievances and motives as on making quid pro quo substantive deals.

- Ask for as many details as possible about the reasons/justification the perpetrators use to explain their actions. The answers will provide criteria that may be useful in other ways later.

- Look for empathetic ways to acknowledge or validate legitimate grievances behind the terrorists' actions while differing with the actions themselves. This will make it harder for them to label you as unreasonable, it will create chances to de-escalate the situation emotionally, and it may help you to create a wedge between their grievances and their actions, which in turn may help them to question the connection.

- Brainstorm with them. Rather than simply trying to stall with the "good cop, bad cop routine," genuinely look for ways to address the more legitimate grievances in ways that do not require unwise, unreasonable, or impossible concessions.
- Make sure someone is looking at the bigger picture, beyond this incident.

In the bigger picture, we must be much more aware that, with our responses to (and within) each incident, we are contributing to longer-term trends and we are teaching the terrorists lessons that will be applied to their future operations. What adaptations are we incentivizing, and what lessons are we teaching them? With each incident, are we contributing to an increase in future lethality, higher numbers of hostages and hostage takers, and less willingness to negotiate? Or are we contributing to more moderation, more communication, and problem solving? At the end of the day, we do not want to be engaged in a contest of wills with people who have a lot less to lose than we do, if we can help to change the game.

For this shift to take place, we must remember that even the most "extreme" terrorists *are not irrational*. We have dealt with members of some of the world's best-known "terrorist" groups—from al Qaida and the Taliban, to HAMAS and Islamic *Jihad*, to the Tamil Tigers and the Provisional IRA. Not once have we met a terrorist we would consider irrational. Without exception, they have been intelligent, highly rational, and often quite articulate. They have simply been willing to engage in actions that most of us find abhorrent—for reasons that they find acceptable, based on the conditions they and their constituents face.

While many of us find this notion unappealing and hard to accept, it is actually good news. If the terrorists truly were irrational, we would have little or no chance of influencing them. But because they are, generally, quite rational, there is a chance that we may influence them . . . and change the way they are trying to influence us. When is it a good time to negotiate with terrorists? The answer is: Always . . . and never.

- *Always* negotiate with terrorists—as long as you know negotiation is about influence (how is not negotiating with them going to help?)
- *Never* negotiate with "terrorists"—negotiate with the *human beings* who, for some reason, have chosen to resort to the tactic of terrorism.

# NOTES

## INTRODUCTION

1. Though we would not necessarily rule it out, prima facie, either.

2. Other famous hostage crises in which terrorists targeted schools include the 1974 Democratic Front for the Liberation of Palestine attack in Ma'alot, Israel, and the 1977 takeover of a school in Bovensmilde, in the Netherlands.

3. Abdul Hameed Bakier, "Lessons from al-Qaeda's Attack on the Khobar Compound," *Terrorism Monitor*, Vol. 4, no. 16 (August 10, 2006), Available at: http://jamestown.org/terrorism/news/article.php?articleid=2370100 (accessed on September 30, 2006).

4. Some of the best pioneering work in CT negotiations has been undertaken by the FBI Critical Incident Negotiation Team, Scotland Yard's Crisis and Hostage Negotiation Unit, New York City Police Department Hostage Negotiation Team, and New South Wales Police Negotiation Unit, among others.

5. Adam Dolnik, "Contrasting Dynamics of Crisis Negotiations: Barricade versus Kidnapping Incidents," *International Negotiation* Vol. 8, no. 3 (2003).

6. Michael McMains and Wayman Mullins, *Crisis Negotiations: Managing Critical Incidents and Hostage Situations in Law Enforcement and Corrections* (Dayton, OH: Anderson Publishing, 2nd ed., 2001), p. 33.

## CHAPTER 1

1. The July 1968, PFLP hijacking of El Al Boeing 707, from Rome to Algeria, which has been credited with being the groundbreaking event that marked the commencement of the age of international terrorism, or 9–11.

2. Adam Dolnik, "Contrasting Dynamics of Crisis Negotiations: Barricade versus Kidnapping Incidents," *International Negotiation*, Vol. 8, no. 3 (2003) p. 60.

3. W. Enders, T. Sandler, and J. Cauley, "U.N. Conventions Technology and Retaliation in the Fight against Terrorism: An Econometric Evaluation," *Terrorism and Political Violence*, Vol. 2, no. 2 (1990) pp. 83–105.

4. Unlike in the past when the official guidelines insisted that hostages should keep calm, comply with the terrorists instructions, and wait for their freedom to be negotiated for, prospective hostages on flights in the post-9-11 world are likely to perceive their chances of survival as slim, and are thus more likely to attempt to overpower the hijackers than in the past. The terrorists' knowledge of this likely outcome has only reinforced the declining attractiveness of skyjackings as a terrorist tool.

5. Brian Michael Jenkins, "Will Terrorists Go Nuclear?" *RAND* Paper P-5541 (1975), 4.

6. Bruce Hoffman, *Inside Terrorism* (New York: Orion Publishing Co., 1998) p. 201.

7. Bruce Hoffman, " 'Holy Terror': The Implications of Terrorism Motivated by a Religious Imperative," *RAND* (1993), 3.

8. Ibid.

9. Ibid.

10. Andrew Tan and Kumar Ramakrishna, *The New Terrorism* (Singapore: Eastern University Press, 2002) p. 7.

11. Ibid.

12. Bruce Hoffman, "The Logic of Suicide Terrorism," *Atlantic Monthly*, Vol. 291, no. 5 (June 2003).

13. It must be noted here that CT negotiation capabilities developed by these world leaders in the field are rapidly proliferating around the world through international cooperation and collaborative training. It is our hope that this book can contribute to this important effort.

14. Dwayne Fuselier and Gary Noesner, "Confronting the Terrorist Hostage Taker," Internet. Available at http://www.emergency.com/host-tkr.htm (accessed on January 29, 2002). Although the authors of this article are the first ones to acknowledge that this particular dynamic has changed, the original paper still remains disproportionately influential among the larger negotiation community.

15. Michael McMains and Wayman Mullins, *Crisis Negotiations: Managing Critical Incidents and Hostage Situations in Law Enforcement and Corrections*, 2nd ed. (Dayton, OH: Anderson Publishing, 2001) p. 231.

16. Thomas Strentz, *Psychological Aspects of Crisis Negotiation* (New York: CRC Press, 2006) p. 8.

17. Ibid., p. 70.

18. Martha Crenshaw, "The Causes of Terrorism," *Comparative Politics*, Vol. 13 (1981) pp. 379–399.

19. Clinton Van Zandt cited in Jayne Docherty, *Learning Lessons from Waco* (Syracuse: Syracuse University Press, 2001) p. 460.

20. Docherty, *Learning Lessons from Waco*, p. 89.

21. Fuselier and Noesner, "Confronting the Terrorist Hostage Taker."

22. James Poland and Michael McCrystle, *Practical, Tactical and Legal Perspectives of Terrorism and Hostage Taking* (Lewiston, NY: Edwin Mellen Press, 2000) p. 26.

23. Edward F. Mickolus, *Transnational Terrorism: A Chronology of Events, 1968–1979* (Westport, CT: Greenwood Press, 1980) p. 367.

24. Fuselier and Noesner, "Confronting the Terrorist Hostage Taker."

25. Perpetrator interviews and victim debriefings show that most of the hostage takers of the 1980s were provided with a list of demands, but only minimal instructions on how to proceed during the standoff with the security forces. See Fuselier and Noesner, "Confronting the Terrorist Hostage Taker."

26. Thomas Strentz, *Psychological Aspects of Crisis Negotiation* (New York: CRC Press, 2006) p. 166.

27. McMains and Mullins,, *Crisis Negotiations*, p. 108.

28. Ibid.

29. Docherty, *Learning Lessons from Waco*, p. 132.

30. Ibid., p. 130.

31. John Stratton, "The Terrorist Act of Hostage Taking: A View of Violence and the Perpetrators," *Police Science and Administration*, Vol. 6, no. 1 (1978).

32. F. Boltz, K. Dudonis, and D. Schultz, *The Counterterrorism Handbook: Tactics, Procedures, and Techniques*, 2nd ed. (Boca Raton, FL: CRC Press, 2002) p. 64.

## CHAPTER 2

1. Steve Rodan, "Poised to Strike," *The Jerusalem Post* (November 12, 1993).

2. Edward F. Mickolus, *Transnational Terrorism: A Chronology of Events, 1968–1979* (Westport, CT: Greenwood Press, 1980) p. 446.

3. Samuel M. Katz, *Israel versus Jibril: The Thirty-Year War against a Master Terrorist* (New York: Paragon House, 1993) p. 54.

4. Wikipedia. Internet. Available at http://en.wikipedia.org/wiki/Maalot_massacre (accessed on December 13, 2006).

5. Ibid., "Terrorism Knowledge Base," Internet. Available at www.tkb.org/Incident.jsp?incID=1275 (accessed on December 13, 2006).

6. Edward F. Mickolus, *Transnational Terrorism: A Chronology of Events, 1968–1979* (Westport, CT: Greenwood Press, 1980) p. 454.

7. John Griffiths, *Hostage: The History, Facts and Reality of Hostage Taking* (London: Andre Deutsch, 2003) pp. 84–85.

8. Ibid.

9. Ibid.

10. Neil Livingstone and David Halevy, *Inside the PLO* (New York: Quill, 1990) p. 186.

11. Edward F. Mickolus, *Transnational Terrorism: A Chronology of Events, 1968–1979* (Westport, CT: Greenwood Press, 1980) p. 454.

12. Ibid., p. 459.

13. Ibid., p. 512.

14. "The Savoy Attack," *Journal of Palestine Studies*, Vol. 4, no. 4 (Summer, 1975) pp. 127–132.

15. Edward F. Mickolus, *Transnational Terrorism: A Chronology of Events, 1968–1979* (Westport, CT: Greenwood Press, 1980) p. 512.

16. "The Savoy Attack," *Journal of Palestine Studies*, Vol. 4, no. 4 (Summer, 1975) pp. 127–132.

17. Steve Coll, *Ghost Wars: The Secret History of the CIA, Afghanistan, and Bin Laden, from the Soviet Invasion to September 10, 2001* (New York: The Penguin Press, 2004) pp. 27–29.

18. Ibid.

19. Edward F. Mickolus, *Transnational Terrorism: A Chronology of Events, 1968–1979* (Westport, CT: Greenwood Press, 1980) p. 890.

20. Sandra MacKey, *The Saudis: Inside the Desert Kingdom* (New York: W W Norton & Co Ltd., 2004) p. 232.

21. Steve Coll, *Ghost Wars: The Secret History of the CIA, Afghanistan, and Bin Laden, from the Soviet Invasion to September 10, 2001* (New York: The Penguin Press, 2004) pp. 27–29.

22. Wikipedia. Internet. Available at http://www.answers.com/topic/grand-mosque-seizure (accessed on December 19, 2006).

23. Robin Wright, *Sacred Rage: The Wrath of Militant Islam* (New York: Touchstone, 2001) p. 152.

24. John Esposito, *Unholy War: Terror in the Name of Islam* (New York: Oxford University Press, 2002) p. 72.

25. Edward F. Mickolus, *Transnational Terrorism: A Chronology of Events, 1968–1979* (Westport, CT: Greenwood Press, 1980) p. 888.

26. Ibid.

27. Sandra MacKey, *The Saudis: Inside the Desert Kingdom* (New York: W W Norton & Co Ltd., 2004) p. 233.

28. John Esposito, *Unholy War: Terror in the Name of Islam* (New York: Oxford University Press, 2002) p. 71.

29. John F. Jr. Murphy, *Sword of Islam: Muslim Extremism from the Arab Conquest to the Attack on America* (New York, Prometheus Books, 2002) p. 146.

30. Malise Ruthven, *Islam in the World* (New York: Oxford University Press, 2006) p. 8.

31. Martha Crenshaw, "Terrorism, Strategies, and Grand Strategies," in Audrey Cronin and James Ludes, *Attacking Terrorism: Elements of a Grand Strategy* (Washington, D.C.: Georgetown University Press, 2004) p. 62.

32. Edward F. Mickolus, *Transnational Terrorism: A Chronology of Events, 1968–1979* (Westport, CT: Greenwood Press, 1980) p. 889.

33. GlobalSecurity.org, "Mecca," Internet. Available at http://www.globalsecurity.org/military/world/gulf/mecca.htm (accessed on January 1, 2007).

34. Jason Burke, *Al Qaeda: Casting a Shadow of Terror* (New York: I.B. Tauris, 2003) p. 54.

35. Sandra MacKey, *The Saudis: Inside the Desert Kingdom* (New York: W W Norton & Co. Ltd., 2004) p. 230.

36. Malcolm Nance, *The Terrorist Recognition Handbook: A Manual for Predicting and Identifying Terrorist Activities* (Guilford, NC: The Lyons Press, 2003) p. 49.

37. Michael Scheuer, *Through our Enemies Eyes* (Dulles, VI: Potomac Books, 2006) p. 35.

38. Wikipedia. Internet. Available at http://www.answers.com/topic/grand-mosque-seizure (accessed on December 19, 2006).

39. Cited in Randall Hamud, *Osama bin Laden: America's Enemy in His own Words* (San Diego, CA: Nadeem Publishing, 2005) p. 186.

40. "The Mahdi and the End Times," Internet. Available at http://www.endoftimes.net/08mahdiandtheendtimes02.html (accessed on December 25, 2006).

41. Harun Yahya International, "The End Times and the Mahdi," Internet. Available at http://www.harunyahya.com/mahdi03.php (accessed on December 25, 2006).

42. Ibid.

43. Ibid.

44. The original plan was to have a simultaneous hostage crisis taking place in Medina as well, but the plan was aborted due to the fact that a large number of government troops were praying there at the time.

45. Edward F. Mickolus, *Transnational Terrorism: A Chronology of Events, 1968–1979* (Westport, CT: Greenwood Press, 1980) p. 888.

46. Hrair R. Dekmejian, *Islam in Revolution: Fundamentalism in the Arab World* (Syracuse, NY: Syracuse University Press, 1985) p. 142.

47. Peter Theroux, *Sandstorms: Day and Night in Arabia Kingdom* (New York: W W Norton & Co Ltd., 1991) p. 92.

48. Edward F. Mickolus, *Transnational Terrorism: A Chronology of Events, 1968–1979* (Westport, CT: Greenwood Press, 1980) p. 888.

49. John Esposito, *Unholy War: Terror in the Name of Islam* (New York: Oxford University Press, 2002) p. 72.

50. The attack was claimed under the name Egyptian Revolution, which was one of the pseudonyms used by ANO for overseas operations. In accordance with the Abu Nidal trademark modus operandi the attack was apparently a part of a synchronized operation, as on the next day a car bomb detonated at the U.S. post exchange in Frankfurt, Germany, injuring thirty-two people.

51. Western hostages were summoned to the front, and all other passengers were seated in the back of the aircraft. It was the first group out of which hostages were selected out for executions.

52. Peter Latham and Patricia Latham, *Terrorism and the Law: Bringing Terrorists to Justice* (Washington, D.C.: JKL Communications: 2002) pp. 39–40.

53. Captain Galal interviewed in National Geographic documentary series *Interpol Investigates*, episode "Terror in the Skies."

54. Jackie Pflug, *Miles to Go before I Sleep: A Survivor's Story of Life after a Terrorist Hijacking* (Center City, MN: Hazelden, 1996) p. 20.

55. Also including three Egyptians and eight Filipino dancers.

56. Maltese official interviewed in National Geographic documentary series *Interpol Investigates*, episode "Terror in the Skies."

57. Jackie Pflug, *Miles to Go before I Sleep: A Survivor's Story of Life after a Terrorist Hijacking* (Center City, MN: Hazelden, 1996) p. 21.

58. Maltese official interviewed in National Geographic documentary series *Interpol Investigates*, episode "Terror in the Skies."

59. John Griffiths, *Hostage: The History, Facts and Reality of Hostage Taking* (London: Andre Deutsch, 2003) p. 87.

60. Ibid., p. 49.

61. Hostage Julie Moldes interviewed by BBC. Internet. Available at http://news.bbc.co.uk/onthisday/hi/dates/stories/november/24/newsid_4356000/4356024.stm (accessed on January 1, 2007).

62. William Smith, "Massacre in Malta," *Time* (June 21, 2005). Available at http://www.time.com/time/magazine/article/0,9171,1074842-2,00.html (accessed on January 1, 2007).

63. Wikipedia. Internet. Available at http://www.answers.com/topic/egyptair-flight-648 (accessed on January 1, 2007).

64. J. Paul de B. Taillon, *Hijacking and Hostages: Government Responses to Terrorism* (Westport, CT: Praeger Studies in Diplomacy and Strategic Thought, 2002) pp. 149–158.

65. Ibid.

66. William Smith, "Massacre in Malta," *Time* (June 21, 2005). Available at http://www.time.com/time/magazine/article/0,9171,1074842-2,00.html (accessed on January 1, 2007).

67. Jackie Pflug, *Miles to Go before I Sleep: A Survivor's Story of Life after a Terrorist Hijacking* (Center City, MN: Hazelden, 1996) p. 26.

68. United States of America versus Omar Mohammed Ali Rezaq. United States Court of Appeals, no. 96–3127 (June 2, 1998). It is interesting to note that one of our sources who had the opportunity to get to know Rezaq during his time in prison has described him as: "very quiet, intelligent and never aggressive in his words and deeds, and always respectful to authorities. I always used to ask, how could such a nice person be involved in such a serious crime?"

69. Jackie Pflug, *Miles to Go before I Sleep: A Survivor's Story of Life after a Terrorist Hijacking* (Center City, MN: Hazelden, 1996) p. 50.

70. At the very least, the poor condition of the plane provided a persuasive argument for forcing the hostage takers to move into another aircraft, making them vulnerable to sniper fire during transit.

71. The attack was again a part of a synchronized operation, as at 9:17 A.M. the next day, a suicide raid took place at the Neve Shalom synagogue in Istanbul, in which twenty-one people were killed and additional four wounded.

72. United States versus Safarini, Docket no. CR-91-504 (January 16, 1991). Available at http://fl1.findlaw.com/news.findlaw.com/hdocs/docs/safarini/ussafariniindct1.pdf (accessed on December 24, 2006).

73. Malcolm, Nance *The Terrorist Recognition Handbook: A Manual for Predicting and Identifying Terrorist Activities* (Guilford, NC: The Lyons Press, 2003) p. 189.

74. Edward F. Mickolus, Todd Sandler and Jean M. Murdock, *International Terrorism in the 1980s: A Chronology of Events, Volume II: 1984–1987* (Ames, IA: Iowa State University Press, 1989) p. 452.

75. Dwayne Fuselier and Gary Noesner, "Confronting the Terrorist Hostage Taker," Internet. Available at http://www.emergency.com/host-tkr.htm (accessed on January 29, 2002).

76. United States versus Safarini, Docket no. CR-91-504 (January 16, 1991). Available at http://fl1.findlaw.com/news.findlaw.com/hdocs/docs/safarini/ussafariniindct1.pdf (accessed on December 24, 2006).

77. Edward F. Mickolus, Todd Sandler, and Jean M. Murdock, *International Terrorism in the 1980s: A Chronology of Events, Volume II: 1984–1987* (Ames, IA: Iowa State University Press, 1989) p. 453.

78. Department of Justice Press Release, May 13, 2004. Available at http://www.fbi.gov/dojpressrel/pressrel04/051304hijacker.htm (accessed on December 24, 2006).

79. Edward F. Mickolus, Todd Sandler, and Jean M. Murdock, *International Terrorism in the 1980s: A Chronology of Events, Volume II: 1984–1987* (Ames, IA: Iowa State University Press, 1989) p. 456.

80. S. Saad, M. Ali, and Usman Shabbir, "Special Service Group (Army)," Pakistan Military Consortium, Internet. Available at http://www.pakdef.info/ pakmilitary/army/regiments/ssg.html (accessed on December 24, 2006).

81. Yossi Melman, *The Master Terrorist* (New York: Avon Books, 1986) p. 226.

82. S. Saad, M. Ali, and Usman Shabbir, "Special Service Group (Army)," Pakistan Military Consortium, Internet. Available at http://www.pakdef.info/ pakmilitary/army/regiments/ssg.html (accessed on December 24, 2006).

83. Edward F. Mickolus, Todd Sandler, and Jean M. Murdock, *International Terrorism in the 1980s: A Chronology of Events, Volume II: 1984–1987* (Ames, IA: Iowa State University Press, 1989) p. 453.

84. S. Saad, M. Ali, and Usman Shabbir, "Special Service Group (Army)," Pakistan Military Consortium, Internet. Available at http://www.pakdef.info/ pakmilitary/army/regiments/ssg.html (accessed on December 24, 2006).

85. Edward F. Mickolus, Todd Sandler, and Jean M. Murdock, *International Terrorism in the 1980s: A Chronology of Events, Volume II: 1984–1987* (Ames, IA: Iowa State University Press, 1989) p. 453.

86. Yossi Melman, *The Master Terrorist* (New York: Avon Books, 1986) p. 227.

87. S. Saad, M. Ali, and Usman Shabbir, "Special Service Group (Army)," Pakistan Military Consortium, Internet. Available at http://www.pakdef.info/ pakmilitary/army/regiments/ssg.html (accessed on December 24, 2006).

88. Wikipedia. Internet. Available at http://en.wikipedia.org/wiki/Pan_Am_Flight_73 (accessed on December 24, 2006).

89. Edward F. Mickolus, Todd Sandler, and Jean M. Murdock, *International Terrorism in the 1980s: A Chronology of Events, Volume II: 1984–1987* (Ames, IA: Iowa State University Press, 1989) p. 456.

90. Patrick Seale, *Abu Nidal: A Gun for Hire* (New York: Random House, 1992) p. 253.

91. Edward F. Mickolus, Todd Sandler, and Jean M. Murdock, *International Terrorism in the 1980s: A Chronology of Events, Volume II: 1984–1987* (Ames, IA: Iowa State University Press, 1989) p. 742.

92. Thomas Sancton, "Anatomy of a Hijack," *Time* (January 9, 1995).

93. Air Crash Investigation Documentary Series, *Hijacked* (Cineflix 2004).

94. Thomas Sancton, "Anatomy of a Hijack," *Time* (January 9, 1995).

95. Edward F. Mickolus, *Terrorism, 1992–1995: A Chronology of Events and a Selectively Annotated Bibliography* (Westport, CT: Greenwood Press, 1997) p. 744.

96. The names of people whose release was demanded allegedly included Sheikh Omar Abdul Rahman, who was jailed in the United States for his involvement in the 1993 World Trade Centre bombing.

97. Ylva Isabelle Blondel, *The Power of Symbolic Power* (Uppsala University PhD Dissertation, 2004) p. 126.

98. Edward F. Mickolus, *Terrorism, 1992–1995: A Chronology of Events and a Selectively Annotated Bibliography* (Westport, CT: Greenwood Press, 1997) p. 742.

99. Ibid.

100. Hassan Zerrouky, "Alger: Meurtre en Direct," *l'Humanité* (December 27, 1994).

101. Edward F. Mickolus, *Terrorism, 1992–1995: A Chronology of Events and a Selectively Annotated Bibliography* (Westport, CT: Greenwood Press, 1997) p. 743.

102. Hassan Zerrouky, "Alger: Meurtre en Direct," *l'Humanité* (December 27, 1994).

103. Thomas Sancton, "Anatomy of a Hijack," *Time* (January 9, 1995).

104. Ylva Isabelle Blondel, *The Power of Symbolic Power* (Uppsala University PhD Dissertation, 2004) p. 127.

105. Wikipedia. Internet. Available at http://en.wikipedia.org/wiki/Air_France_Flight_8969 (accessed on January 1, 2007).

106. Joshua L. Gleis, "Connecting the Dots: Osama bin Laden and al Qaeda Involvement in Terrorism Prior to 9-11." Internet. Available at http://www.teachingterror.net/resources/AQ%20Involvement%20in%20Terror%20Prior%20to%20911.doc (accessed on December 28, 2006).

107. Wikipedia. Internet. Available at http://en.wikipedia.org/wiki/Air_France_Flight_8969 (accessed on January 1, 2007).

108. The plane was allegedly short on fuel because the Auxiliary Power Unit (APU) which supplies power to the aircraft had been running since day one. Since the APU on a Boeing 300 consumes about three tons of fuel per day, about six tons of fuel was allegedly missing.

109. Edward F. Mickolus, *Terrorism, 1992–1995: A Chronology of Events and a Selectively Annotated Bibliography* (Westport, CT: Greenwood Press, 1997) p. 743.

110. Ibid.

111. Ibid.

112. Rohan Gunaratna, *Inside al Qaeda* (New York: Columbia University Press, 2002) p. 123.

113. Thomas Sancton, "Anatomy of a Hijack," *Time* (January 9, 1995).

114. Wikipedia. Internet. Available at http://en.wikipedia.org/wiki/Air_France_Flight_8969 (accessed on January 1, 2007).

115. Edward F. Mickolus, *Terrorism, 1992–1995: A Chronology of Events and a Selectively Annotated Bibliography* (Westport, CT: Greenwood Press, 1997) p. 743.

116. Sancton, Thomas Sancton, "Anatomy of a Hijack," *Time* (January 9, 1995).

117. Peter Lance, *Cover Up: What the Government is Still Hiding about the War on Terror* (New York: Harper-Collins Publishers, 2004) p. 179.

118. Edward F. Mickolus, *Terrorism, 1992–1995: A Chronology of Events and a Selectively Annotated Bibliography* (Westport, CT: Greenwood Press, 1997) p. 743.

119. Evan Kohlmann, "Missed Opportunities: The December 1994 Air France Hijacking," Internet. Available at http://www.globalterroralert.com/pdf/0105/airfrancehijack.pdf (accessed on January 1, 2007).

120. Ibid.

121. Sergei Topol, *Budyonnovsk: Reportazh pod Pritselom* (Moscow: De Fakto, 2005) p. 9.

122. John Arquilla and Theodore Karasik, "Chechnya: A Glimpse of Future Conflict?" *Studies in Conflict and Terrorism*, Vol. 22 (July–September 1999).

123. Sergei Topol, *Budyonnovsk: Reportazh pod Pritselom* (Moscow: De Fakto, 2005) p. 22.

124. Aukai Collins, *My Jihad* (New York: Pocket Star Books, 2002) p. 80.

125. John Giduck, *Terror at Beslan* (Golden, CO: Archangel Group Inc., 2005) p. 68.

126. Paul J. Murphy, *The Wolves of Islam: Russia and the Faces of Chechen Terror* (Dulles, VA: Brasseay's Inc, 2005) p. 21.

127. Sergei Topol, *Budyonnovsk: Reportazh pod Pritselom* (Moscow: De Fakto, 2005) p. 27.

128. Ibid., p. 35.

129. Agentura.ru, "Buddyonovsk," Internet. Available at http://www.agentura.ru/timeline/1995/basaev/ (accessed on November 18, 2006).

130. Sergei Topol, *Budyonnovsk: Reportazh pod Pritselom* (Moscow: De Fakto, 2005) p. 30.

131. Ibid., p. 36.

132. Ibid., p. 44.

133. More specifically the presence of Organization for Security Cooperation in Europe (OSCE).

134. Edward F. Mickolus, *Terrorism, 1992–1995: A Chronology of Events and a Selectively Annotated Bibliography* (Westport, CT: Greenwood Press, 1997) pp. 823–24.

135. Sergei Topol, *Budyonnovsk: Reportazh pod Pritselom* (Moscow: De Fakto, 2005) p. 56.

136. Cited in ibid., p. 61.

137. John Arquilla and Theodore Karasik, "Chechnya: A Glimpse of Future Conflict?" *Studies in Conflict and Terrorism*, Vol. 22 (July–September 1999).

138. Sergei Topol, *Budyonnovsk: Reportazh pod Pritselom* (Moscow: De Fakto, 2005) p. 77.

139. Ibid., p. 98.

140. Ibid., pp. 100–101.

141. Ibid., p. 104.

142. Rudayev died on December 15, 2002 of "internal bleeding" while serving a life sentence in Solikamsk prison in the Urals.

143. Paul J. Murphy, *The Wolves of Islam: Russia and the Faces of Chechen Terror* (Dulles, VA: Brasseay's Inc, 2005) p. 51.

144. Edward F., Mickolus, *Terrorism, 1996–2001: A Chronology* (Westport, CT: Greenwood Press, 2002) p. 5.

145. Agentura.ru, "Kizlyar-Pervomayskoe," Internet. Available at http://www.agentura.ru/timeline/1996/pervomay/ (accessed on December 16, 2006).

146. Ibid.

147. Edward F. Mickolus, *Terrorism, 1996–2001: A Chronology* (Westport, CT: Greenwood Press, 2002) pp. 5–7.

148. Ibid.

149. The original deadline would later be extended by one day.

150. For instance, one of the Russian units did actually succeed in reaching the location where the hostages were held but was forced to retreat due to friendly fire from a Russian helicopter.

151. Wikipedia. Interent. Available at http://en.wikipedia.org/wiki/Kizlyar_raid (accessed on December 16, 2006).

152. Edward F. Mickolus, *Terrorism, 1996–2001: A Chronology* (Westport, CT: Greenwood Press, 2002) pp. 5–7.

153. Interview with one of the hijackers (Azerbaijan, summer 2006).

154. Ibid.

155. After Mecca.

156. Preetam Bora, "Terrorist Attack on Parliament: Striking at the Heart of Indian Democracy," SAPRA INDIA report (December 26, 2001) Internet. Available at http://www.subcontinent.com/sapra/research/terrorism/terrorism20011226a.html (accessed on December 25, 2006).

157. Interview with Neeraj Kumar, at the time Director of Special Cell of New Delhi police, in charge of investigation of the attack. (New Delhi, February 14, 2002).

158. Preetam Bora, "Terrorist Attack on Parliament: Striking at the Heart of Indian Democracy," SAPRA INDIA report (December 26, 2001) Internet. Available at http://www.subcontinent.com/sapra/research/terrorism/terrorism20011226a.html (accessed on December 25, 2006).

159. On October 1, 2001, at 1:58 P.M., three men in police uniforms attacked the Jammu and Kashmir Assembly in Srinagar, just moments after their colleague rammed an explosive-laden truck into a security bunker at the main gate. The terrorists used this diversion to enter the compound, and shooting indiscriminately they took more than twenty officials and other employees of the Legislative Council hostage. A five-hour battle followed in which thirty-eight people were killed and over eighty injured.

160. Interview with IG Kabu, BSF, Operations (New Delhi, February 22, 2002).

161. Preetam Bora, "Terrorist Attack on Parliament: Striking at the Heart of Indian Democracy," SAPRA INDIA report (December 26, 2001) Internet. Available at http://www.subcontinent.com/sapra/research/terrorism/terrorism20011226a.html (accessed on December 25, 2006).

162. K. Bushan and G. Katyal, *Attack on Parliament* (New Delhi: APH Publishing Corp. 2002) p. 4.

163. Edward F. Mickolus, *Terrorism, 1996–2001: A Chronology* (Westport, CT: Greenwood Press, 2002) p. 430.

164. Interview with Neeraj Kumar, Director of Special Cell of New Delhi Police, in charge of investigation of the attack. (New Delhi, February 14, 2002).

165. Preetam Bora, "Terrorist Attack on Parliament: Striking at the Heart of Indian Democracy," SAPRA INDIA report (December 26, 2001) Internet. Available at http://www.subcontinent.com/sapra/research/terrorism/terrorism20011226a.html (accessed on December 25, 2006)

166. K. Bushan and G. Katyal, *Attack on Parliament* (New Delhi: APH Publishing Corp. 2002) p. 16.

167. Interview P.K. Mishra, BSF, DIG, in charge of parliament security during the time of the attack (New Delhi, February 20, 2002).

168. Interview with Neeraj Kumar, at the time Director of Special Cell of New Delhi police, in charge of investigation of the attack. (New Delhi, February 14, 2002); K. Bushan, and G. Katyal *Attack on Parliament* (New Delhi: APH Publishing Corp. 2002) p. 4.

169. Reuters, "Saudis Rescue Hostages, Arrest Militants," Internet. Available at http://www.theage.com.au/articles/2004/05/30/1085855422319.html?from=storylhs (accessed on December 25, 2006).

170. CNN, "Witness: Attackers Hunted Westerners" (May 30, 2004). Available at http://edition.cnn.com/2004/WORLD/meast/05/30/saudi.eyewitness/index.html (accessed on December 25, 2006).

171. Caroline Faraj, "Saudis Blame al Qaeda for Attack," CNN (May 31, 2004). Available at http://edition.cnn.com/2004/WORLD/meast/05/30/saudi.shooting/index.html (accessed on December 25, 2006).

172. Middle East Media Research Institute, Special Dispatch Series, no. 731, Internet. Available at http://www.memri.org/bin/articles.cgi?Area=sd&ID=SP73104 (accessed on December 25, 2006).

173. Reuters, "Saudis Rescue Hostages, Arrest Militants." Internet. Available at http://www.theage.com.au/articles/2004/05/30/1085855422319.html?from=storylhs (accessed on December 25, 2006).

174. BBC, "Saudi Commandos Rescue Hostages" (May 30, 2004). Available at http://news.bbc.co.uk/2/hi/middle_east/3761263.stm (accessed on December 25, 2006).

175. Middle East Media Research Institute, Special Dispatch Series, no. 731, Internet. Available at http://www.memri.org/bin/articles.cgi?Area=sd&ID=SP73104 (accessed on December 25, 2006).

176. Caroline Faraj, "Saudis Blame al Qaeda for Attack," CNN (May 31, 2004). Available at http://edition.cnn.com/2004/WORLD/meast/05/30/saudi.shooting/index.html (accessed on December 25, 2006).

177. Abdul Hameed Bakier, "Lessons from al-Qaeda's Attack on the Khobar Compound," *Jamestown Foundation Terrorism Monitor*, Vol. 4, no. 16 (August 10, 2006). Available at http://jamestown.org/terrorism/news/article.php?articleid=2370100 (accessed on September 30, 2006).

178. BBC, "Saudi Commandos Rescue Hostages" (May 30, 2004). Available at http://news.bbc.co.uk/2/hi/middle_east/3761263.stm (accessed on December 25, 2006).

179. Abdul Hameed Bakier, "Lessons from al-Qaeda's Attack on the Khobar Compound," *Jamestown Foundation Terrorism Monitor*, Vol. 4, no. 16 (August 10, 2006). Available at http://jamestown.org/terrorism/news/article.php?articleid=23701 00 (accessed on September 30, 2006).

180. Intel Centre, "Al Qaida in Saudi Arabian Peninsula," Internet. Available at http://www.intelcenter.com/AQAP-SHK-PUB-v1-1.pdf (accessed on September 30, 2006).

181. "Gunmen Kill 22 People at Saudi Facility Associated with Halliburton," Internet. Available at http://www.halliburtonwatch.org/news/hostages_taken.html (accessed on September 30, 2006).

182. Full translation of the statement is available at Intel Centre, "Al Qaida in Saudi Arabian Peninsula," Internet. Available at http://www.intelcenter.com/AQAP-SHK-PUB-v1-1.pdf (accessed on September 30, 2006).

183. SITE Institute, "As-Sahab Video Production of the 2004 Attack in Khobar, Saudi Arabia," Internet. Available at http://siteinstitute.biz/bin/articles.cgi?ID=publications191506&Category=publications&Subcategory=0 (accessed on September 30, 2006).

184. Thomas Strentz, *Psychological Aspects of Crisis Negotiation* (New York: CRC Press, 2006) p. 166.

185. The mutually positive relationship between the hostages and the hostage takers. The dynamics of the Stockholm syndrome are discussed in greater detail in Chapter 3.

**CHAPTER 3**

1. Some of the material in this chapter was first published in Adam Dolnik and Richard Pilch, "The Moscow Theater Hostage Crisis: The Perpetrators, Their Tactics, and the Russian Response," *International Negotiation*, Vol. 8, no. 3 (Leiden, Netherlands: Brill Academic Publishers 2003).

2. Gregory Feifer, "Russia: Murky Information Complicates Hostage-Crisis Conclusions," Radio Free Europe. Available at http://www.rferl.org/nca/features/2002/11/12112002163511.asp (accessed on July 3, 2003).

3. Nabi Abdullaev, "Picture Emerges of How They Did It," *Moscow Times* (10/06/02).

4. C. Huang, "The Moscow Massacre," *Maxim* (March 2003). Available at http://web1.maximonline.com/articles/index.aspx?a_id=5086 (accessed on December 12, 2006).

5. Yevgeny Kolesnikov, "Lessons Learned from the Nord-Ost Terrorist Attack in Moscow from the Standpoint of Russian Security and Law Enforcement Agencies," in *Terrorism: Reducing Vulnerabilities and Improving Responses: U.S.–Russian Workshop Proceedings* (Washington D.C.: National Academic Press, 2004).

6. Natalia Yefimova, Torrey Clark, and Lyuba Pronina, "Armed Chechens Seize Moscow Theater," *Moscow Times* (October 24, 2002).

7. Yevgeny Kolesnikov, "Lessons Learned from the Nord-Ost Terrorist Attack in Moscow from the Standpoint of Russian Security and Law Enforcement Agencies," in *Terrorism: Reducing Vulnerabilities and Improving Responses: U.S.–Russian Workshop Proceedings* (Washington, D.C.: National Academic Press, 2004).

8. Not everyone heard these instructions. As hostage Svetlana Gubareva explained: "We sat in the 17th row and didn't know what was happening below … the sound carried poorly. I understood that they were letting kids out only when they were at the exit, and by then it was already too late." This also explains why the Azeri hostages were not released until the last day.

9. He himself was twelve when the first Chechen war started.

10. Pravda.ru. Details of the Crisis in Moscow. Internet. Available at http://english.pravda.ru/main/2002/10/24/38602.html (accessed on November 14, 2006).

11. This was reported to journalists by Aslanbek Aslakhanov. According to him, the terrorists have so far not communicated with him and negotiations have not been started yet. The terrorists' demands were transmitted to him via released hostages.

12. Kavkaz Centre, "Protest Demonstration of Chechen Refugees in Baku," Internet. Available at http://www.kavkazcenter.com/eng/content/2002/10/24/548.shtml (accessed on October 28, 2002).

13. L. Burban, S.Gubareva, T. Karpova, N. Karpov, V., Kurbatov, D. Milovidov, and P. Finogenov, "Nord-Ost: Investigation Unfinished…" Internet. Available at http://www.pravdabeslana.ru/nordost/nordost.htm (accessed on October 11, 2006).

14. Pravda.ru. Details of the Crisis in Moscow., Internet. Available at: http://english.pravda.ru/main/2002/10/24/38602.html (accessed on November 14, 2006).

15. Natalia Yefimova, Torrey Clark, and Lyuba Pronina, "Armed Chechens Seize Moscow Theater," *Moscow Times*, October 24, 2002.

16. C. Huang, "The Moscow Massacre," *Maxim* (March 2003). Available at http://web1.maximonline.com/articles/index.aspx?a_id=5086 (accessed on December 12, 2006).

17. Kavkaz Centre, "Protest Demonstration of Chechen Refugees in Baku," Internet. Available at http://www.kavkazcenter.com/eng/content/2002/10/24/548.html

18. L. Burban, S. Gubareva, T. Karpova, N. Karpov, V. Kurbatov, D. Milovidov, and P. Finogenov, "Nord-Ost: Investigation Unfinished..." Internet. Available at http://www.pravdabeslana.ru/nordost/nordost.htm (accessed on October 11, 2006).

19. Svetlana Gubareva, "Description of the Events during the Seizure of the Dubrovka Theater in Moscow, October 23–26, 2002," Internet. Available at http://www.geocities.com/svetlana.gubareva/other/opisanie_gubareva_1_eng.html (accessed on October 1, 2006).

20. Kevin O'Flynn, "Up to 65 Foreigners Still Held in Theater," *St Ptersburgh Times* (October 25, 2002).

21. "Chechen Hostage Takers Urge Talks, Refuse to Release Foreigners," *People's Daily* (October 24, 2002). Available at http://english.people.com.cn/200210/24/eng20021024_105617.shtml (accessed on October 1, 2006).

22. Michael Wines, "Kremlin on Edge after Chechens Threaten to Kill Hostages," *New York Times* (October 25, 2002).

23. Lyuba Pronina, Oksana Yablokova, and Andrei Jr. Zolotov, "One Dead in Theater, 8 Walk Free" *Moscow Times* (October 25, 2002). Available at http://www.eng.yabloko.ru/Publ/2002/papers/moscow-times-251002.html (accessed on October 1, 2006).

24. According to Russian authorities, however, the operation was carried out with Maskhadov's blessing. This seems to be confirmed by the fact that one of the rebels encouraged the negotiators to speak directly to Maskhadov.

25. *Al Jazeera* tape.

26. NEWSru.com, "Zhurnalisty NTV zapisali interviu s Movsarom Barayevym," Internet. Avaliable at: http://www.newsru.com/russia/25oct2002/review.html (accessed on October 1, 2006).

27. BBC,"Seven Hostages Freed in Moscow Siege" (October 25, 2002). Available at http://news.bbc.co.uk/2/hi/world/europe/2359491.stm (accessed on October 1, 2006).

28. C. Huang, "The Moscow Massacre," *Maxim* (March 2003). Available at http://web1.maximonline.com/articles/index.aspx?a_id=5086 (accessed on December 12, 2006).

29. http://www.gazeta.ru/2002/10/25/15hostagesre.shtml

30. "And you know it's simply not true that the Chechens demanded relatives of the hostages to go out on Red Square and demonstrate. What he said was, when people claimed that they were against the war, Barayev replied: "Well, you don't act like you're against the war, you don't go out onto Red Square and demand they stop the war!' A few hours after these words a lady got up from the front row and said: 'You see, the government's not going to do anything? Our lives our in

our own hands! Come on, let's call our relatives and tell them to go have a meeting out on Red Square to stop the war!' Barayev merely shrugged his shoulders. 'Go ahead and call if you want' and told his people to hand out the cell phones." Interview with Karagandan Svetlana Gubareva. Available at http://www.geocities.com/svetlana.gubareva/02.html (accessed on December 12, 2006).

31. *Gazeta.Ru* (October 25, 2006).

32. Ibid.

33. Hostage Anna Andrianova interviewed in *Moskovskaya Pravda* (October 26, 2002).

34. C. Huang, "The Moscow Massacre," *Maxim* (March 2003). Available at http://web1.maximonline.com/articles/index.aspx?a_id=5086 (accessed on December 12, 2006).

35. Telephone interview with Anna Politkovskaya (March 19, 2002).

36. Alex Nicholson, "Yavlinsky Describes his Role in Crisis," *Moscow Times* (November 4, 2002).

37. Some accounts claim the deadline was set to midnight (i.e., HBO: "Terror in Moscow"); however the telephone call in which the terrorists conveyed this threat through a hostage actually specified 6:00 A.M. as the deadline for executions.

38. CTV News, "Moscow Standoff Ends as Soldiers Storm Theatre," Internet. Available at http://www.ctv.ca/servlet/ArticleNews/story/CTVNews/20021026/moscow_hostages_chechens_021025?s_name=&no_ads= (accessed on November 11, 2006).

39. "Azerbaijan: Daily publishes pre-assault interview with Chechen hostage-taker," *Baku Zerkalo* (10/ 26/2002) FBIS ID# CEP20021026000120

40. "Russian Special Services Link Saudi Arabia, UAE, Turkey to Moscow Terrorist Act,"*Moscow Trud* (October 29, 2002).

41. BBC, "How Special Forces Ended Siege" (October 29, 2002); "A Man, A Bottle, A Shot, Then Gas," *The Moscow Times* (October 28, 2002); CNN, "Tantrum' Sparked Theatre Raid" (October 28, 2002).

42. Some accounts suggest that this was the same bullet, which had continued on after passing through the man's head.

43. "A Man, A Bottle, A Shot, Then Gas," *The Moscow Times* (October 28, 2002); BBC, "Hostages Speak of Storming Terror" (October 26, 2002).

44. Natalya Galimova, Denis Belikov, Marat Khayrullin, and Yuriy Gavrilov, "Was Assault Scheduled as Far Back as Wednesday? Hostages' Bodies Piled up," *Moskovskiy Komsomolets* (October 28, 2002); Susan B. Glasser, and Peter Baker, "Russia Seizes Theater from Rebels," *Washington Post* (October 27, 2002).

45. Natalya Fomina, "A Karagandan at 'Nord-Ost': One Year Later," *Novy Vestnik* (October 22, 2003). Also available at http://www.geocities.com/svetlana.gubareva/02.html (accessed on October 22, 2006).

46. Ibid.

47. BBC, "How Special Forces Ended Siege" (October 29, 2002); Steven Lee Myers, "From Anxiety, Fear and Hope, the Deadly Rescue in Moscow," *New York Times* (November 1, 2002).

48. Irina Borogan, Andrei Soldatov, "Coverage of the Storm of the Theatre," Internet. Available at http://www.agentura.ru/timeline/2002/nord-ost/reportbrit/ (accessed on October 25, 2002).

49. Anna Politkovskaya, "Inside a Moscow Theatre with the Chechen Rebels," International Women's Media Foundation. Internet. Available at http://www.iwmf.org/features/anna (accessed on November 21, 2002); Natalya Galimova, Denis Belikov, Marat Khayrullin, and Yuriy Gavrilov, "Was Assault Scheduled as Far Back as Wednesday? Hostages' Bodies Piled up," *Moskovskiy Komsomolets* (October 28, 2002).

50. Steven Lee Myers, "From Anxiety, Fear and Hope, the Deadly Rescue in Moscow," *New York Times* (November 1, 2002).

51. Andrei Soldatov, e-mail correspondence (March 26, 2003); Steven Lee Myers, "From Anxiety, Fear and Hope, the Deadly Rescue in Moscow," *New York Times* (November 1, 2002); BBC, "How Special Forces Ended Siege" (October 29, 2002). It has alternatively been suggested that the release of the gas and initiation of the assault in fact took place simultaneously. Telephone interview with Anna Politkovskaya (March 19, 2002).

52. A Man, A Bottle, A Shot, Then Gas," *The Moscow Times* (October 28, 2002); Andrei Soldatov,, e-mail correspondence (March 26, 2003); Steven Lee Myers, "From Anxiety, Fear and Hope, the Deadly Rescue in Moscow," *New York Times* (November 1, 2002).

53. Again, reports conflict: some hostages claim to have smelled the gas, some to have seen it, others to have felt its effects (namely, disorientation, dizziness, and euphoria), and still others to have lost consciousness without any recognition whatsoever.

54. The Chechens had disabled the air-conditioning system early on in the raid. Tom Newton Dunn, "Moscow Siege," *The Mirror* (October 28, 2002) p. 11; BBC, "How Special Forces Ended Siege" (October 29, 2002).

55. These respirators likely offered only minimal protection against the gas, but some protection nonetheless. Tom Newton Dunn, "Moscow Siege," *The Mirror* (October 28, 2002) p. 11; BBC, "How Special Forces Ended Siege" (October 29, 2002).

56. Areas removed from the influx of the gas are thought to include the corridor and balcony.

57. Natalya Galimova, Denis Belikov, Marat Khayrullin, and Yuriy Gavrilov "Was Assault Scheduled as Far Back as Wednesday? Hostages' Bodies Piled up," *Moskovskiy Komsomolets* (October 28, 2002).

58. These so-called "temporal associations" reflect the relative timing, based on witness descriptions, of gunfire, explosions, and actions, both outside and within the theater.

59. Natalya Kozlova, "Interview in Rossiyskaya Gazeta's Editorial Office with Five Officers of the Alfa and Vympel Special Subunits," *Rossiyskaya Gazeta* (October 12, 2002); "Soldiers of Last Resort. Fighters from the Alfa and Vympel Special Subunits Answer Our Newspaper's Questions," taken from HTML version of source provided by ISP (FBIS); BBC, "Hostages Speak of Storming Terror" (October 26, 2002).

60. Steven Lee Myers, "From Anxiety, Fear and Hope, the Deadly Rescue in Moscow," *New York Times* (November 1, 2002). One witness claimed that when the shots were first heard, those rebels still conscious told the hostages to take cover in their seats, a confusing action if the intention was to detonate the bombs and kill

those same hostages upon identification of a hostile force within the theater. BBC, "How Special Forces Ended Siege" (October 29, 2002). Another hostage claimed that the reaction of the rebels did not in any way suggest a desire to inflict harm on the hostages. BBC, "Hostages Speak of Storming Terror" (October 26, 2002).

61. Natalya Kozlova, "Special Liberation Detachment. One of Chiefs of Staff for Liberation of Hostages Gives Exclusive Interview," *Rossiyskaya Gazeta* (October 29, 2002) FBIS ID# CEP20021030000064.

62. Natalya Kozlova, "Soldiers of Last Resort. Fighters From the Alfa and Vympel Special Subunits Answer Our Newspaper's Questions," *Rossiyskaya Gazeta* (October 12, 2002) FBIS ID# CEP20021114000199.

63. Susan B. Glasser, "Rescue Ended Days of Horror and Uncertainty," *Washington Post* (October 27, 2002) p. A1.

64. Johanna McGeary and Paul Quinn, "Theatre of War," *Time Europe* (November 4, 2002).

65. BBC, "How Special Forces Ended Siege" (October 29, 2002).

66. Michael Wines, "Russia Names Drug in Raid, Defending Use," *New York Times* (October 30, 2002). It should be noted, however, that the fentanyl derivative may have been delivered into Dubrovka theater in combination with another chemical, and further that a fentanyl derivative may in fact have not been used at all. Toxic analyses and insider accounts have named multiple other agents in the assault; some have denied the use of fentanyl altogether. The authors have accepted the official Russian declaration in this case but have formulated conclusions independent of the type of gas used.

67. A.k.a. Movsar Suleimanov.

68. Chris Kline, and Mark Franchietti, "The Woman behind the Mask," *Timesonline.* Available at http://www.timesonline.co.uk/printFriendly/0,,1-3505-469538,00.htlm (accessed on March 24, 2003).

69. He also reportedly ordered the beheading of three Britons and one New Zealander in 1998 who were building a cell phone network in Chechnya.

70. Telephone interview with Anna Politkovskaya (March 19, 2002).

71. Two killed was the figure presented by the Russians. The Chechens claimed the blast had killed twenty-nine.

72. Maria Tsvetkova, "Chechen Women to Drive Killer Trucks," Gazeta.ru, Internet. Available at http://www.gazeta.ru/2002/10/29/Chechenwomen.shtml (accessed July 3, 2003).

73. Abu Bakar was also a pseudonym for Barayev's close associate Yusupov, who however was supposedly killed two years earlier.

74. Shamil Basayev, "Murder of Deputy Has Something to Do with My Letter..." Internet. Availale at: http://www.kavkazcenter.com/eng/content/2003/04/27/1269.shtml (accessed on November 17, 2006).

75. Telephone interview with Anna Politkovskaya (March 19, 2002).

76. Natalya Kozlova, "Special Liberation Detachment. One of Chiefs of Staff for Liberation of Hostages Gives Exclusive Interview," *Rossiyskaya Gazeta* (October 29, 2002) FBIS ID# CEP20021030000064.

77. Yuri Senatorev, "Nord-Ost Zakhvatil Banker," *Izvestia* (October 26, 2004) Also available at http://www.compromat.ru/main/chechya/baraevelmurzaev.htm (accessed on November 17, 2006).

78. RAS was originally set up by Basayev as an ad hoc, one-time group for the Nord-Ost operation. However, following the unanticipated lack of support from the international community after the attack, Basayev decided to establish RAS as a permanent group designated for high-profile suicide operations against civilians. More details about RAS are discussed in Chapter 4.

79. When the reporters were talking on the radio about how many Chechens had seized the theater, Barayev was walking by, and said: "Twenty, thirty, forty … they don't even know how many of us came to the theater! There's fifty-four of us here, fifty-four!" (see Svetlana Gubareva, "Description of the Events During the Seizure of the Dubrovka Theater in Moscow, October 23–26, 2002," Internet. Available at http://www.geocities.com/svetlana.gubareva/other/opisanie_gubareva_1_eng.html (accessed on October 1, 2006).

80. FBIS, "Russian Source Talks of 'Pause' in Developments Surrounding Hostage Crisis," Internet. Available at (accessed on October 24, 2006). FBIS ID# CEP20021024000569.

81. Anna Politkovskaya, "Nord-Ost: Where Did 12 Terrorists Go?" *Novaya Gazeta* (November 18, 2004).

82. Ben Venzke and Aimee Ibrahim, *The al-Qaeda Threat: An Analytical Guide to al-Qaeda's Tactics and Targets* (Alexandria, LA: Tempest Publishing, 2004) p. 78

83. Nabi Abdullaev, "Picture Emerges of How They Did It," *Moscow Times* (November 6, 2002).

84. Abu Bakar interviewed on NTV.

85. Adam Dolnik, and Richard Pilch, "The Moscow Theater Hostage Crisis: the Perpetrators, their Tactics, and the Russian Response," *International Negotiation*, Vol. 8, no. 3 (2003).

86. Nabi Abdullaev, "Picture Emerges of How They Did It," *Moscow Times* (November 6, 2002).

87. Shamil Basayev, "Murder of Deputy Has Something To Do with My Letter…" Internet. Availale at: http://www.kavkazcenter.com/eng/content/2003/04/27/1269.shtml (accessed on November 17, 2006).

88. Adam Dolnik and Richard Pilch, "The Moscow Theater Hostage Crisis: The Perpetrators, Their Tactics, and the Russian Response," *International Negotiation*, Vol. 8, no. 3 (2003).

89. Anne Speckhard, Nadejda Tarabrina, Valery Krasnov and Khapta Akhmedova, "Research Note: Observations of Suicidal Terrorists in Action," *Terrorism and Political Violence*, Vol.16, no.2 (Summer 2004), pp. 305–327.

90. Natalya Kozlova, "Soldiers of Last Resort. Fighters from the Alfa and Vympel Special Subunits Answer Our Newspaper's Questions," *Rossiyskaya Gazeta* (October 12, 2002) FBIS ID# CEP20021114000199.

91. FBIS, "Russian Source Talks of 'Pause' in Developments Surrounding Hostage Crisis," Internet. Available at (accessed on October 24, 2006) FBIS ID# CEP20021024000569.

92. Roman Shleinov on his role in the crisis in *Novaya Gazeta* (October 28, 2002).

93. Johanna McGeary and Paul Quinn, "Theatre of War," *Time Europe* (November 4, 2002).

94. It seems that the group was keen on attacking a theater in Moscow from the very beginning, supported by the fact that a videotape indicating the Moskovky

Dvorets Molodyozhi (MDM) Theater as another possible target was recovered from one of the dead hostage takers. Nabi Abdullaev, "Picture Emerges of How They Did It," *Moscow Times* (November 6, 2002).

95. Abu Bakar for NTV.

96. Tickets for the show were not cheap, selling for 450 to 1000 Rubles (approximately 14 to 42 US dollars). At the same time, the musical had played long enough for the celebrities and the rich toalready attend the show.

97. Svetlana Gubareva, "Description of the Events During the Seizure of the Dubrovka Theater in Moscow, October 23–26, 2002," Internet. Available at http://www.geocities.com/svetlana.gubareva/other/opisanie_gubareva_1_eng.html (accessed on October 1, 2006).

98. Adam Dolnik, "Die and Let Die: Exploring Links between Suicide Terrorism and Terrorist Use of Chemical, Biological, Radiological, and Nuclear Weapons," *Studies in Conflict and Terrorism*, Vol. 26, no. 1 (January–February 2003) pp. 17–35.

99. In fact, the Chechen groups especially have a history of using suicide-truck bombings with the principal goal of solidifying the fighters' morale.

100. In the interview with Azeri TV prior to the rescue operation, Abu Said was asked whether the terrorists expected an attack. He replied: "Yes, they will definitely attack. We are waiting for this attack." (*Baku Zerkalo*, October 26, 2002).

101. BBC, "Non-stop Nightmare for Moscow Hostages" (October 25, 2002). It should be noted that while the hostages were not free to move around on the first day, the rules became more lax as the incident progressed and as the hostages started moving around and settling closer to their friends or relatives.

102. Thomas Strentz, "The Cyclic Crisis Negotiations Time Line," *Law and Order* (March 1995) pp. 73–75.

103. The same does not necessarily apply to kidnapping scenarios however, as the beheading practice in Iraq and Saudi Arabia has shown us. But the key difference here is that in the kidnapping scenario the terrorists have the freedom to kill their hostages without sanction.

104. Even before the Moscow hostage incidents, groups in Chechnya had conducted at least seven suicide-truck-bombings, with the most significant operation being a coordinated attack of five suicide-truck bombers, who blew up military checkpoints and a police dormitory in 2000, killing 33 people and injuring 84.

105. For instance, many of the terrorists spoke to Politkovskaya in a confessional mode and sometimes asked her to pass messages on to their families. According to Politkovskaya, the hostage takers also performed traditional Chechen preparations for death.

106. According to negotiator Irina Khakamada: "From my negotiations with terrorists in the Theatrical Center and from the later developments I came to believe that it had not been in the plans of the terrorists to blow up the Theatrical Center," Internet. Available at http://grani.ru/Politics/Russia/President/m.56704.html (accessed on November 18, 2006).

107. Svetlana Gubareva, "Description of the Events During the Seizure of the Dubrovka Theater in Moscow, October 23–26, 2002," Internet. Available at http://www.geocities.com/svetlana.gubareva/other/opisanie_gubareva_1_eng.html (accessed on October 1, 2006).

108. William Zartman, "Negotiating Effectively with Terrorists" in Barry Rubin, ed., *The Politics of Counterterrorism* (Washington, D.C.: The Johns Hopkins Foreign Policy Institute, 1990) p. 163–188.

109. James Poland and Michael McCrystle, *Practical, Tactical and Legal Perspectives of Terrorism and Hostage Taking* (Lewiston, NY: Edwin Mellen Press, 2000) p. 24.

110. Michael McMains and Wayman Mullins, *Crisis Negotiations: Managing Critical Incidents and Hostage Situations in Law Enforcement and Corrections*, 2nd ed. (Dayton, OH: Anderson Publishing, 2001) p. 167.

111. Interview with Karagandan Svetlana Gubareva. Available at http://www.geocities.com/svetlana.gubareva/02.html (accessed on December 12, 2006).

112. Anne Speckhard, Nadejda Tarabrina, Valery Krasnov, and Khapta Akhmedova, "Research Note: Observations of Suicidal Terrorists in Action," *Terrorism and Political Violence*, Vol.16, no.2 (Summer 2004).

113. Svetlana Gubareva, "Description of the Events During the Seizure of the Dubrovka Theater in Moscow, October 23–26, 2002," Internet. Available at http://www.geocities.com/svetlana.gubareva/other/opisanie_gubareva_1_eng.html (accessed on October 1, 2006).

114. Ibid.

115. Anne Speckhard, Nadejda Tarabrina, Valery Krasnov, and Khapta Akhmedova, "Research Note: Observations of Suicidal Terrorists in Action," *Terrorism and Political Violence*, Vol.16, no.2 (Summer 2004).

116. Georgy Vasiliev interviewed in HBO documentary "Terror in Moscow."

117. Anne Speckhard, Nadejda Tarabrina, Valery Krasnov, and Khapta Akhmedova, "Research Note: Observations of Suicidal Terrorists in Action," *Terrorism and Political Violence*, Vol.16, no.2 (Summer 2004).

118. Thomas Strentz, "The Cyclic Crisis Negotiations Time Line," *Law and Order* (March 1995) pp. 73–75.

119. Ekho Moskvy, "Interview with Terrorists in the Nord-Ost Auditorium" (October 24, 2002). Also available at http://www.vokruginfo.ru/news/news2784.html (accessed on November 13, 2006).

120. Vyacheslav Ismailov, "The Drama Behind 'Nord-Ost'," *Perspective*, Vol. 13, no. 2 (November–December 2002).

121. Telephone interview with Anna Politkovskaya (March 19, 2002).

122. Dwayne Fuselier, "What Every Negotiator Would Like His Chief to Know," *FBI Law Enforcement Bulletin* (March 1986).

123. The existence of this shared misery is very clear from statements made by both captives and captors. For instance, one hostage claimed: "We were speaking with one of the Chechens saying we can understand their position and their pain, that their children are in war, but at the same time we said these methods are not good to solve war. The Chechen told us that our government feels nothing for us and doesn't care to save us." Another hostage recalls the Barayev's angry reaction to claims of ill treatment of hostages in a radio broadcast: "Do you hear how they lie? That's just how they fool you about Chechnya!"

124. Politkovskaya, for instance, had to fly in from the United States, where she was receiving a prestigious journalist award. Among the other individuals with whom the terrorists demanded to speak was Yavlinsky, who at the time was in Tomsk.

125. Svetlana Gubareva, "Description of the Events During the Seizure of the Dubrovka Theater in Moscow, October 23–26, 2002," Internet. Available at http://www.geocities.com/svetlana.gubareva/other/opisanie_gubareva_1_eng.html (accessed on October 1, 2006).

126. Xenia Kaspari, "Interview with Altynbek Sarsenbayev" (March 21, 2005).

127. Kevin O'Flynn, "Up to 65 Foreigners Still Held in Theater," *St Ptersburgh Times* (October 25, 2002).

128. Svetlana Gubareva, "Description of the Events During the Seizure of the Dubrovka Theater in Moscow, October 23–26, 2002," Internet. Available at http://www.geocities.com/svetlana.gubareva/other/opisanie_gubareva_1_eng.html (accessed on October 1, 2006).

129. L. Burban, S. Gubareva, T. Karpova, N. Karpov, V. Kurbatov, D. Milovidov, and P. Finogenov, "Nord-Ost: Investigation Unfinished . . . " Internet. Available at http://www.pravdabeslana.ru/nordost/nordost.htm (accessed on October 11, 2006).

130. Interview with hostage Anna Andrianova featured in *Moskovskaya Pravda* (October 26, 2002).

131. Telephone interview with Anna Politkovskaya (March 19, 2002).

132. Interview with Karagandan Svetlana Gubareva, Available at http://www.geocities.com/svetlana.gubareva/02.html (accessed on December 21, 2006).

133. For instance, responding to the question: "Do your parents know that you are here?" the terrorists replied. "Many of us don't have parents. They are dead. Killed in this war. And our brothers and sisters, wives and children." See Jenny Norton, "Talking to the Moscow Gunmen," BBC. Available at http://news.bbc.co.uk/1/hi/programmes/from_our_own_correspondent/2391627.stm (accessed on December 11, 2006).

134. L. Burban, S. Gubareva, T. Karpova, N. Karpov, V. Kurbatov, D. Milovidov, and P. Finogenov, "Nord-Ost: Investigation Unfinished . . . " Internet. Available at http://www.pravdabeslana.ru/nordost/nordost.htm (accessed on October 11, 2006); Yavlinsky, Yastrazhebsky, Politkovskaya, Nemtsov interviews.

135. Alex Nicholson, "Yavlinsky Describes His Role in Crisis," *Moscow Times* (November 4, 2002).

136. Such procedural agreement was indeed reached between Abu Bakar and Boris Nemtsov on the second day: for each peaceful day in Chechnya the terrorists agreed to release hostages. One peaceful day—the children; another one—the women, and so on. According to Nemtsov, the "rebels liked that idea. And the day before yesterday was indeed a peaceful day. But when I reminded Abu Bakar about our agreements, he sent me to the devil and said that one should talk with either Basaev or Maskhadov." In conversations with Politkovskaya immediately after this phone call, Abu Bakar justified his reaction by pointing a report he had received from Vedeno district that the mop-up operations had not seized as claimed, but had in fact been only intensified. This suggested that had the agreement actually been followed through on the ground, additional release of hostages was at least a possibility.

137. According to the negotiators, the hostage takers were not firm in their discussions and had problems formulating their demands. For instance, Yavlinsky described the reaction of the terrorists to his efforts to make them specify their

demands in the following way: "First they were confused, then they became nervous, then they became angry, because they didn't know how to do this." Alex Nicholson, "Yavlinsky Describes His Role In Crisis," *Moscow Times* (November 4, 2002).

CHAPTER 4

1. Although the number of repeat offenders is rising steadily even in the category of nonterrorist incidents.

2. Obviously, even in cases involving first-time offenders, the subject may use his knowledge of movies or highly medialized past cases to draw an expectation of how the responders might proceed in the standoff. This may raise many fears and suspicions, which however, can be dispelled relatively easily throughout the course of negotiations.

3. "Interest-based negotiation" refers to the pragmatic approach to negotiation developed at the Harvard Negotiation Project, by Professor Roger Fisher and his colleagues. The approach is simply based on the assumption that people do what they perceive to be in their best interests, and that strategies to exercise influence with others should also be based on this assumption.

4. Some of the material in this chapter was first published in Adam Dolnik, *Understanding Terrorist Innovation: Technology, Tactics and Global Trends* (London: Routledge, 2007) pp. 104–126.

5. Statistic accurate as of December 2006.

6. The number of Israelis killed in this time period was 331. Jewish Virtual Library, "Decline in Terror Fatalities in 2004," Internet. Available at http://www.jewishvirtuallibrary.org/jsource/Terrorism/stats2004.html (accessed on February 25, 2005).

7. Paul J. Murphy, *The Wolves of Islam: Russia and the Faces of Chechen Terror* (Dulles, VA: Brasseay's Inc, 2005) p. 20.

8. Anna Kolchak, "The Development of Chechen Terrorism," Internet. Available at http://english.pravda.ru/main/18/87/347/10444_chechen.html (accessed on February 23, 2005).

9. ITAR-TASS, "Antiterrorist Center Official Says CIS Countries May Experience Suicide Attacks." FBIS ID #CEP20030703000288; Reuven Paz, "Suicide Terrorist Operations in Chechnya: An Escalation of the Islamist Struggle," *Middle East Intelligence Bulletin*. Vol.2 no.6 (2000).

10. Fred Weir, "Chechen Rebels Go Kamikaze," *Christian Science Monitor* (June 7, 2000).

11. Paul J. Murphy, *The Wolves of Islam: Russia and the Faces of Chechen Terror* (Dulles, VA: Brasseay's Inc, 2005) p. 177.

12. Pravda RU, "Chechen Terrorist Planned to Seize Parliament's Building in Moscow," Internet. Available at http://newsfromrussia.com/accidents/2003/06/20/48458.html (accessed on October 19, 2004).

13. Shamil Basayev, "Statement of Chief of the Military Council of State Defense Council <<Majlis al-Shura>> of Chechen Republic of Ichkeria Abdullah Shamil Abu-Idris Concerning the Events of October 23–26, 2002 in Moscow," Internet. Available at http://62.212.121.113/www.kavkazcenter.com/eng/articlebe27.html?id=605 (accessed on October 19, 2004).

14. RAS letter, "To heads of NATO Member States, to International Organizations: the UN, the OSCE, the Parliamentary Assembly of the Council of Europe, and the European Union" (November 22, 2002) Internet. Available at http://www.kavkazcenter.com/eng/content/2002/11/22/640.shtml (accessed on October 19, 2004).

15. Ibid.

16. ITAR-TASS: "Russia Steps up Security at Chechen Administration Building," FBIS ID#: CEP20021024000297.

17. Paul J. Murphy, *The Wolves of Islam: Russia and the Faces of Chechen Terror* (Dulles, VA: Brasseay's Inc, 2005) p. 211.

18. Pravda, "Explosives Were Smuggled into Znamenskoye as Construction Materials," Internet. Available at http://newsfromrussia.com/accidents/2003/05/14/46910.html (accessed on October 19, 2004).

19. Moskovskiye Novosti: "Recent Terrorist Acts in Chechnya Apparently Aimed at Specific Individuals,"FBIS ID# CEP20030521000291.

20. Paul J. Murphy *The Wolves of Islam: Russia and the Faces of Chechen Terror* (Dulles, VA: Brasseay's Inc, 2005) p. 211.

21. "School Hostage-Takers Released from Prison," *The Russia Journal* (September 7, 2004).

22. Aleksander Shvarev, "'Man with a Gun' from Engenoy," *Vremya Novostey* (September 16, 2004).

23. Yekaterina Blinova and Anton Trofimov, "Beslan Hostage Takers May Have Included Arrested Terrorist, Basayev Link Likely," *Nezavisimaya Gazeta* (September 8, 2004).

24. Zaur Farniev, "Who Should We Kill Now, Zarema?" *Kommersant* (December 24, 2005).

25. "Professional Terrorists," *Vremya Novostey* (September 17, 2004).

26. Paul J. Murphy *The Wolves of Islam: Russia and the Faces of Chechen Terror* (Dulles, VA: Brasseay's Inc, 2005) p. 231.

27. Ibid., p. 232.

28. *Vremya Novostey*: "Russian Law Enforcement Identifies Beslan Ringleader as Chechen Ruslan 'The Colonel' Khuchbarov," FBIS ID#: CEP20040910000096.

29. Dmitry Zaks, "Chechens Wary as Kadyrov Wins by Landslide," *Agence France Presse* (October 7, 2003).

30. Boaz Ganor, "Analysis: Train, Remote Detonation, Suicide Attack—Chechen Terrorists Kill 44," *Center for Tactical Counterterrorism Bulletin* (December 19, 2003).

31. Lawrence Uzzell, "Basayev Claims Responsibility for Terrorist Bombings," *Chechnya Weekly*, Vol. 5, no. 1 (Jamestown Foundation, 2004).

32. Paul J. Murphy *The Wolves of Islam: Russia and the Faces of Chechen Terror* (Dulles, VA: Brasseay's Inc, 2005) p. 235; However, in the atypical absence of Basayev's claim of responsibility there is some uncertainty about RAS involvement.

33. *Startfor Analysis*, "Islamist Militants at Work: A Study of the Kadyrov Assassination" (June 24, 2004).

34. Paul J. Murphy *The Wolves of Islam: Russia and the Faces of Chechen Terror* (Dulles, VA: Brasseay's Inc, 2005) p. 239.

35. Kavkaz-Tsentr News Agency: "Basayev Says 'Special Operations' Prepared for 'Occupying Forces'," FBIS ID#: CEP20040617000031.

36. RFE/RL Fact Box: "Major terrorist Incidents Tied to Russian–Chechen War," Internet. Available at http://www.rferl.org/featuresarticle/2004/09/d981dd2d-8b08-41ff-a2e2-ada25338093c.html (accessed on October 19, 2006).

37. Uwe Buse, Ullrich Fichtner, Mario Kaiser, Uwe Klussmann, Walter Mayr, and Christian Neef, "Putin's Ground Zero," *Der Spiegel* (December 27, 2004).

38. In an informal chat, several policemen who were also Sagopshi residents denied the existence of the camp, as well as the discovery of the weapons and shootout with Tsechoyev. But the body language and inconsistency in their story have led the author to conclude that they were lying. This is no surprising as some of the Beslan terrorists were their childhood friends and fellow policemen.

39. C. J. Chivers, and Steven Lee Meyers, "Chechen Rebels Had Precise Plan," *New York Times* (September 6, 2004).

40. On February 21, 1970, the PFLP-GC detonated two barometric pressure bombs on board Swissair flight 330 and an Australian Airlines flying from Frankfurt to Vienna. Forty-seven were killed.

41. The other two cases being the 1994 Ansar Allah attack on a twin engine plane in Panama, and the 2001 Richard Reid, the shoe bomber, attempt.

42. Julius Strauss, "Chechnya 'Black Widows' Linked to Sabotage of Russian Jets," *Daily Telegraph* (August 28, 2004).

43. Nick Paton Walsh and Peter Beaumont "When Hell Came Calling at Beslan's School no. 1," *The Observer* (September 5, 2004).

44. Anna Politkovskaya, *A Small Corner of Hell* (Chicago: University of Chicago Press, 2003) p. 142.

45. Quoted in Paul J. Murphy *The Wolves of Islam: Russia and the Faces of Chechen Terror* (Dulles, VA: Brasseay's Inc, 2005) p. 91.

46. Ibid., pp. 90–91.

47. Ibid., p. 11.

48. Ibid., p. 99.

49. Basayev quoted in Anne Nivat, *Chienne De Guerre* (New York: PublicAffairs, 2001) p. 41.

50. Kavkaz Center, "Interview with Chechen Commander Amir Ramzan, the Commander of One of Chechen Jama'ats Operating against Russian Forces in the Northern Caucasus" (November 28, 2003).

51. Anne Nivat, *Chienne De Guerre* (New York: PublicAffairs, 2001) p. 22.

52. Barayeva's Martyrdom video; Khava was the cousin of Budyonnovsk team member Arbi Barayev and the aunt of Dubrovka team leader Movsar Barayev.

53. Kavkaz Center, "Transcript of Shamil Basayev Interview for Channel 4 News," Internet. Available at http://kavkazcenter.com/eng/article.php?id=3500 (accessed on August 4, 2005).

54. Svetlana Gubareva, "Description of the Events During the Seizure of the Dubrovka Theater in Moscow, October 23–26, 2002," Internet. Available at http://www.geocities.com/svetlana.gubareva/other/opisanie_gubareva_1_eng.html (accessed on January 10, 2006).

55. Interview with Larisa Mamitova, Beslan (November 2005).

56. Major Sultan Gurashev, an Ingush police officer, encountered and single-handedly tried to stop the suspicious vehicles near the village of Khurikau. He was disarmed and tied up in one of the cars. The terrorists left him there as they stormed to school.

57. Basayev's interview for Prima News Agency (May 2002). Cited in Paul J. Murphy *The Wolves of Islam: Russia and the Faces of Chechen Terror* (Dulles, VA: Brasseay's Inc, 2005) p. 170.

58. Kavkaz Center, "Statement of Chief of the Military Council of State Defense Council <<Majlis al-Shura>> of Chechen Republic of Ichkeria Abdullah Shamil Abu-Idris Concerning the Events of October 23–26, 2002 in Moscow," Internet. Available at http://62.212.121.113/www.kavkazcenter.com/eng/articlebe27.html?id=605 (accessed on April 8, 2005).

59. *The Guardian*, "Transcript of Osama bin Laden's 'Letter to the American People'," Internet. Available at http://observer.guardian.co.uk/worldview/story/0,11581,845725,00.html (accessed on April 4, 2005).

60. Kavkaz Center, Transcript of Shamil Basayev's Interview for Channel 4 News. Internet. Available at http://kavkazcenter.com/eng/article.php?id=3500 (accessed on April 8, 2005).

61. Ibid.

62. Not only can such an analysis provide an insight into the terrorists' calculus behind the attack, it can also generate precedents set by past agreements that can be used in the upcoming discussions as objective criteria.

63. In Dubrovka two hostages were also executed, but this was a measure necessary to maintain control of the auditorium, not one designed to pressure the authorities at a deadline. And while the moral responsibility for the killing of people is the same, from a negotiator's perspective these different circumstances carry different implications.

64. On the evening of the second day of the crisis in Dubrovka, the terrorists received a phone call from General Kazantsev, who promised to come to Moscow to negotiate on the next day. The terrorists were happy and relieved, calling off their deadline for executions of hostages and letting their guard down. Several hours later, the rescue operation was launched.

65. This prediction was expressed by one of the authors of this book in an interview with Reuters on the first day of the crisis: "The Russians will assault the school without a doubt, they have done it in every single case … They will likely stall for time in order to get enough intelligence about the location, they will search for ways in and they will prepare a plan. I would expect the assault within the next two days, if history is anything to go by." See Mosnews, "Analysts Say School Storming Possible Despite Putin's Statement" (September 2, 2004). Available at http://mosnews.com/news/2004/09/02/analysts.shtml (accessed on October 10, 2005).

66. Kulayev trial provides new Beslan details. Jamestown Foundation *Chechnya Weekly*, Vol. 6, no. 23 (June 16, 2005).

## CHAPTER 5

1. Some of the material in this chapter was first published in "Negotiating the Impossible: The Lessons of the Beslan Hostage Crisis" by Adam Dolnik. RUSI Whitehall Report 2-07 (London: Royal United Services Institute, 2007).

2. Henry Plater-Zyberk, "Beslan—Lessons Learned?" Conflict Studies Research Centre (November 2004).

3. Betrozov's use of the Ossetian language broke the ground rules set by the terrorists, forbitting anoyne from speaking in another language other than Russian.

4. Uwe Buse, Ullrich Fichtner, Mario Kaiser, Uwe Klussmann, Walter Mayr, and Christian Neef, "Putin's Ground Zero," *Der Spiegel* (December 27, 2004) pp. 65–101.

5. Testimony of Vitalii Zangionov at the Nur-Pashi Kulayev trial, Vladikavkaz (January 26, 2006).

6. There is no public record of the actual talks, but hostages who sat in Ali's proximity, agree on the responses he provided.

7. This conversation was heard by several hostages sitting in Ali's proximity.

8. "Chief Beslan Gunman Described," *Caucasian Knot* (August 4, 2005).

9. Aslanbek Aslakhanov interviewed in Kevin Sim's documentary "Beslan: Siege of School no. 1." (Wide Angle, 2005).

10. Further, the other terrorists immediately afterward prayed by the bodied of their dead colleagues, which is something that wouldn't happen if they were considered traitors.

11. This incident is discussed in more detail in Part IV.

12. Uwe Buse, Ullrich Fichtner, Mario Kaiser, Uwe Klussmann, Walter Mayr, and Christian Neef, "Putin's Ground Zero," *Der Spiegel* (December 27, 2004).

13. Ibid.

14. Iznaur Kodzoyev would later be killed—not in September 2004 in Beslan, but instead, in his native village of Al'tievo, in April 2005. This suggests that either Kodzoyev was either really not present in the school, or that he got away.

15. C.J. Chivers, "The School: The Inside Story of the 2004 Attack in Beslan" *Esquire*, Vol. 145, no. 6 (June 2006).

16. RIA: Inquiry Finds Chechen Separatist Leader Was Given Chance to Intervene at Beslan, March 3, 2005.

17. Author's interview with Ruslan Aushev, Moscow (November 2005).

18. Henry Plater-Zyberk, "Beslan—Lessons Learned?" Conflict Studies Research Centre (November 2004).

19. Author's interview with Ruslan Aushev, Moscow (November 2005).

20. Aslanbek Aslakhanov interviewed in Kevin Sim's documentary "Beslan: Siege of School no. 1." (Wide Angle, 2005).

21. Author's interview with Larisa Kudzieva, Beslan (November 2005).

22. Author's interview with Larisa Mamitova, Beslan (November 2005).

23. The terrorists had a book that was rigged as a switch to the explosive daisy chain. One terrorist always had his foot on this book. If he lifted the foot, detonation would occur.

24. Author's interview with Larisa Kudzieva, Beslan (November 2005).

25. Uwe Buse, Ullrich Fichtner, Mario Kaiser, Uwe Klussmann, Walter Mayr, and Christian Neef, "Putin's Ground Zero," *Der Spiegel* (December 27, 2004).

26. Alexander Khinstein, "Rab Allaha Basayev ego peroskhoditelstvu Putinu . . . ," *Moskovski Komsomolets* (September 11, 2004).

27. According to Zakayev, the very first person to contact him was journalist Anna Politkovskaya.

28. Uwe Buse, Ullrich Fichtner, Mario Kaiser, Uwe Klussmann, Walter Mayr, and Christian Neef, "Putin's Ground Zero," *Der Spiegel* (December 27, 2004).

29. Interview with Israil Totoonti, Vladikavkaz (November 2005).

30. "New Details Emerge on Maschadov's Bit to Mediate in Beslan," Jamestown Foundation *Chechnya Weekly*, Volume 7, no. 1 (January 5, 2006).

31. Mayak Radio, "Russia: Beslan Inquiry Chief Says Maskhadov Missed Chance To Be True Leader" (April 2, 2005).

32. Maschadov was then killed on March 8, 2005 in the village of Tolstoy-Yurt, near Grozny.

33. This included Ali.

34. Kulayev's testimony, Vladikavkaz (May 31, 2005).

35. Basayev's Interview for Channel 4 News (April 2, 2005).

36. According to Senator Alexander Torshin who heads the federal investigative committee, the terrorists also had a backup school that would be easier to attack then Beslan in the village of Nesterovskaya in Ingushetia, on the road to which the terrorist would not have to travel from Ingushetia across checkpoints.

37. Henry Plater-Zyberk, "Beslan—Lessons Learned?" Conflict Studies Research Centre (November 2004).

38. William Zartman, "Negotiating Effectively with Terrorists" in Barry Rubin, ed., *The Politics of Counterterrorism* (Washington, D.C.: The Johns Hopkins Foreign Policy Institute, 1990).

39. Interview with Larisa Kudzieva (Beslan, November 2005).

40. Basayev's interview for Channel 4 News (April 2, 2005).

41. Nur Pasha Kulayev interviewed on Russian NTV station (April 9, 2005).

42. "Šéf teroristů z Beslanu uniká, tvrdí tisk," *Idnes* (September 10, 2004).

43. Anne Nivat, *Chienne De Guerre* (New York: Public Affairs, 2001) p. 92.

44. Interviews with local residents, Beslan and Nazran (November 2006).

45. Henry Plater-Zyberk, "Beslan—Lessons Learned?" Conflict Studies Research Centre (November 2004).

46. The official number is the result of thirty-one bodies being found with one terrorist being captured alive. The hostages, however, report seeing between 50–70 hostages, suggesting that some were able to escape. In addition only 17 of the bodies were positively identified, and consequently, only a limited profiling sample is available.

47. Yekaterina Blinova and Anton Trofimov, "Beslan Hostage Takers May Have Included Arrested Terrorist, Basayev Link Likely," *Nezavisimaya Gazeta* (September 8, 2004).

48. Thomas Strentz, "13 Indicators of Volatile Negotiations," *Law and Order* (1991).

49. Nick Paton Walsh, "Mystery Still Shrouds Beslan Six Months on: Theories and Rumors Fuel Relatives' Doubt and Anger," *The Guardian* (February 16, 2005).

50. MosNews, "New Drugs Used by Beslan Terrorists Puzzle Russian Experts" (October 19, 2004). Available at http://www.mosnews.com/news/2004/10/19/smoking.shtml (accessed on October 10, 2006).

51. This would not be inconsistent with past cases, as the Kremlin has always attempted to portray Chechen militants as drug addicts, bandits, and alcoholics.

52. John B. Dunlop. "Beslan: Russia's 9/11?" The American Committee for Peace in Chechnya and The Jamestown Foundation (October 2005).

53. See for instance "They Knifed Babies, They Raped Girls,"*Sunday Mirror* (09/05/04). Available at http://www.freerepublic.com/focus/f-news/1208007/ posts (accessed on October 10, 2006).

54. Author's interview with Larisa Kudzieva, Beslan (November 2005).

55. Ibid.

56. Author's interview with Aneta Gadieva, Vladikavkaz (July 2005).

57. Mark Franchetti, and Matthew Campbell, "How a Repressed Village Misfit Became the Butcher of Beslan", *The Sunday Times* (September 12, 2004). Available at http://www.timesonline.co.uk/article/0,,2089-1257953_1,00.html (accessed on July 4, 2005).

58. Ibid.

59. Testimony of hostage Svetlana Dzheriyeva at the Kulayev trial.

60. MosNews, "Beslan Hostage-Takers Did Not Want to Die—Former Ingush President Ruslan Aushev" (September 28, 2004).

61. Author's interview with Larisa Mamitova, Beslan (November 2005).

62. Mamitova did in fact know Khodov's mother, but never met the son before.

63. Similarly, when on the second day Larissa Kudzieva approached Khodov with a request to wash her blood soaked skirt, he replied. "You'll wash it at home."

64. Thomas Strentz, "The Cyclic Crisis Negotiations Time Line," *Law and Order* (March 1995) pp. 73–75.

65. Author's interview with Ruslan Aushev, Moscow (July 2005).

66. RIA: Russian Official Reveals Evidence Uncovered by Beslan Investigation. (February 4, 2005).

67. Kulayev Trial Provides New Beslan Details, Jamestown Foundation, *Chechnya Weekly,* Vol. 6, no. 23 (June 16, 2005).

68. Madina Khuzmieva testimony in the Kulayev Trial, attended by author, Vladikavkaz (07/19/05).

69. RFE/RL, "Basaev Claims Beslan Attacks." (September 17, 2004).

70. Author's interview with Regina Revazova, Beslan (July 2005).

71. Author's interview with Andrei Soldatov, Moscow (July 2005).

72. Plater-Zyberk, Henry, "Beslan—Lessons Learned?" Conflict Studies Research Centre (November 2004).

73. Author's interview with Madina Shavlokhova, Beslan (July 2005).

74. "Controversial Evidence in Kulayev Case," *Caucasian Knot* (January 17, 2006).

75. Author's interview with Fatima Dudiyeva, Beslan (November 2005).

76. Author's interview with Ala Ramonova, Beslan (July 2005).

77. Lenta.RU: "Saniperam meshalo specialnoe otsteklenie v beslanskoi shkole" (August 12, 2005). Internet. Available at http://lenta.ru/news/2005/08/12/ sniper/ (accessed on December 8, 2005).

78. For instance, according to the investigation of Yuri Savelyev, a weapons and explosives expert and a member of Russia's parliamentary commission investigating the Beslan events, the initial explosions were allegedly caused by rocket-propelled grenades fired onto the roof from the outside. His conclusions seem to be supported by an anonymous video posted on Youtube in July 2007, which can be found at: http://www.pravdabeslana.ru/video.htm

79. Lawrence Uzzell, "Reporter Puts Forward Another Version of Events," Jamestown Foundation, *Chechnya Weekly*, Vol. 5, no. 35 (September 15, 2004).

80. Elena Milashina, "Eyewitnesses: 'The Roof Caught Fire When They Began Shooting Shells At It'," *Novaya Gazeta* (October 7, 2004).

81. "Newspaper Provides Fresh Beslan Details," Jamestown Foundation, *Chechnya Weekly*, Vol. 6, no. 21 (June 1, 2005).

82. "Controversial Evidence in Kulayev Case," *Caucasian Knot* (January 17, 2006)

83. Author's interview with Israil Ttoonti, Beslan (November 2005).

84. Author's interview with the head of the Beslan Mother's Committee Susanna Duadyieva and local journalist and witness Murag Kaboev, Beslan (July 2005).

85. "Newspaper Provides Fresh Beslan Details," Jamestown Foundation, *Chechnya Weekly*, Vol. 6, no. 21 (June 1, 2005).

86. Kavkaz Center, "Statement of Chief of the Military Council of State Defense Council <<Majlis al-Shura>> of Chechen Republic of Ichkeria Abdullah Shamil Abu-Idris Concerning the Events of October 23–26, 2002 in Moscow," Internet. Available at http://62.212.121.113/www.kavkazcenter.com/eng/articlebe27.html?id=605 (accessed on August 4, 2005).

87. Ibid.

88. Kavkaz Center Transcript of Shamil Basayev Interview for Channel 4 News. Internet. Available at http://kavkazcenter.com/eng/article.php?id=3500 (accessed on August 4, 2005).

89. Not surprisingly, the causes of the explosion remain a subject of much speculation. While the federal security services have claimed credit for eliminating Basayev, in a "special operation," Chechen sources inists that the explosion occurred as an accident after the truck hit a pothole. Other sources speculate that Basayev faked is own death, and is still alive.

90. Laura Mansfield, "Chechen Terrorists Follow al-Qaida Manual," Internet. Available at http://www.worldnetdaily.com/news/article.asp?ARTICLE_ID=40298 (accessed on December 12, 2004).

## CHAPTER 6

1. Abu Musab al Zarqawi's practice of beheading of hostages on video represents a slightly different phenomenon because it occurred in a kidnapping scenario in which the location of hostages and hostage takers was unknown. In such a setting, negotiation options become much more limited, as the terrorists have the liberty to execute their hostages without sanction.

2. There were some questions with regards to the hostage taker's Fumio Kutsumi's relation to the cult, as Aum officially denied involvement, and the perpetrator himself, allegedly also denied that he was a Aum member (Mickolus p. 826).

3. Kaplan, p. 283.

4. Dwayne Fuselier and Gary Noesner, "Confronting the Terrorist Hostage Taker," Internet. Available at http://www.emergency.com/host-tkr.htm (accessed on January 29, 2002).

5. Thomas Strentz, *Psychological Aspects of Crisis Negotiation* (New York: CRC Press, 2006) p. 164.

6. It must be emphasized here that there is a huge difference between the training and capabilities of one of the thousands of police departments in the United States and around the world, and the FBI and other top agencies mentioned earlier. While the lead expert agencies do emphasize the principle of flexibility and the need to avoid "cookie cutter" approaches in their training, the general negotiation guideliness they offer are frequently applied by less experienced bodies in a "bible-like" manner.

7. Ibid., p. 221.

8. See, for instance, Frederick Lanceley, *On-Scene Guide for Crisis Negotiators*, 2nd ed. (Boca Raton, FL: CRC Press, 2003) p. 127.

9. Thomas Strentz, *Psychological Aspects of Crisis Negotiation* (New York: CRC Press, 2006) p. 221.

10. Jayne Docherty, *Learning Lessons from Waco* (Syracuse: Syracuse University Press, 2001) p. 91.

11. Statistics show that containment and negotiation have had a 95 percent success rate. See Michael McMains, and Wayman Mullins, *Crisis Negotiations: Managing Critical Incidents and Hostage Situations in Law Enforcementand Corrections*, 2nd ed. (Dayton, OH: Anderson Publishing, 2001) p. 33.

12. Some demands in crisis negotiations are referred to as non–negotiable, either because of official policy or because of the potential of making the situation more volatile. In barricade situations, for instance, additional weapons will not be given to the hostage taker under any circumstances, as the suspect might be using a fake or a nonfunctional weapon; satisfying his or her demand would only provide the tools necessary for a violent exchange. Other non-negotiable demands in a barricade situation also include supplying the hostage taker with alcohol or drugs, as these substances have the potential of escalating the suspect's violent behavior. See Michael McMains and Wayman Mullins, *Crisis Negotiations: Managing Critical Incidents and Hostage Situations in Law Enforcementand Corrections*, 2nd ed. (Dayton, OH: Anderson Publishing, 2001) pp. 117–118.

13. Michael McMains and Wayman Mullins, *Crisis Negotiations: Managing Critical Incidents and Hostage Situations in Law Enforcementand Corrections*, 2nd ed. (Dayton, OH: Anderson Publishing, 2001) p. 116.

14. Ibid., p. 118.

15. Thomas Strentz, "The Cyclic Crisis Negotiations Time Line," *Law and Order* (March 1995) pp. 73–75.

16. James Poland and Michael McCrystle, *Practical, Tactical and Legal Perspectives of Terrorism and Hostage Taking* (Lewiston, NY: Edwin Mellen Press, 2000) p. 59.

17. Jayne Docherty, *Learning Lessons from Waco* (Syracuse: Syracuse University Press, 2001) pp. 155–56.

18. The Iranian hostage crisis which lasted for 444 days is not considered here, because it did not constitute a classical barricade hostage incident occurring on friendly territory, and thus lacked the threat of instantaneous forceful resolution.

19. It is not the intention here to take anything away from the special unit responsible for the Lima raid, but it must be mentioned that many of the hostages only escaped the gunfire simply because they tripped over the carpets in the building. Had it not been for this incalculable development, the number of fatalities among the hostages would have likely been higher than one.

20. Thomas Strentz, *Psychological Aspects of Crisis Negotiation* (New York: CRC Press, 2006) p. 189.

21. Ibid., p. 186.

22. F. Boltz, K. Dudonis, and D. Schultz, *The Counterterrorism Handbook: Tactics, Procedures and Techniques*, 2nd ed. (Boca Raton, FL: CRC Press, 2002) p. 64.

23. Cited in Yagil Henkin, "From Tactical Terrorism to Holy War: The Evolution of Chechen Terrorism, 1995–2004." *Central Asian Survey* Vol. 25 no. 1–2 (March–June 2006).

24. F. Boltz, K. Dudonis, and D. Schultz, *The Counterterrorism Handbook: Tactics, Procedures and Techniques*, 2nd ed. (Boca Raton, FL: CRC Press, 2002) p. 118.

25. Ibid.

26. John Griffiths, *Hostage: The History, Facts and Reality of Hostage Taking* (London: Andre Deutsch, 2003) p. 120.

27. Charles M. Sennott, "Abbas: Klinghoffer Created Troubles So We Killed Him," *The Boston Globe* (June 26, 1998).

28. E-mail communication with Gary Noesner, Chief, FBI Crisis Negotiation Unit, retired (August 28, 2007).

29. F. Boltz, K. Dudonis, and D. Schultz, *The Counterterrorism Handbook: Tactics, Procedures and Techniques*, 2nd ed. (Boca Raton, FL: CRC Press, 2002) p. 67.

30. E-mail communication with Gary Noesner, Chief, FBI Crisis Negotiation Unit, retired (August 28, 2007).

31. Ibid., 140.

32. Ibid.

33. F. Boltz, K. Dudonis, and D. Schultz, *The Counterterrorism Handbook: Tactics, Procedures and Techniques*, 2nd ed. (Boca Raton, FL: CRC Press, 2002) p. 56.

34. Such as giving up on negotiations or immediately fulfilling the terrorists' demands (after an execution).

35. Thomas Strentz, *Psychological Aspects of Crisis Negotiation* (New York: CRC Press, 2006) p. 107.

36. Michael McMains and Wayman Mullins, *Crisis Negotiations: Managing Critical Incidents and Hostage Situations in Law Enforcementand Corrections*, 2nd ed. (Dayton, OH: Anderson Publishing, 2001) p. 50.

37. J.R Corsi, "Terrorism as a Desperate Game—Fear, Bargaining, and Communication in the Terrorist Event," *Journal of Conflict Resolution*, Vol. 25, no.1 (1981).

38. William Zartman, "Negotiating Effectively with Terrorists" in Barry Rubin, ed., *The Politics of Counterterrorism* (Washington, D.C.: The Johns Hopkins Foreign Policy Institute, 1990) p. 170.

39. Arthur A. Slatkin, *Communications in Crisis and Hostage Negotiations* (Springfield, IL: Charles C. Thomas Publishers, 2005) p. 87.

40. Anthony Hare "Training Crisis Negotiators: Updating Negotiation Techniques and Training," in Rogan, Randal, Hammer, Mitchell and Van Zandt, Clinton, *Dynamic Processes of Crisis Negotiation*, (Westport, CT: Praeger, 1997) p. 152.

41. Thomas Strentz, *Psychological Aspects of Crisis Negotiation* (New York: CRC Press, 2006) pp. 34–36.

42. Arthur A. Slatkin, *Communications in Crisis and Hostage Negotiations* (Springfield, IL: Charles C Thomas Publishers, 2005) p. 11.

43. Dwayne Fuselier, "What Every Negotiator Would Like his Chief to Know," *FBI Law Enforcement Bulletin* (March 1986); Thomas Strentz, *Psychological Aspects of Crisis Negotiation* (New York: CRC Press, 2006) p. 32.

44. This holds only for cases where the terrorists have actually made such a demand. As we have seen in the Egypt Air flight 648 hijacking, the involvement of top politicians in cases where terrorist have not made any demands of a political nature is likely to be counterproductive (see Chapter 2).

45. Thomas Strentz, *Psychological Aspects of Crisis Negotiation* (New York: CRC Press, 2006) p. 23.

46. McMains and Mullins describe how the negotiator can suggest taking a lunch break and continuing the discussion later. The mentioning of food has the potential of reminding the hostage taker of his primary needs.

47. This is similar to the effects of the aforementioned availability of surveillance technology that can potentially aid the terrorists in eavesdropping on communication channels used by the security forces. If the terrorists can listen to the communications and find out that the negotiator's intentions are genuine, this could help in reducing some of the tension, making the negotiation process less challenging.

48. United States versus Crosby, 1983; State versus Sands, 1985.

49. Richard Hayes, "Negotiations with Terrorists" in Victor Kremenyuk, *International Negotiation* (San Francisco: Jossey-Bass, 2001) p. 422.

50. Mitchell, R. Hammer and Randall G. Rogan, "Negotiation Models in Crisis Situations: The Value of a Communication-Based Approach," in Rogan, Randal, Hammer, Mitchell and Van Zandt, Clinton, *Dynamic Processes of Crisis Negotiation* (Westport, CT: Praeger, 1997) p. 9.

51. The most relevant references to this issue in the Koran include:

[2:190–192] *"And fight in the cause of Allah with those who fight with you, and do not exceed the limits, surely Allah does not love those who exceed the limits. And kill them wherever you find them, and drive them out from where they drove you out, and persecution is severer than slaughter, and do not fight with them at the Sacred Mosque (in Makkah) until they fight with you in it, but if they do fight you, then slay them; such is the reward of the unbelievers. But if they desist, then surely Allah is Forgiving, Merciful. And fight with them until there is no persecution, and religion should be only for Allah, but if they desist, then there should be no hostility except against the oppressors."*

[2:178] *"O you who believe! the law of equality is prescribed to you in cases of murder: the free for the free, the slave for the slave, the woman for the woman. But if any remission is made by the brother of the slain, then prosecution (for the bloodwit) should be made according to usage, and payment should be made to him in a good manner; this is an alleviation from your Lord and a mercy; so whoever exceeds the limit after this he shall have a painful chastisement."*

[42:40–43] *"The recompense for an injury is an injury equal thereto (in degree): but if a person forgives and makes reconciliation, his reward is due from Allah: for (Allah) loves not those who do wrong. But indeed if any do help and defend themselves after a wrong (done) to them, against such there is no cause of blame. The blame is only against those who oppress men and insolently transgress beyond bounds through the land, defying right and justice: for such there will be a grievous penalty. And whoever is patient and forgiving, these most surely are actions due to courage."*

52. For full text of the statement see "Transcript of Osama bin Laden's 'Letter to the American People'," *The Guardian*, Internet. Available at http://observer. guardian.co.uk/worldview/story/0,11581,845725,00.html (accessed on April 4, 2005).

# SELECTED BIBLIOGRAPHY

Antokol, Norman and Nudell, Mayer. *No One a Neutral: Political Hostage Taking in the Modern World*. Medina, OH: Alpha Publications, 1990.

Aston, Clive C. *A Contemporary Crisis: Political Hostage-Taking and the Experience of Western Europe*. Westport, CT: Greenwood Press, 1982.

Bandura, Albert. "Mechanisms of Moral Disengagement." In Walter Reich, editor, *Origins of Terrorism: Psychologies, Ideologies, Theologies, States of Mind*, 2nd ed. Washington, D.C.: Woodrow Wilson Center Press, 1998.

Boltz, F., Dudonis, K., and Schultz, D. *The Counterterrorism Handbook: Tactics, Procedures and Techniques*, 2nd ed. Boca Raton, FL: CRC Press, 2002.

Clutterbuck, Richard. *Kidnap & Ransom: The Response*. London: Faber and Faber, 1978.

Corsi, J.R. "Terrorism as a Desperate Game—Fear, Bargaining, and Communication in the Terrorist Event." *Journal of Conflict Resolution*, Vol. 25, no. 1 (1981), pp. 47–86.

Crenshaw, Martha. "Terrorism, Strategies, and Grand Strategies." In Audrey Cronin and James Ludes, editors, *Attacking Terrorism: Elements of a Grand Strategy*. Washington, D.C.: Georgetown University Press, 2004.

Davidson, Thomas M. *To Preserve Life: Hostage-Crisis Management*. San Rafael, CA: Cimacom, 2002.

Docherty, Jayne. *Learning Lessons from Waco*. Syracuse, NY: Syracuse University Press, 2001.

Dolnik, Adam. "Contrasting Dynamics of Crisis Negotiations: Barricade versus Kidnapping Incidents." *International Negotiation*, Vol. 8, no. 3 (2003), pp. 53–84.

———. *Negotiating the Impossible: The Beslan Hostage Crisis*. London: Royal United Services Institute for Defence and Security Studies (RUSI) Whitehall Report 2-07, 2007.

Dolnik, Adam and Pilch, Richard. "The Moscow Theater Hostage Crisis: The Perpetrators, Their Tactics, and the Russian Response." *International Negotiation*, Vol. 8, no. 3 (2003), pp. 135–169.

Fisher, Roger and Ury, William. *Getting to Yes: Negotiating Agreement without Giving In*, 2nd ed. New York: Penguin Books, 1991.

Fuselier, Dwayne. "What Every Negotiator Would Like His Chief to Know." *FBI Law Enforcement Bulletin*, March 1986.

Fuselier, Dwayne and Noesner, Gary. "Confronting the Terrorist Hostage Taker." Available at http://www.emergency.com/host-tkr.htm (accessed on January 29, 2002).

Greenstone, James L. *The Elements of Police Hostage and Crisis Negotiations: Critical Incidents and How to Respond to Them.* Binghamton, NY: Haworth Press, 2005.

Griffiths, John. *Hostage: The History, Facts and Reality of Hostage Taking.* London: Andre Deutsch, 2003.

Hassel, Conrad V. "The Hostage Situation: Exploring the Motivation and the Cause." *Police Chief*, Vol. 42, no. 9 (September 1975), pp. 55–58.

Hayes, Richard. "Negotiations with Terrorists." In Victor Kremenyuk, editor, *International Negotiation.* San Francisco, CA: Jossey-Bass, 2001.

Hoffman, Bruce. *Inside Terrorism.* New York: Orion Publishing Co., 1998.

Jenkins, Brian M., Johnson, Janera, and Ronfeld, David. *Numbered Lives: Some Statistical Observations from 77 International Hostage Episodes.* Santa Monica, CA: Rand Corporation, 1977.

Laceley, Frederick. *On-Scene Guide for Crisis Negotiators*, 2nd ed. Boca Raton, FL: CRC Press, 2003.

McMains, Michael and Mullins, Wayman. *Crisis Negotiations: Managing Critical Incidents and Hostage Situations in Law Enforcement and Corrections*, 2nd ed. Dayton, OH: Anderson Publishing, 2001.

Poland, James and McCrystle, Michael. *Practical, Tactical and Legal Perspectives of Terrorism and Hostage Taking.* Lewiston, NY: Edwin Mellen Press, 2000.

Rogan, Randal, Hammer, Mitchell, and Van Zandt, Clinton. *Dynamic Processes of Crisis Negotiation.* Westport, CT: Praeger, 1997.

Slatkin, Arthur A. *Communications in Crisis and Hostage Negotiations.* Springfield, IL: Charles C. Thomas Publishers, 2005.

Stratton, John. "The Terrorist Act of Hostage Taking: A View of Violence and the Perpetrators." *Police Science and Administration*, Vol. 6, no. 1 (1978), pp. 1–9.

Strentz, Thomas. "13 Indicators of Volatile Negotiations." *Law and Order* (1991).

———. "The Cyclic Crisis Negotiations Time Line." *Law and Order* (1995).

———. *Psychological Aspects of Crisis Negotiation.* New York: CRC Press, 2006.

Taillon, J. Paul de B. *Hijacking and Hostages: Government Responses to Terrorism.* Westport, CT: Praeger, 2002.

Topol, Sergei. *Budyonnovsk: Reportazh pod Pritselom.* Moscow: De Fakto, 2005.

Wardlaw, Grant. *Political Terrorism.* London: Cambridge University Press, 1982.

Wilson, M. and Smith, A. "Roles and Rules in Terrorist Hostage Taking," in D. Canter and L. Alison, editors, *The Social Psychology of Crime: Groups, Teams and Networks.* Aldershot, U.K: Ashgate, 1999.

Zartman, William. "Negotiating Effectively with Terrorists." In Barry Rubin, editor, *The Politics of Counterterrorism.* Washington, D.C.: The Johns Hopkins Foreign Policy Institute, 1990.

———. *Negotiating with Terrorists.* Leiden, Netherlands: Martinus Nijhoff Publishers, 2006.

# INDEX

## ABOUT THE AUTHORS

Dr ADAM DOLNIK is the Director of Research Programs and Senior Fellow at the Centre for Transnational Crime Prevention (CTCP) at the University of Wollongong in Australia. Formerly he has served as chief trainer at the International Centre for Political Violence and Terrorism Research (ICPVTR) in Singapore, and as a researcher at the Weapons of Mass Destruction Terrorism Research Project at the Monterey Institute of International Studies in California and at the United Nations Terrorism Prevention Branch in Vienna. Dolnik regularly lectures for various governmental and nongovernmental organizations and agencies around the world, and has also conducted field research on terrorist networks in conflict zones. He is the author of *Understanding Terrorist Innovation: Technologies, Tactics, and Global Trends* (Routledge, 2007) and has also written over forty reports and articles on terrorism-related issues.

KEITH M. FITZGERALD is Managing Director of Sea-Change Partners and Director of the Asian Programme on Negotiation and Conflict Management (APNCM) at the S. Rajaratnam School of International Studies in Singapore. He is a former Associate of the Harvard Negotiation Project at Harvard Law School and at the Conflict Management Group in Cambridge, Massachusetts, and a former Teaching Fellow at Harvard's John F. Kennedy School of Government. He is also a member of the Council for Emerging National Security Affairs (CENSA), a virtual policy advisory think-tank based in Washington, DC. Fitzgerald lectures widely on negotiation, conflict management, crisis leadership, and negotiating with "terrorists." As a practitioner, he has trained and advised parties and facilitated negotiations in dozens of peace processes, hostage, barricade, and crisis negotiations in over sixty-five countries worldwide.